# Listening for Madeleine

MADELEINE L'ENGLE AT HER SEVENTIETH
BIRTHDAY CELEBRATION, 1988

# Listening
## for
# Madeleine

✳

A PORTRAIT OF

MADELEINE L'ENGLE

IN MANY VOICES

## Leonard S. Marcus

FARRAR, STRAUS AND GIROUX   NEW YORK

Farrar, Straus and Giroux
18 West 18th Street, New York 10011

Distributed in Canada by D&M Publishers, Inc.
Printed in the United States of America
First edition, 2012

Frontispiece photograph taken by and used with permission from Dana Catharine;
photograph of Hugh and Madeleine at Crosswicks taken by and used with permission
from Luci Shaw. All other photographs are courtesy of Madeleine L'Engle Papers (SC-3),
Wheaton College Special Collections, Wheaton, Illinois, and appear with the permission
of Crosswicks, Ltd., in cooperation with McIntosh and Otis, Inc.

Library of Congress Cataloging-in-Publication Data
Listening for Madeleine : a portrait of Madeleine L'Engle in many voices / [edited by]
Leonard S. Marcus.
 p.  cm.
 ISBN 978-0-374-29897-5 (hardback)
 1. L'Engle, Madeleine—Friends and associates.  2. Authors, American—20th
century—Biography.  3. Women authors, American—Biography.  I. Marcus,
Leonard S.

PS3523.E55 Z73 2012
813'.54—dc23
[B]

                                        2012009144

Designed by Abby Kagan
Title page hand lettering and star by Vivienne Flesher

www.fsgbooks.com

1  3  5  7  9  10  8  6  4  2

*To the memory*

*of my father, who said, "Talk to people,"*

*and*

*of my mother, who taught me to listen*

WITH HER MOTHER,
MADELEINE HALL
BARNETT CAMP,
1918 OR EARLY 1919

SKIING AT CHAMONIX-MONT-BLANC,
AGE TWELVE

AT THE BEACH IN JACKSONVILLE
WITH HER GRANDMOTHER CAROLINE
L'ENGLE BARNETT, C. 1923

THE FRANKLINS, 1963: (FROM LEFT) BION, MARIA,
JOSEPHINE, MADELEINE, AND HUGH

HUGH AND MADELEINE AT CROSSWICKS, 1982

# CONTENTS

CONTENTS

## MATRIARCH

## MENTOR

## FRIEND

# CONTENTS

## ICON

# Listening
## for
# Madeleine

# INTRODUCTION

For any reasonably self-reflective and intelligent individual in the modern age personal identity is not a birthright but a conquest. If we are successful it is because gradually we learn to tell ourselves a story about who we are . . . that others can judge as in some sense "true to the facts." —LAIRD M. EASTON, ED., *Journey to the Abyss: The Diaries of Count Harry Kessler, 1880–1918*

I don't understand how and why I come to *be* only as I lose myself, but I know from long experience that this is so.
—MADELEINE L'ENGLE, *The Irrational Season*

She was born in New York City on November 29, 1918, the only child of Charles Wadsworth Camp and Madeleine Hall Barnett Camp. Her parents, whom she ruefully described as "Olympian," had both grown up in privileged circumstances—Charles at Hilton, a rambling old house in Crosswicks, New Jersey; Madeleine in Jacksonville, Florida, where her family owned the largest bank. Her parents lived an elegant if far from opulent beau monde life, with Charles, a Princeton man and veteran of World War I, plying his trade as a journalist and mystery writer, while the elder Madeleine, a classically trained pianist who shunned the professional limelight, looked after the family finances, a task for which she proved to be as well suited as any Barnett. The couple was married in 1906 in Jacksonville, Florida, where the bride's family lived and Charles's parents had taken to spending the winter. Charles, having cut his teeth out of college as a beat reporter for the New York *Sun*, worked for *McClure's* and *Metropolitan* magazines and, for a time, traveled the world as a foreign correspondent while also dabbling in fiction. On at least one occasion, Madeleine Camp accompanied her husband on his far-flung adventures.

At home in New York, the Camps dressed for dinner, attended the theater and the opera, and entertained their friends in the arts. When in the eleventh year of their marriage their daughter was born following an unusually difficult pregnancy, the couple kept up their busy social schedule as before, with young Madeleine consigned to the care of an English nanny—the salt-of-the-earth "Mrs. O." (short for Mary O'Connell) of Liverpool. A succession of boarding schools would later serve the same purpose of freeing the Camps to maintain their gilded routine.

Madeleine's poor-little-not-quite-rich-girl status did have advantages. By the time she was ten, she had met George Gershwin—and Gershwin's mistress, the gifted musician and composer Kay Swift—and heard them play the piano in a school friend's opulent drawing room; listened as members of the Metropolitan Opera Company sang for their friends in the Camps' own parlor, accompanied by her mother; and frequented the galleries—a short walk from her parents' East Eighty-second Street apartment—of the Metropolitan Museum of Art. Exposure to the arts spilled over into the summer months when, before she was old enough for sleepaway camp, her parents brought her along to the Cornish Art Colony, a popular New England retreat founded by the American sculptor Augustus Saint-Gaudens, whose dashing art-world-grandee son, Homer, had been a wartime comrade-in-arms of Charles's. To a shy, ungainly, keenly observant young child, a steady diet of experiences such as these was more than enough to confirm the world of culture as the most desirable of realms, even if it did little to balance out the near-total lack of regular playmates or her overbusy parents' serial lapses of attention. It was then that Madeleine learned to fill the emotional hollows in her life by seeking solace in books and, from the age of eight, by writing in the pages of a journal. Books, she decided, were more reliable companions than people. For decades afterward, L'Engle would work feverishly to prove herself wrong about this.

She had a disastrous first experience of school. At her mother's insistence, the Camps enrolled Madeleine at Brearley, an academically rigorous private girls' school catering to the cream of New York society, where her teachers pigeonholed her as at best an average student and she dreaded having to participate in athletics. When it became clear how unhappy she was there, her mother sympathized with her and, over Charles's protestations, transferred her to the next of a series of city day schools. Then, in 1930, when Madeleine was eleven, the Camps left New York for France and took up residence in a picture-postcard alpine château as the guests of family friends. They did so ostensibly for the sake of Charles's health but more likely to trim the family's expenses as the Great Depression made it harder for him—now a freelance writer with only modest success to show for his efforts—to earn a living. When fall came, Madeleine's parents, up to their old tricks, delivered their daughter without warning to a Swiss boarding school, introduced her to the matron in charge, said their goodbyes, and drove away. Madeleine remained there for the next three years. Reading and writing off the menu of the school curriculum once again sustained her amid the demands of a rigidly structured, insular world in which she did not feel appreciated. It was then, L'Engle recalled, that she burnished her powers of concentration and mastered the ability to "write anywhere," disciplines that afterward served her as a writer with young children at home and as a sought-after lecturer with a frenetic travel schedule.

After three years abroad, the Camps, having received the news that Madeleine's maternal grandmother, Caroline Hallowes L'Engle Barnett, of Jacksonville, had fallen ill, returned to the United States. Charles and his wife now settled in Jacksonville and arranged for Madeleine to enroll in Ashley Hall, a girls' boarding school in Charleston, South Carolina. It must have astonished no one more than Madeleine herself that Ashley Hall suited her so perfectly. It was there that her formal education and her fugitive efforts to prepare herself for a writing career finally converged in an exhilarating blast of encouragement for her passion for literature. At Ashley Hall, she went so far as to question her harsh self-assessment as a socially and physically awkward girl, even mustering the courage to take on the lead role in school plays. Madeleine now added stage acting to reading and writing in the arsenal of her tried-and-true escape-and-rescue strategies. The prodigious internal growth she experienced at this time prepared her well for Smith College.

Madeleine was in her senior year at Ashley Hall when in October 1936 she received an urgent message concerning her father's health. Days earlier, on a whirlwind visit up north, Charles Camp had looked hale and hearty to his old college friends at a Princeton reunion and to fellow members of New York's Players Club. But by the time he was home in Jacksonville, he had come down with a bad case of pneumonia, and his condition deteriorated with terrifying speed. Armed with a copy of *Jane Eyre*, Madeleine boarded a train bound for Florida but arrived too late to see her father alive one last time.

The death of Charles Camp, as L'Engle described it in *The Summer of the Great-Grandmother*, shook her to the core—perhaps as much due to as despite the fact that her relationship with her father, the mystery writer in professional (and one suspects emotional) decline throughout the years of her childhood and adolescence, had been such a distant one. "In the long dream of her fiction," Cynthia Zarin observed in *The New Yorker*, "the search for the father is central." In later years, L'Engle would turn nightly to mystery fiction for a pleasurable escape that must also, at times, have stirred unsettling memories of the great absent figure in her life.

In the mid-1940s, as a young married woman with dreams of raising a large, close-knit family, L'Engle placed another reminder of Charles Camp in her path when she accepted her mother's suggestion to give the name Crosswicks to the only house that she and her husband, Hugh, would ever own. Crosswicks was familiar to them as the name of the village in Chesterfield Township, New Jersey, where Charles Wadsworth Camp, the youngest of ten children, had been raised. In this way, L'Engle made her home a monument of sorts to her father's memory.

Then, twenty-five years later, when L'Engle was looking for a title for her first volume of memoirs—the book she finally called *A Circle of Quiet*—she considered calling it "Crosswicks" as well. In a meditation on the power of names found in that book, she described her search for the perfect title, noting the appeal of "Crosswicks" as a companionable old word meaning "where the two roads meet"—although in what language she did not say. It is not known where L'Engle got this mistaken notion. Had her mother, Madeleine Barnett Camp, who had lived with her husband for a time at Hilton, told her this? Historians trace the origins of "Crosswicks" to "Crossweeksung," the name of a Lenape Indian tribal village once located in the vicinity of present-day Crosswicks, New Jersey. The Quakers who arrived in the region in the 1660s gave an Anglicized form of the Lenape original to their own village and to nearby Crosswicks Creek. So much for the language of origin; what about its meaning? All too ironically for a name chosen by L'Engle to stand for family togetherness, "Crossweeksung" translates not as "where the two roads meet" but as "house of separation."

In *A Wrinkle in Time*, L'Engle casts Meg's father as a brilliant

scientist engaged in a top secret government project. When ma-
levolent cosmic forces, threatened by Dr. Alex Murry's work, im-
prison him in another part of the universe, it falls to the daughter
character, who loves her father dearly, to undertake the impossible
task of bringing him home. Meg succeeds brilliantly at her mission as well as at the additional task of rescuing her younger brother.
Or, to put this in the language of L'Engle's theology, she triumphs
as completely as only someone armed with the power of love can
do. Charles Camp's own story ended rather less happily, with pneumonia the immediate cause of death but long-term alcoholism the
presumed underlying factor in the unraveling of his health. As the
self-appointed keeper of the family history, L'Engle in her four-
volume Crosswicks Journal would assign to her father a less troubling and more praiseworthy death, that of a victim of a wartime
mustard gas attack that slowly but surely ravaged his lungs. During World War I, Charles Camp had indeed served as a U.S. Army
second lieutenant, seeing action in France at Baccarat and in the
Oise-Aisne Offensive. But obituaries and Princeton alumni rec-
ords, among other sources, do not bear out L'Engle's account of
her father's illness and death. Then and with regard to any number of other emotionally charged personal matters, L'Engle seems
simply to have told the story she needed to tell, without concern
for the facts.

As a member of the Smith College class of 1941, she continued
to hone her literary craft in classes taught by the novelists Mary
Ellen Chase and Leonard Ehrlich. She lived in French House,
earned good grades, and edited *The Smith College Monthly*, where
her tenure turned surprisingly stormy when fellow staff members,
led by Bettye Goldstein—the future Betty Friedan—succeeded in
transforming the literary magazine Madeleine cared about into a
political forum for debating the rapidly deteriorating world situation. In the course of agitating for curriculum reform, L'Engle
herself may have alienated members of the college administration

or faculty. She implied as much when in *A Circle of Quiet* she recalled having missed election to Phi Beta Kappa for reasons of "behavior." Perhaps posting defiant lines from Plato on her dorm room door had had something to do with it: "All learning which is acquired under compulsion has no hold upon the mind."

Dead at fifty-seven, Charles Camp missed by nearly a decade his daughter's first literary triumphs, the publication in the December 1944 *Mademoiselle* of a short story titled "Vicky" and, in that same month, a translation from the French of a story in the Grinnell College literary journal, *The Tanager*. The following February, *The Tanager* published another original story begun as a writing exercise at Smith. The latter piece, the semiautobiographical "Evening of a Governess," evoked the perfumed atmosphere and stiflingly status-conscious social order of the Madeleine character's school friend's household. Like Madeleine herself but on a far grander scale, the child of this wealthy family rarely sees her parents at home, dwelling almost entirely within the orbit of the staff. Dialogue was the strong suit of the journeyman effort, which dramatized the resentment felt by a young girl's governess toward her brusquely condescending employer, on the one hand, and the seemingly ungrateful child in her charge, on the other. It was a fragile piece of work but one that evinced definite talent and an alluringly sophisticated background. Queried by her first editors about how she wished her name to appear in print, the young writer took the opportunity to decide the question once and for all, choosing to be known not as Charles Wadsworth Camp's talented daughter but rather, in a cleaner victory for her, as "Madeleine L'Engle."

By then she was living in New York and pursuing a stage career in no small part because, as she later observed, she considered the theater "the best school for a writer." She may well have known all along that her big-boned, taller-than-average five-foot-nine-inch frame, slight limp, and sundry other minor physical imperfections stood to bar her from major success as an actor. By 1944, she had, in any case, won a coveted spot in the Theatre Guild acting troupe led by Eva Le Gallienne and Margaret Webster, albeit as an understudy and member of the ensemble destined for walk-on roles. It fell to her as well to serve as Miss Le Gallienne's personal secretary. The high point for L'Engle came in 1945 when she was chosen for both the Broadway and the touring company productions of *The Cherry Orchard*. Adding to her jubilation that year, she published her first novel, for which she garnered generally favorable reviews. *The New York Times*, noting *The Small Rain* as the work of a "young actress [who had] somehow managed to compose [it] during the hurry and bustle of a road tour," concluded that the novel presented "evidence of a fresh new talent." Sales were strong and steady enough to cover the author's living expenses for the next several years.

Rounding out this fateful time, Madeleine while on tour with *The Cherry Orchard* fell in love with a fellow cast member, the lanky, debonair Hugh Franklin, originally of Muskogee, Oklahoma. They married in Chicago in January 1946 and settled into an apartment in Greenwich Village where Leonard Bernstein was an upstairs neighbor. Untroubled by the curse of writer's block that commonly besets a second-time novelist, she published her next book, *Ilsa*, exactly one year after the first. The new novel did not fare nearly so well as had its predecessor; still, L'Engle had planted her flag as a writer. Now embarked on two challenging careers, and with an accomplished husband who shared her desire for children, L'Engle—the young Mrs. Franklin—had much to be proud of and doubtless more to look forward to from the new life she had forged on her own terms.

Taking a lead from theater friends, the Franklins in the summer after their wedding purchased a large tumbledown colonial-era farmhouse in Goshen, Connecticut, just over a hundred miles northeast of Manhattan. They continued to call New York home while the drafty old house was gradually made ready for year-round living. Along with countless baby boom–era couples, the Franklins had concluded that the city was no place to raise a family. Four years later, when they finally gave up their apartment and moved to Goshen full-time, Madeleine and Hugh were the parents of a three-year-old daughter named Josephine.

Other considerations may well have influenced the couple's decision to leave New York, including Hugh Franklin's apparent wish—or need—for a more dependable, less nerve-racking alternative to a life in the theater. The decade of the 1950s would coincide almost exactly with the long intermission in the taciturn Franklin's acting career, an interlude that, curiously, he spent operating Goshen's only general store (a business he purchased one day, seemingly on a whim, without prior experience and without first discussing the matter with his wife) and immersing himself, alongside Madeleine, in the community life that centered on the local Congregational church. On occasion Hugh even preached a Sunday morning sermon at the church, where Madeleine directed the choir. The Franklins of Oklahoma were born-and-bred Baptists, the Camps and L'Engles Episcopalians, but both Madeleine and Hugh were comfortable enough, in the company of their new friends, as congregants in what in any case was the only Protestant church of any description in town. Their family grew in 1952 with the birth of their son, Bion—named for Bion Barnett, cofounder of the Barnett Bank and the husband of Madeleine's grandmother Caroline L'Engle. Then, in 1956, Madeleine and Hugh adopted a third child, Maria, whose parents, who were friends of the couple, had both recently died. Four years later in *Meet the Austins*, L'Engle published a fictionalized account of the conflict-ridden changes in the family dynamic—for Hugh and Madeleine and the children alike—brought on by the adoption. *Meet the Austins* was her first juvenile novel (*And Both Were Young*, published in 1949, and *Camilla Dickinson*, published two years later, had both been released as novels for teens) and received some of the best reviews of any of the five novels that had followed *The Small Rain* at irregular intervals and at such great effort, given L'Engle's growing family responsibilities.

L'Engle's time of professional discouragement was far from over, however. In later years, she never wearied of recounting the protracted search for a publisher for her seventh work of fiction, *A Wrinkle in Time*. In characteristic fashion, she transformed the pivotal episode of her publishing history into mythic material, varying the number of rejections she had endured—had it been twenty-six? thirty-six?—with each retelling. A novelist for adults of the 1950s was far more likely than a writer for children to enjoy the benefit of professional representation. L'Engle was already a client of Theron Raines, then of the Ann Elmo Agency, when she presented him with the manuscript of her highly idiosyncratic juvenile novel about time travel, preteen female heroism, and cosmic redemption. Raines sent the manuscript out to editors in the usual way. Nonetheless, L'Engle had at least two more dramatic stories about how the manuscript finally found a home at Farrar, Straus and Giroux. In *A Circle of Quiet* she credited her initial contact with John Farrar, a partner in the firm, to the concerned intervention of an old friend of her mother's. And in one of her last interviews, she detailed a scenario that had the ring of a Christian miracle tale. In this latter version, one Sunday morning John Farrar was leaving Manhattan's Church of the Resurrection, where he and Madeleine both worshipped at the time, when he happened to spy the envelope containing the manuscript on a pew bench. By then, the book had received numerous rejections. That morning, L'Engle recalled, she had not so much forgotten the packet as finally resigned herself to the fact that no publisher would ever want the book. It thus was miraculous indeed for a publisher to come along at just the right moment and save the manuscript from oblivion. Or had he? The younger of L'Engle's two granddaughters, Charlotte Voiklis, who worked closely with her grand-mother on literary matters in the latter's later years and who then emerged as the chief custodian of L'Engle's literary estate, had heard her tell this improbable story before and doubted its authenticity.

For most of her adult life, Madeleine L'Engle enjoyed a stage actor's fine powers of recall and took casual pride, in the manner of the well-read men and women of her own and earlier generations, in seasoning her writing and conversation with lines from the immortals. "George MacDonald," she confided to readers of *Walking on Water*, a book of reflections on art and spirituality, "gives me renewed strength during times of trouble—times when I have seen people tempted to deny God—when he says, 'The Son of God suffered unto death, not that men might not suffer, but that their sufferings might be like his.'" In *A Circle of Quiet*, she noted, "Paul Klee said, 'Art does not reproduce the visible. Rather, it makes visible'" and "I think it was Toynbee who said that we are a sick society because we have refused to accept death and infinity." In *Walking on Water*, she recalled, "What I remember from Ruskin is the phrase: *the cursed animosity of inanimate objects*, which I mutter under my breath when I get in a tangle of wire coat hangers." Quoting T. S. Eliot, she admonished students, fellow writers, and librarians, among others, to "dare [to] disturb the universe."

L'Engle in turn was among the most quotable of writers. She could be acutely perceptive on the subject of human vulnerability. In *A Circle of Quiet*, a book in which she also cataloged the joys of country living and family togetherness, she wondered aloud: "But where, after we have made the great decision to leave the security of childhood and move on into the vastness of maturity, does anybody ever feel completely at home?"

She had a notable flair as well for the orphic and revelatory, writing, in *A Stone for a Pillow*: "I take the Bible too seriously to take it all literally"; and in *Many Waters*: "Some things have to be believed to be seen." And she could be endlessly droll. "It was not until I was nearly forty," she declared with tongue firmly in cheek in *The Irrational Season*, "that I discovered that higher math is easier than lower math." Arguing in *A Circle of Quiet* for the paradoxically liberating power of strict adherence to demanding literary forms such as the sonnet, she observed: "The amoeba has a minimum of structure, but I doubt if it has much fun." Art forms were, to her, no different in this regard from the structures of domestic life, and in particular family and marriage, the latter of which she so deftly analogized as a "two-part invention."

With a wink to the reader, she chose for the opening line of *A Wrinkle in Time*, her most audaciously original work of fiction, one of the hoariest of clichés: "It was a dark and stormy night." L'Engle herself was certainly aware of the old warhorse's literary provenance as line one, page one of Edward Bulwer-Lytton's much-maligned, much-parodied repository of Victorian purple prose, *Paul Clifford* (1830). Young readers were less likely to get the joke, but critics were sure to do so. And as L'Engle most certainly knew, critics were bound at a minimum to find *A Wrinkle in Time* something of a challenge, and the purists among them might well be put off by its aggressively unorthodox mongrelization of the genres of realism, science fiction, quest fantasy, and religious allegory. Of these four distinctive literary strands, only the first posed no obvious potential for controversy. Until that time, novels of contemporary or (more often) historical realism routinely triumphed at Newbery Medal time. Science fiction, on the other hand—the little of it that was published for the juvenile market—bore the stigma of all down-market pulp magazine fiction and thus had few champions in publishing or at the libraries. Juvenile fantasy literature, with certain, primarily British exceptions, had a dubious reputation among educators as a source of potential confusion in impressionable young people. As for fiction with a religious or spiritual subtext, recent state court and U.S. Supreme

Court rulings banning school prayer had left educators and children's book publishers alike feeling wary of any book that might ignite a similar controversy. Challenges to *A Wrinkle in Time* on grounds of its being un-Christian lay decades in the future.

L'Engle was fortunate in the timing of the book's release. *A Wrinkle in Time* debuted just one year after another, albeit very different, work of juvenile fantasy fiction overcame the initial skepticism of publishers to win near-universal critical and popular acclaim. As much a work of genre-bending originality as *A Wrinkle in Time*, *The Phantom Tollbooth* by Norton Juster, illustrated by Jules Feiffer, had the madcap manner and acrobatic wordplay of a Marx Brothers free-for-all—or of Lewis Carroll's *Alice's Adventures in Wonderland*. Its salty mix of verbal cleverness and brain-teasing philosophical gamesmanship asked of readers not so much that they willingly suspend their disbelief—as did L'Engle's more emotionally intense and plot-driven book—as that they simply go along for the ride.

Yet *The Phantom Tollbooth*'s resemblance to *A Wrinkle in Time* was also striking. Milo—like Meg—is a bored, unhappy, misunderstood preteen who struggles with schoolwork, with fitting in, and ultimately with the meaning of life. Feeling stifled in a world run largely by and for the benefit of grown-ups, Milo and Meg make their way to different worlds and undertake heroic quests that would seem to be well beyond their powers to complete, and complete them anyway. They return from their adventures emotionally strengthened, more knowing about the moral and intellectual challenges that growing up entails, and more at home with themselves. Since the time of their initial publication, three generations of young people have found the reading of these two books to be mind-expanding, life-changing experiences.

L'Engle won the Newbery Medal for *A Wrinkle in Time* in the same year that Ezra Jack Keats was awarded the Caldecott Medal for his picture book *The Snowy Day*. In both instances, the

American Library Association awards committee had chosen not to play it safe. The idyllic story line of Keats's picture book about a young child's adventures in a snow-covered urban landscape gave no hint of the provocative subtext embedded in its illustrations. The artist had chosen to depict Peter, the boy out playing in the snow, as an African-American child and had done so in an entirely offhand way, as much as to say that to do so was the most natural thing in the world. In reality, the gesture set Keats's picture book apart from nearly every American picture book that had come before it. By honoring that book within months after the forced integration of the University of Mississippi at Oxford and the submission by Congress to the states of the Twenty-fourth Amendment to the Constitution, abolishing poll taxes in federal elections, the all-white world of children's literature took a big step of its own toward integration.

The great—and greatly surprising—success of *A Wrinkle in Time* in the Newbery Medal competition was hardly less momentous for the future course of American children's literature. Together with *The Phantom Tollbooth*, it opened the American juvenile tradition to the literature of What if? as a rewarding and honorable alternative to realism in storytelling. Within a few short years, the fantasy and science fiction writers Lloyd Alexander, Susan Cooper, Ursula K. Le Guin, and Robert C. O'Brien had all launched their careers.

For L'Engle herself, winning the Newbery Medal proved to be a liberating experience on several counts. It gave her the professional validation she had been hungering for throughout the years of self-imposed exile in Goshen. It cemented her relationship with Farrar, Straus and Giroux, a distinguished literary house where she would have the freedom to experiment across genres and readerships. It substantially boosted both her current income and her long-term financial prospects, and as invitations to speak at library conventions and schools all around the country began to pour in, it gave her a new platform from which to perform in public and a whole new world of librarian and educator friends. It showed once and for all that she would not be heir to her mother's legacy of unrealized creative ambitions or even to her father's more mixed legacy of genuine accomplishment tinged with failed expectations. For the next four decades she published on average a book a year.

A second turning point in L'Engle's career came with the publication in 1972 of her memoir *A Circle of Quiet*. In an appreciative, though far from unreservedly favorable, review in *The New York Times*, Polly Longsworth offered a canny appraisal of the undeniable appeal of the award-winning author's first work of adult nonfiction. "Anyone," she began, "who has read many of Madeleine L'Engle's excellent novels for young people must hanker to know something about *her*, to find out why beautiful mothers and radiantly warm family life recur in her books, and why her female characters achieve fuller dimension than her male, and how she dares champion the forces of good in these dark times. The chance to know her comes on like a Newfoundland puppy in 'A Circle of Quiet.'"

For L'Engle, the very writing of this book, which she had undertaken with some trepidation, had combined aspects of a comfortable old experience and a thrilling new one: *A Circle of Quiet* represented both a variant on her lifelong practice of journal keeping and a bold extension of that practice into the public realm. Volume one of what came to be known collectively as the Crosswicks Journal was published when L'Engle was fifty-three and the first readers of *A Wrinkle in Time* were entering their twenties, graduating from college, and perhaps also struggling, as L'Engle had done at their age, with the competing demands of work and family. For young women who as preteen girls a decade earlier had caught compelling reflections of themselves in the out-of-sorts yet stupendously purposeful character Meg, the new book came just in time to offer some guidance through the minefields of mid-twentieth-century American womanhood.

L'Engle's memoir was book-ended, philosophically, by two earlier bestsellers by women she knew. L'Engle had met Jean Kerr, the author of *Please Don't Eat the Daisies* (1957), through Hugh, who had known Jean's husband, the theater critic Walter Kerr, since their student days together at Northwestern University. Kerr's breezy comic essays about coping with rambunctious children, temperamental interior decorators, and high-maintenance pets were, on the whole, far lighter in tone than L'Engle's ruminations about home and family and were firmly grounded in the sun-splashed world of postwar middle-class American suburban living. L'Engle wrote about the lighter side of home life as well, but she did not stop there. In her own review of *A Circle of Quiet*, Jean Kerr, after anointing it her "favorite" of all L'Engle's books, went on to suggest that the author's reflections on love, work, community life, the Cold War threat of nuclear annihilation, religious faith, and self-discovery held the promise of "great consolation" for "ordinary people" who wonder "why they bother to get out of bed in the morning." In an often bleak and sometimes menacing world, L'Engle, it seemed, had the rare ability to find hope and significance everywhere.

The second bookend was the work of L'Engle's Smith College schoolmate and sometime antagonist—a member of the class of 1942—Betty Friedan. Published in 1963, *The Feminine Mystique* issued a forceful critique of the status of women in American society, and in particular of the social pressures that systematically encouraged women to seek fulfillment only as wives and mothers rather than also as professionals in the workplace. Friedan's book became a major bestseller and propelled its author to fame and a leadership role in what soon afterward came to be known as the women's movement's second wave. While L'Engle clearly shared Friedan's hope that women would learn to define their self-worth as much from their success in the world of work as by their domestic relationships, she insisted that she herself was an "apolitical creature" and remained wary of movements and causes. L'Engle preferred—and one suspects that many of the readers who embraced her book did so as well—to negotiate life on her own terms rather than within the framework of a group effort. She bristled at the notion of herself as a member of an oppressed minority by virtue of her gender, a view that begged the question, of course, of whether she had not all her life enjoyed certain advantages available only to the privileged few. In defense of her aversion to political or social movements of any kind, she cited E. M. Forster, who in *Two Cheers for Democracy* had written: "I hate the idea of causes, and if I had to choose between betraying my country and betraying my friend, I hope I should have the guts to betray my country."

The one movement she passionately associated herself with was the church. It is unclear when L'Engle's religious faith first came to matter deeply to her. In *Two-Part Invention* she recalls frequenting a Greenwich Village Episcopal parish church during her eventful first years of living on her own. Church community life helped sustain her during the difficult Goshen decade. Then, a few years after her family's return to New York, she had one of the fateful encounters of her life when she met Edward Nason West, the canon sacrist at the Cathedral Church of St. John the Divine. From then until his death in January 1990, West was many things to L'Engle: her confessor and spiritual adviser, her alter ego, her office neighbor at the cathedral, and one of her closest friends.

West was the ranking authority on Anglican Church iconography and liturgy and a showman down to his bones. The pageantry of the cathedral Mass as meticulously choreographed by him appealed greatly not only to L'Engle's spiritual longings but to her theatrical instincts as well. It is no wonder that in *The Arm of the Starfish*, *The Young Unicorns*, *Dragons in the Waters*, and *Certain Women* she could not resist playfully turning West into fiction as the powerful and tantalizingly mysterious canon John Tallis. The name she had chosen for him was a typically nimble play on words, a mirror reference to the name of a well-known sixteenth-century liturgical composition, "Tallis's Canon."

Ultimately, L'Engle regarded herself as a church of one, a spiritual quester whose faith alternately flagged and soared in a manner that left her ever mindful of her vulnerability. The God she sought and often found was generous, all loving, and equipped with an earthy sense of humor. "I like some saints," she told an interviewer, "because they're funny. St. Theresa of Avila, for instance, who was out in her carriage and got stuck in the mud. God said, 'This is how I treat my friends, Theresa.' To which she replied, 'No wonder you have so few.'"

The interviews that follow draw on memories of Madeleine L'Engle that reach as far back as her childhood years. More often it is the adult L'Engle who is recalled in these pages, starting from her time as a young New York stage actress and novelist and ending with her death, in 2007, at the age of eighty-eight, after a long illness. During most of those last sixty years, she maintained regular contact with a large and ever-expanding circle of friends, professional colleagues, and acquaintances while also placing herself at the center of her own extended family, which for a time spanned four generations. By the 1970s she had become a well-known public figure, a celebrity of sorts and a peripatetic speaker on the literary, college, and Christian lecture circuits. The list of honors conferred on her grew and grew: the 1978 University of Southern Mississippi Medallion for her lifetime contribution to children's literature; the 1980 American Book Award for *A Swiftly Tilting Planet*; a 1981 Newbery Honor for *A Ring of Endless Light*;

the 1984 Regina Medal of the Catholic Library Association for distinguished contributions to children's literature; an honorary Doctor of Literature from Wheaton College in 1984; an honorary Doctor of Letters from her alma mater, Smith College, in 1986; the University of Minnesota's 1990 Kerlan Award in children's literature; and the American Library Association's 1998 Margaret A. Edwards Award for lifetime achievement in writing for the teen ages; among others. She received seventeen honorary degrees in all. In 1976 her collected papers were archived at Wheaton College. During the mid-1980s she was elected to a two-year term as president of the Authors Guild. And in a curious sidebar to all this, from 1970 to 1983 L'Engle also found herself the wife of a television star, Hugh Franklin having crossed the threshold of national celebrity in the role of Dr. Charles Tyler on the daytime soap opera *All My Children.*

The last years of her life were marked by periods of great sadness and loss that in all likelihood hastened L'Engle's physical and mental decline: the death in 1986 of Hugh Franklin, the death less than four years later of Edward West, and in 1999 the death of her son, Bion, of long-term alcoholism, at the age of forty-seven. About two years after the loss of Bion, she suffered a stroke that left her aware but diminished and put an end to her travels and her literary life.


In pursuit of a fully rounded portrait of Madeleine L'Engle from living memory, it seemed essential to hear not only from as many as possible of the people who knew her most intimately but also from some whose more fleeting encounters were representative of those of the thousands of students, teachers, librarians, aspiring writers, neighbors, and others who crossed her path in the course of a richly complex life enacted largely in public view.

The portrait that emerges is—and was bound to be— impressionistic in nature. The principal reason for this is that

L'Engle carefully departmentalized her vast and densely populated universe. People important to her in one sphere of her life typically did not meet those important to her in the others. The inveterate fan and sometime practitioner of the mystery genre knew very well how to scatter the clues to her own story, an overwhelmingly admirable tale that at times, however, bore scant resemblance to the placid domestic idyll of *A Circle of Quiet* and its sequels, as a controversial profile of L'Engle published in *The New Yorker*, in April 2004, made clear. Some of the most deep-seated family conflicts also proved to be among the longest lived. Regrettably, L'Engle's adopted daughter, Maria, was among the few people approached about an interview for this book who declined.

All but three of the interviews were recorded in person or by telephone. Two (those with James Cross Giblin and Mary Pope Osborne) were done via e-mail. One (Lee Kingman's) was completed by letter. In several instances where the reminiscences and remarks of an interview subject seemed naturally to coalesce into a continuous narrative, I opted to edit myself out of the exchange. In every instance, my aim has been to maintain absolute fidelity to the substance and context of my interviewees' words.

On June 1, 2002, I traveled by bus from New York City to Goshen, Connecticut, to interview Madeleine L'Engle for a book for young readers called *The Wand in the Word: Conversations with Writers of Fantasy*. I had hesitated about asking for an interview, having heard vague rumors of the author's ill health. A publicist forwarded my request to L'Engle's granddaughter Charlotte, who offered to make the arrangements, provided I understood that her grandmother had "good days and bad days" and that the interview might well have to be cut short or canceled.

I decided to take my chances and began to sketch out my questions for a writer who had been interviewed so many times before.

I had of course read and admired a great many of her books and had heard L'Engle speak at a PEN American Center forum years earlier. I had once even chatted briefly with her at a party in her honor. On the latter occasion I asked L'Engle if she had known the late Ursula Nordstrom, the visionary publisher of Harper Junior Books, who shared her theater background and iconoclastic spirit and whose letters I had edited. To my surprise, she reacted to the mere mention of Nordstrom's name as an irritant. Catching herself, she explained that Nordstrom, like so many of her fellow editors, had rejected *A Wrinkle in Time*. Oh dear, I thought, and feeling suddenly out of place, I wished her a good evening and slipped back into the crowd.

That party had been a good five years earlier. When the bus pulled in at Goshen, Charlotte was waiting for me. It was a short drive to Crosswicks, where, attended by Charlotte and a professional caregiver, L'Engle greeted me from her wheelchair in the big, open kitchen of the airy, light-filled one-story cottage, just across the road from the main house, that had become her full-time residence. As we began to talk, I sensed a distinct remoteness in her tone and manner. She felt unreachable. Try as I might to make her laugh, or to pique her interest by showing her some snapshots I had brought along of the Cathedral of St. John the Divine, nothing was working. She responded to each of my questions but only with a perfunctory sentence or two. After half an hour of this, her caregiver wheeled her away for a nap, and I was escorted to the sunroom, where it was suggested that I might read the paper until it was time for the bus back to the city. Well, Charlotte had warned me.

As it turned out, my day with Madeleine L'Engle was far from over, however. The real interview began when, an hour or so later, the sunroom door burst open and, unaccompanied, L'Engle wheeled herself up to me and in the vigorous voice of a very different person asked, "Want to talk some more?" I switched on my recorder, and we immediately fell into animated conversation. What followed was an utterly remarkable performance, and an act of generosity that must have drawn on every ounce of her strength and determination. I recognized, from the published interviews I had prepped on, her responses to some of my questions. But much of what she said, I thought, was new. When I asked her about the mail she received from readers, L'Engle told the story of a young reader of *A Wrinkle in Time* who ended what had seemed a typical fan letter with the news that he was ill with cancer. "We corresponded," she said, "until he died. It was hard and wonderful both." Then L'Engle said, "My books are not bad books to die with." As she uttered this extraordinary remark, a chill ran up my spine.

"What do you mean?" I asked her.

"What I mean," she said, "is that when I read a book, if it makes me feel more alive, then it's a good book to die with. That," said L'Engle, "is why certain books last."

# MADELEINE

## IN THE

# MAKING

Mary "Sister" L'Engle Avent was born and raised in Jacksonville, Florida. She and Madeleine L'Engle were cousins.

*Q: How did you meet Madeleine L'Engle?*

A: Her grandmother Caroline Hallowes L'Engle Barnett was my aunt—the sister of my father, Camillus Saunders L'Engle. Madeleine was two years older than me and about six years old when I first knew her. She and her parents would occasionally come down to Jacksonville, Florida, from New York by train. They would come to visit her grandfather and her grandmother, who by then had separated. It was a very ugly kind of situation.

What happened was that Mr. Bion Hall Barnett, having sired four children, told my aunt—Madeleine's grandmother, whom I called Aunt Lina—that he wanted a divorce.* Her answer to him was "We don't get a divorce in this family." She flat out refused to divorce him. "You will be my husband," she told him, "until I die." Mr. Barnett had fallen in love with a young Frenchwoman. When Aunt Lina said no to a divorce, he took the new love of his life and her two daughters and went with them to live in France.

---

*In 1877, Caroline Hallowes L'Engle's husband, Bion Hall Barnett, co-founded the Jacksonville-based Barnett Bank, which grew to be the largest bank in Florida.

After a while, the future Mrs. Barnett, who was a devout Catholic, got tired of living with Mr. Barnett as a companion, and so he adopted her as his daughter! Then, when Aunt Lina finally died, he did marry her, but not before opening a very large account with the pope in order to "unclaim" her as an adopted daughter. Eventually, Mr. Barnett and his new wife moved back to Jacksonville. She died before he did. This was a great scandal in the 1920s in a small city like Jacksonville. Everyone in Jacksonville knew the story, and it hung like a cloud over Madeleine's head, because people felt very sorry for her grandmother. It was a very embarrassing situation.

My earliest impressions of Madeleine were not very favorable. She didn't know how to play like the rest of us girls. For example, she didn't know how to ride a bicycle, which was a favorite thing for us girls to do. Her grandfather lived at the Park Lane Apartments, which was located in a beautiful setting along the banks of the St. Johns River, by a park that was a good place for bicycling. Both her parents would say to Madeleine, "You've got to play with Sister"—Sister was my nickname—"this afternoon." Well, that wasn't what she wanted to do. My mother would say, "Cousin Madeleine [Madeleine's mother] wants you to come down and be with Madeleine." And I would say, "Oh, yuck, Mom. I don't want to do that!" She was such a loner, always writing or reading. Her father was a New York theater critic, and when they were up north, her parents were often out at night, leaving her alone or with her nanny. As I later realized, her behavior was due in part to her having spent so much time by herself during her early life while her mother and father were out seeing plays.

Jacksonville was a small, quiet, beginning-to-come-up town. Florida had not been found yet, really. Henry Flagler had built the Florida East Coast Railway through Jacksonville on its way to Miami. The banks in town were very strong, as was the practice of law. Lumber was big and the port was good. Jacksonville sits on the St. Johns River, which flows into the Atlantic Ocean about eighteen miles away. It's a huge river, and so shipping was good. About forty miles away, St. Augustine was quite a place of note as a vacation resort. In the summer, the men in Jacksonville all wore white linen suits. When seersucker suits became fashionable, my father would call them his "downtown pajamas."

Jacksonville had a garden club and two country clubs—one group had gotten mad at the other and built a little farther out of town. There was the side of the river that you lived on and the other side, which had not yet been developed. In 1933, when Madeleine's parents returned from living in Europe, they bought a house in Jacksonville. It was a nice house but not very grand, and it was on the wrong side of the river. It was not in Riverside or Avondale, which were considered the two good neighborhoods, but closer to town, and it was not far from her grandmother's beach house.

Madeleine was very close to her grandmother, who had her own apartment in the Park Lane Apartments as well as a great house down at what is now called Jacksonville Beach. We called it Pablo at the time. Madeleine loved to go there, in part because it was a good place to be alone. The house, which was named Red Gables and which I think is gone now, was one of our favorite, favorite places. It was right on the ocean, along a part of the beach that had not yet been "found." It was a comfortable, rambling old wooden house with big porches and long windows because you counted on the breeze to cool it. It was furnished informally with wicker furniture, that kind of thing. Very few people lived at the beach all year round and Red Gables was Aunt Lina's summer house, but she would stay there a great deal of the time, and Madeleine would go down there a great deal, too.

Madeleine's mother was the oldest daughter of four in her

family, very nice-looking but a little on the shy side, very pleasant but not really warm. She spoke in a quiet voice with a southern accent. She had been raised in Jacksonville but long before my time. Then she married this gentleman from the North who had been badly hurt during World War I, and they had lived together in New York in circumstances completely unlike anything here in Jacksonville. So Madeleine's mother knew two different worlds, and I think she may have felt about New York the same way that Madeleine felt about Jacksonville.

As a New Yorker, Madeleine was completely oblivious to the southern customs of the time. She was always polite, but she was also shy. Between one thing and another, she had a very hard time with us and we with her. When we girls were in our late teens and were all making our debuts and being introduced into the hierarchy of society, Madeleine remained very much the outsider. She would be invited to many of the parties, and she would always say that she couldn't stand the food. We had lots of luncheons, at which chicken salad was always served. Madeleine said she didn't like chicken salad. She was just completely out of place at that time and in that part of the world.

Her one close friend in Jacksonville was Pat Collins [later Cowdery], and they were very close.* Pat was a delightful, lovely person, very cordial, very open, and she was exactly Madeleine's age. When Madeleine's family moved to Jacksonville, Madeleine was sent to boarding school in Charleston, South Carolina. But prior to going off to Smith College, in order to prepare for some entrance or placement exams she was going to take, Madeleine enrolled in summer courses at the Bartram School for Girls, which was a small local private school, and I think that that is where she

---

*Patricia Collins Cowdery became a medical doctor and in 1972 was the first woman to be appointed head of Jacksonville's Department of Health, Welfare, and Bioenvironmental Services.

and Pat became good friends. She and Madeleine remained close even late in life.

As a grown-up, Madeleine would sometimes come down to Jacksonville by herself and head straight for Orange Park, where Pat's family had a house. Orange Park is a small community out on the St. Johns River, ten miles out of town, where the houses are spread far enough apart that you have no near neighbors. We say it is "in town but out of town." When you are in Orange Park, you feel completely away from everything. Out there, Madeleine had no social obligations. She didn't have to be anyplace that she didn't want to be or listen to other people discuss among themselves what they had had that day for lunch. She could just be herself and be with Pat and relax. Madeleine might be there for ten days or two weeks without anybody knowing it.

My grandparents John Claudius L'Engle and Susan Philippa Fatio had eleven children, all of whom were born and lived in the Jacksonville area. So the woods were full of L'Engles. If your name was L'Engle, it was generally something to be very proud of. But then you could have killed some of the others who were also named L'Engle. We would say, "He might be my cousin, but I don't know him!" So you would pick and choose.

My father's younger sister, my aunt Tracy L'Engle, was very much intrigued by the theater.* She had vague fantasies about being an actress and thought she should have been accepted immediately. She wrote poetry as well, but I would say that all in all she was far better known for her temper. Tracy lived in New York for

---

*Katherine Tracy L'Engle Angas, the daughter of Camille Saunders and Carrie Hubbard L'Engle, pursued a variety of careers in the arts. She wrote for and performed on radio, lectured on fashion, edited encyclopedias, dabbled in fiction writing, directed amateur theatricals, and self-published a memoir and a book of poems. Her papers, which are archived at the University of Florida's George A. Smathers Libraries, include correspondence with Madeleine L'Engle, H. L. Mencken, Zora Neale Hurston, and others.

quite some time, although I don't think she pursued her dream of the theater too seriously while there.

Tracy was a character, and Madeleine knew her well. They probably met when Madeleine was in her teens, which would have been in the late 1930s. Madeleine was very comfortable with my aunt, who had graduated from Wellesley and had a mind of her own. She was haughty. Her two brothers were older than she, and come World War I, they were married with children. When neither of the brothers offered their services to their country, Tracy said, "By damn, if you all are such weaklings, I'm going to go!" And so she did, running military canteens, giving the soldiers their mail, that kind of thing. She had a uniform and was proud of it. And she was very ashamed that her two brothers hadn't enlisted in the service. She was very strong and adventurous; in fact, "strong" is a very weak word for Tracy! At one time when she was still quite young, she became so upset with her father after he had reprimanded her that she moved out and never spoke to him again. After that incident, she lived with us instead. Madeleine looked up to her. She and Tracy were very much alike. They were very determined to do things their way, and to hell with what anybody else said.

There is a saying in the L'Engle family that refers to the fact that we're all stubborn and that we have all got our own ways. You might say to one of your relatives: "You have certainly inherited a lot of the L'Engle-arities!" Madeleine had all of the L'Engle-arities. The Barnetts were pretty strong themselves, so you can imagine what that added up to. Mrs. Barnett—Madeleine's grandmother—was a L'Engle too, so she got it on both sides.

Madeleine's name was a combination of her mother's name and her grandmother's name. She named her own son after her grandfather Bion Barnett. Madeleine also had an uncle named Bion, who was her mother's youngest brother. *That* Bion Barnett was a writer and an artist, although I don't think he made a living by either.* His oil paintings—landscapes and beach scenes, scenes from around the river—were lovely, and he did sell them on occasion. But people liked his paintings because the scenes were familiar, and his banker father paid his bills. He too married a French girl. I'm sure that he and Madeleine knew of each other. Bion's oldest daughter wanted to be a writer as well.

I had not seen Madeleine for a long time when she and I got together for a very brief visit, in New York, probably in 1941. This was the one and only time I saw her in New York. She spoke about wanting to be on the stage. We chatted and asked each other what we were doing, and then we said goodbye. It was a very brief visit. She was not the friendly type, and I still couldn't understand her aloofness. She couldn't understand how I could be so flighty and gregarious. Her life and mine were just so different. By then we had at least become mature enough to acknowledge each other's differences. As far as she was concerned, I was a cousin from Jacksonville. As far as I was concerned, she was a cousin from New York.

In later life—I would say during the 1970s—I saw Madeleine twice in Jacksonville. Once she gave a graduation talk at Bartram, the school where she had done her summer studies. She gave another talk at Bolles, which started out as a military school for boys and which later merged with Bartram. Madeleine had become very friendly with Bartram's two headmistresses. I went to hear her speak on both occasions and was completely mesmerized. She was very cool and calm, with a little bit of a sophisticated humor. The audience all loved her. They saw her as a good writer who had once lived here and had come back to town.

---

*Son of the co-founder of the Barnett Bank, Bion H. Barnett Jr. was a painter living in France when he met his wife, Yvonne Charnott Barnett, who was an accomplished pianist. Following the outbreak of World War II, the couple and their three daughters resettled in Bion Barnett's native Jacksonville.

I have most of Madeleine's books. I bought them myself. You'll get a lot of Madeleine's history from *The Summer of the Great-Grandmother*, which I thought was an accurate description. There are still several Barnetts here. But I guess I am the last of the L'Engles of Jacksonville.

# NANCY BRUCE

Nancy Bruce's older sister was the late Dr. Patricia Collins Cowdery, Madeleine L'Engle's closest friend from her Jacksonville, Florida, years.

*Q: How did you meet Madeleine L'Engle?*

A: I knew Madeleine, but mainly it was my sister, Pat, who knew her well. They were best friends, starting back in the late 1930s, when Madeleine and Pat were at a small girls' school together in Jacksonville, Florida, called Glynlea and later renamed Bartram. My sister was enrolled as a student at Glynlea, and Madeleine spent a short time there to be tutored for her college entrance exams. It all worked out well because Madeleine went on to Smith and my sister went to Vassar. The story was that four years later, at her college graduation, Madeleine was so unenthusiastic about the ceremony that she marched in at the very back of the line, dressed in a raincoat rather than an academic gown.

After college, Pat went to medical school in Philadelphia, married, and returned to Jacksonville. Madeleine moved to New York to work in Eva Le Gallienne's acting company. I saw Madeleine there when she had an apartment on West Tenth Street. I was a student at Vassar, and Pat was teaching at Barnard for a year. Madeleine had a roommate from Jacksonville named Frances Burnett, who was a talented pianist. Unfortunately for Frances, she suffered from stage fright and for that reason was never able to have a career.

I had followed Pat to Bartram, where—to give you an idea of my small group—my best friend was Selden Kirby-Smith, who married Lawrence Ferlinghetti. Her grandfather was Edmund Kirby-Smith, the last Confederate general to surrender!* I saw Selden and Lawrence a lot. But Pat wouldn't have been interested in them. My sister and I were not all that close until much later in our lives. Another of my classmates, Palmer Daniels, was a cousin of Madeleine's. Madeleine had lots of cousins in Jacksonville.

I would say that Jacksonville was very . . . *warm*. It was not a place I would have returned to, as my sister, Pat, did. It was a very class-conscious place, and of course it was segregated. As young people, we were all so used to segregation that I don't think we gave it any thought at the time.

My mother taught Sunday school and gave piano lessons. My father was a lawyer who worked in real estate. He and the other men all went hunting. Hunting is what the men of Jacksonville did. We children used to get little animals and skin them and make dolls' clothes out of the hides. Not Madeleine, however.

My father was one of eight boys, and one of my uncles was a man named Charles Wallace Collins. I don't think that Madeleine ever met Charles Wallace, but Pat may have told her about him. He was a well-known lawyer during the Franklin Roosevelt era, a prominent southern Democrat and states' rights advocate, and the author of a book called *Whither Solid South?* He lived outside of Washington, D.C., in a historic house known as Harmony Hall,

---

*Edmund Kirby-Smith was the Confederate general in command of the Trans-Mississippi Department of the Confederacy following the fall of Vicksburg. Kirby-Smith negotiated the surrender of his department on May 26, 1865, well over a month after Robert E. Lee's surrender to Ulysses S. Grant at Appomattox, Virginia.

which he was responsible for restoring. It was an impressive house but not all that harmonious from what I heard! There were one or two other Charles Wallaces in the family down through the generations. It was a family name, and I think that Madeleine liked the sound of it. My father's twin brother was Littlebury Calhoun Collins. I'm surprised Madeleine didn't use that name!

Pat and Madeleine were like sisters, I guess. It's hard to know just why. Pat was not religious. As a doctor, she was, of course, interested in science. The main thing about them was that they were both sort of odd! They were both loners. Madeleine didn't like Jacksonville society, and maybe that's why she and my sister got along. They did not fit in within the social group.

Later, Madeleine would visit Pat in Jacksonville. My sister's house there was beyond help. Madeleine would tell Pat, "Your house is getting to be more than ratty." She would have notes to herself pinned all over. Her boys shared a room with a dresser that was propped up with paperback books. There was a bed for the dog. Madeleine wanted her to spruce it up and gave her a quilt as a present for the bed that guests slept on. It was such a contrast to the "good life" that Madeleine's mother knew in her later years in Jacksonville, with her live-in maid named Dinah. I do recall Mrs. Camp as a lovely woman without a trace of snobbishness. Eventually, she bought Dinah a house of her own. And that was when Mrs. Camp moved up to Goshen to live with Hugh and Madeleine at Crosswicks.

In their later years Pat and Madeleine would sometimes travel together. Madeleine was in London in 1995 and got Pat to come over and join her. My sister had never had a passport! Madeleine and she also went to the Caribbean together. Pat would go up to New York for Madeleine's book parties. When she went to Crosswicks, she would have to chauffeur Madeleine around to parties. When Hugh was quite ill, she would go to Goshen frequently just to keep Madeleine intact. One time, my husband, Victor, and

I picked Pat up at Crosswicks. Madeleine was fond of my husband, who was a scientist and a professor at Princeton—an expert on circadian rhythms. Madeleine liked to ask him questions about his research.

Our neighbor on Martha's Vineyard was Bishop Paul Moore of the Episcopal Diocese of New York, and I got the distinct impression that Madeleine disliked Moore's liberal politics when I had a political discussion with her at Crosswicks. Paul Moore was a limousine liberal and was a well-known figure on the cocktail circuit on Martha's Vineyard. I was more of a regular liberal who marched in Washington and New York against the Vietnam War. I kept marching and marching! During that conversation with Madeleine, I discovered that she was neither kind of liberal, politically speaking. Let's just say that it came to my attention that she was not one of my group!

## LEE KINGMAN

Lee Kingman headed Houghton Mifflin's children's book department during the mid-1940s. She is the author of more than thirty books for children and teens as well as an editor of reference works about juvenile literature.

While I was at Smith in 1939–40, a writing seminar was conducted by Leonard Ehrlich, author of *God's Angry Man*, a book published in 1932 that gave him enough of a reputation as a writer to be recruited by a college. As I remember him, he was a bit shy—perhaps just not at ease with a dozen gabbling girls—but he did not mind criticizing our writing.

We met in what must have been Ehrlich's living quarters at the college—in a very small room with dim lighting, a few chairs, and a carpet to sit on. All of us eager-to-be-published writers were seniors, except for one, a junior—Madeleine Camp. We were impressed—a junior daring to advance to a seminar with seniors? She must have used strong powers of persuasion with the liberal arts department to let her take that seminar—or maybe the indomitable Mary Ellen Chase ordered Ehrlich to do so.*

I do remember Madeleine as a bit tall and leggy, and she was

*From 1926 until her retirement in 1955, the novelist, memoirist, and literary scholar Mary Ellen Chase taught popular courses at Smith College on the English novel and the King James Bible.

often demoted by the seniors in the group to floor sitting. She was quiet as we listened to Ehrlich read bits and pieces from our stories, essays, and articles, but she wasn't afraid to ask lots of questions. Maybe she had read *God's Angry Man*—and knew that it had been praised by critics as Literature. Clifton Fadiman, in his foreword to the Readers Club edition, pontificated about Ehrlich's writing, noting that it had two rare qualities: "the quality of moral passion [and] the quality of tragic imagination." Now, as I think of Madeleine L'Engle's books, I wonder how much she absorbed from Ehrlich, the qualities of his own writing, and that seminar experience. Her books for the young—and the old!—do have both qualities that Fadiman found in our teacher's writing.

I do still have a feeling about that Madeleine Camp—that in some sense she was apart from us, the group of hopeful gabblers. To say she seemed "otherworldly" doesn't quite define it, but none of us knew what a difficult childhood she had had, which I learned about only from the *New Yorker* profile piece—"The Storyteller," by Cynthia Zarin. I doubt that any of us in that seminar had a clue to her past—or to what she might become.

## GAY JORDAN

Gay Jordan is a retired actress.

In 1951, I toured as a cast member in S. N. Behrmann's *I Know My Love*, starring Alfred Lunt and Lynn Fontanne. The play had opened on Broadway in November 1949 at the Shubert Theatre, where it ran for 247 performances. Hugh Franklin was a member of the original Broadway cast, and he toured with the show too. We started in New Haven and ended in San Francisco, with stops at a great many cities in between. I got my part by reading onstage for Miss Fontanne after a performance. She was sitting in the audience as I read. Afterward, she said, "My dear, you don't look a bit like me from up front, but from out front you could be another Lynn Fontanne!" I was speechless and thrilled.

My memory of our New Haven opening is that my shoes had not been scratched, which meant that I had a tendency to go slipping and sliding offstage. Later, when I went to apologize to Miss Fontanne for all the noise I had been making, I thought she might fire me on the spot. Instead, all she said was "I heard you hurtling around back there." She and her husband were absolutely wonderful people.

In Bangor, Miss Fontanne tripped coming out of the hotel on her way to the theater and broke her arm. Without skipping a beat, she said, "Gay wore a scarf to the theater. I'll need that scarf for my third-act sling." Then she sent somebody around to borrow the scarf from me. She was incredible! That evening, Mr. Lunt came out in front of the curtain before the performance to announce that we'd had an accident, but that everything was fine. The show would go on! He joked that if *he* had had the accident, things might have been quite different. He closed by inviting everyone to "ignore the cast and enjoy the play."

Hugh was what we called a "featured player." He was a wonderful actor and a very charming, handsome man. In *I Know My Love*, he played Daniel Talbot, the manager of a factory that had once been run by Mr. Lunt's father. He was a soft-spoken man with a baritone voice. On the train, he would go around and sit with various members of the cast. He was always outgoing and giving.

You never knew what might happen on the road. In Pittsburgh, my hometown, we had a blizzard, and I almost didn't make it from my parents' house to the theater on time. From there we went to Detroit. Because of the snow, the scenery and costumes hadn't arrived for opening night, so we all put on our most colorful outfits. Mr. Lunt made a speech to that audience too, and then, to make up for the lack of scenery, he gave the audience a running commentary, sort of like the stage manager in *Our Town*. It was quite a memorable evening of theater.

The critics always praised the Lunts. *They* were the reason that audiences came to see the show. The reviewers treated the rest of us as incidental. Still, it was a great experience to work with them, especially for someone just starting out like me. And the Lunts were extremely loyal to the people they worked with. Actors would work in play after play of theirs.

Mr. and Mrs. Lunt had their own bedroom on the train, but the rest of us had uppers and lowers with curtains across. We might stay for a week or two in a city, or just three days and then go on for another three days somewhere else. We lived out of our trunks and cooked in our rooms whenever we could. Mr. Lunt said once, "The top of a toilet is the best breadboard you'll ever find."

If you were married, your husband or wife generally didn't come along on tours, so you might be separated for a year. On tour, Hugh was very much the married man and would often talk about his family. There was no hanky-panky that I know of! Madeleine joined Hugh briefly when we played Chicago. We didn't socialize much, but she must have made a meal for some of us because I recall thinking at the time that Madeleine was a "very good hotel cook."

KATHARINE WEBER

Katharine Weber is a novelist and the author of a family memoir, *The Memory of All That*.

*Q: Tell me how you met Madeleine L'Engle.*

A: I met Madeleine in June 1987, on assignment to interview her for a magazine. I went up to see her at her home in Connecticut. This was less than a year after her husband, Hugh Franklin, had died. In the course of the conversation, I asked her a question that I often liked to ask writers: What was her first published work of fiction? She described a story about two privileged little girls and the rich household in which one of them lived and the very brittle housekeeper who was observing them.* Madeleine had written the story as a senior at Smith College. Her writing teacher had said, "Now write it again from the point of view of the governess," instead of from that of the little girl who was visiting the rich household. So she rewrote it from the point of view of the governess, and it was that second version of the story, "Evening of a Governess," that was published in *The Tanager* soon after she was graduated from Smith. Madeleine talked about how the story had been inspired by visiting her own best friend, in her family's splendid New York household, when she was very young.

---

*The story referred to here, "Evening of a Governess," was among L'Engle's first publications, but not the very first. See Introduction, page 9.

I already had an inkling that Madeleine had a connection to members of my family, and now something made me ask her: "What was the name of your best friend, the rich little girl?" Madeleine said, "April Warburg." And that was when it connected for me. I said, "That's my aunt April."* April Warburg is my mother's older sister. Madeleine looked at me and said, "Oh, you're Andrea's daughter." She could see it in my face. She had known my mother as well. But April had been in Madeleine's class at the Brearley School in New York in the early 1920s, and Madeleine had spent quite a lot of time with April in that household. Knowing all this sort of derailed the literary profile. It made the article harder to write. We kept returning to personal matters that were a distraction from what I was there to do, and portions of our conversation were not recorded. But that was the beginning of my friendship with Madeleine. The family connection made it seem as if we already knew each other in a way. There were all these common points of reference. The mother in Madeleine's story, putting on her makeup as the girls sat on the bed and watched, was my grandmother! I put her in touch with my aunt April, and they had lunch. They were both in their seventies by then, and I think they found that they no longer had very much in common. But they had a fond reunion after all those years.

After discussing her first story in *The Tanager*, she told me she would look for the manuscript, which she thought she must have filed somewhere. A few days later, in the mail, came the original typescript of the story, with a note telling me I could keep it. It was startling, how casually she could give away the manuscript of her first published story, and it felt, if I may say this without seeming self-important or pretentious, like a benediction of sorts.

*April Warburg was the eldest daughter of James Paul Warburg, a prominent New York banker and adviser to President Franklin D. Roosevelt.

During that same five-hour lunch at Crosswicks, we also discovered another odd point of connection in the fact that her husband, Hugh Franklin, had for many years played Dr. Tyler on *All My Children*, and my father's first wife, Fran Heflin, had played Mona Kane, his television wife. So my father's first wife was the woman who the public thought was Madeleine's husband's wife! When Madeleine found this out, she laughed and said, "We're practically family!" She encouraged me to be in touch with Fran Heflin, and I was just getting up my nerve to do that when Fran died. It had been a bitter divorce, and I'm not so sure that she would have wanted to talk to me, but I would have liked to talk to her, even if she had told me only terrible, terrible things about my father. It had been a short marriage, the whole of it taking place within the two-year Broadway run of *I Remember Mama*, in which Fran played Christine. Madeleine had such a theater background, and I think she had known Fran from before *All My Children*.

*Q: What did Madeleine tell you about her childhood?*

A: She told me that her mother was a gifted pianist. My grandmother Kay Swift, who had started out as Katharine Faulkner Swift and then married my grandfather James Warburg, in 1918, was a very gifted classical pianist.* She met my grandfather when she was the pianist in a classical trio that was the hired musical entertainment at a Warburg family tea. Kay at this time was also just beginning to write popular music. In the late 1920s, she and George Gershwin started their ten-year romance.

Once, Madeleine recalled, she was playing with April at the Warburg house on Seventieth Street when her mother came to pick her up. Her mother was sent upstairs, and apparently she

---

*Katharine Faulkner "Kay" Swift was a musician and composer who divorced James Paul Warburg after becoming romantically involved with George Gershwin.

stopped outside the living room and stood there listening as my grandmother played the piano. She just stood there listening, too shy to go in, or perhaps just not wanting to interrupt. This was Madeleine's mother. And then her mother did go in, and still she hung back. Apparently, my grandmother knew that Madeleine's mother was a pianist—perhaps Madeleine herself had told her—and she asked to hear her play. My grandmother even offered to arrange for George Gershwin to hear her play. Madeleine's mother never would take her up on the offer, whether it was because she was shy or afraid, I don't know. But I do know that it had been a genuine offer. It was the kind of thing that my grandmother, who was not a self-important person, did all the time. She was always helping people with talent to get ahead. So that story was particularly poignant to me.

*Q: What do you think drew April and Madeleine together as children?*

A: They were both wildly imaginative girls who saw a great deal and on whom nothing was wasted. My aunt April was going to study opera but ended up marrying her much older voice teacher. She derailed at that point, never pursuing a career. But as a child, she was enormously bright and observant. She grew up in very odd circumstances, with the George Gershwin affair permeating every corner of family life. And I think that she and Madeleine, whether it was spoken about or not, would have been onto everyone and everything. Each would also have been drawn to the other's humor and imagination. And then there was just the fact of being in the same class at Brearley.

Madeleine was a funny-looking kid—gawky, tall—and self-conscious about it. In conversations with me she said that she thought she looked like a grand ostrich. She always felt most at home in books. *Anne of Green Gables* and Lucy Maud Montgomery's other books—especially *Emily of New Moon*—were very important to Madeleine, in part because it was in a way *her* childhood that they described. That was the world she lived in imaginatively. Madeleine referred more than once to Anne of Green Gables as having been one of her childhood friends, and she and April would have had Anne in common.

The Warburg house was a house full of books, and certainly Madeleine was drawn to April for that reason too. April was a very well-read girl. My grandmother came from a very literate family, and I have on my shelves her childhood copies of books by Howard Pyle, Katharine Pyle, E. Nesbit, E. F. Benson's *David Blaize and the Blue Door*—children's books from the 1880s and 1890s, some of which are now obscure, and on through my mother's childhood books from the 1920s. Madeleine talked about my grandmother reading to the girls at teatime, which might be the only time she spent with the children during the day if she was going out to a dinner party in the evening.

The three Warburg sisters were poor little rich girls raised by a governess. My mother was the middle one. April was the oldest. The other two sisters were adorable children, cute as buttons, and they were always dressed alike, which was to April's disadvantage. She would tell the story about how people would always react on seeing the three of them. "*Ooooh*, look how cute! There's Kay," someone would say. And then, "*Ooooh*, look how adorable! There's Andrea." Then inevitably there would come the disappointed sigh. "Oh. There's April." That's how April would tell the story. Some of that becomes self-fulfilling. When April was an adult and at the peak of her beauty, she looked like Ava Gardner! But in her mind she was always the odd man out in that family.

*Q: Did Madeleine's family move in the same circles of New York society as the Warburgs?*

A: No. But before my grandmother married into the Warburg family—the first mixed marriage for both families—her life would have been a lot like that of Madeleine and her parents. My grandmother was born into a genteel, educated family, and she grew up in a fourth-floor walk-up on the Upper West Side. Her father was a music and art critic for New York newspapers. Her mother was English and very cultured. It was a house filled with music and literature and not much money. All in all, it was a very similar sort of background to Madeleine's, I would say.

The atmosphere and culture of the household my mother grew up in was very much set by her mother. Her father, Jimmy Warburg, was so eager to get off the "Warburg anthill" that he wouldn't allow very much that was Warburgian into the house, and he made it clear that whatever Katharine Faulkner Swift Warburg wanted was fine with him, starting with a Christmas tree and Easter celebrations. It would have been a more moneyed version of what Madeleine knew.

My mother grew up not knowing she was Jewish until one day Florence Straus, her classmate at Brearley, happened to remark, "We're the two Jews." Of course, it would be a Straus and a Warburg that a school like Brearley would have! A visit to my grandmother's house would not have been much like walking into the Felix Warburgs' much fancier and much more Jewish home—the mansion that today houses the Jewish Museum, at 1109 Fifth Avenue. At Kay and Jimmy Warburgs' the emphasis was on music and books, all of which Madeleine would have been at home with, even with all the servants around, who had obviously got her attention since that is what her short story is about. It is a story about all these servants coming and going.

*Q: Madeleine's father took her to the opera when she was quite young.*

A: And by the time my grandmother was five or six, she had heard every major opera. Her father would take her. She was a musical prodigy, and at six she could come home and sit at the piano and play whatever she had just heard. Anything she heard she *knew*, which is why later on she was so invaluable to George Gershwin. Well into her eighties she could play the entire uncut four-hour-long *Porgy and Bess* original score from memory—flawlessly. She even knew all the variations that had been cut and never performed. She knew it all. I did feel that as a child Madeleine had had a particular interest in my grandmother. It is not that she spent so much time with her, but she saw that she was a lot of fun and that she was deeply interested in music and books.

*Q: Apart from Madeleine's own father, Kay Swift must have been the first person from the world of culture whom Madeleine knew.*

A: Yes, and as I said, she and April were very similar, odd little girls and very much observers of their own lives as they were experiencing them.

In "Evening of a Governess," there is a character named Mrs. Warburton—a giant leap away from Warburg! My grandmother had an Irish maid named Kitty Ford, who also appears in the story with a different name. The governess from whose point of view the story is told was in reality a very troubled, difficult person who I believe was absolutely obsessed with my mother and her sisters and was in her way quite abusive. She gave them enemas every day, which at the time was considered just over-caretaking. Madeleine may have picked up something about this lonely, angry, disturbed person in the household. In the story, the Madeleine character, Emily, is so upset in the governess's presence that she flees the dinner table into her own nanny's waiting arms.

*Q: What are some of your later memories of seeing Madeleine?*

A: I stayed in touch with her. I was an unpublished fiction writer and was doing a lot of journalism and book criticism and literary profiles. Madeleine was immensely kind and encouraging to me. In a way, she treated me as an equal. She proposed me for membership in the Authors Guild, read things of mine, and gave me a blurb for my first novel. I probably chatted with her on the phone once every two or three months and saw her once or twice a year, almost always at Crosswicks, until close to the end of her life.

I would go up with her into the Tower at Crosswicks, where she worked and where she had a computer. She was a very early adapter. Early on she encouraged me to get a machine like the one she was using for writing when she was on the go. It was called a Canon Typestar, and it was an electronic typewriter, which was a transitional technology. It was a typewriter with a memory. It was a big, heavy thing, although in those days it was considered amazingly portable. Later, Madeleine was one of the first people I knew to use word processing comfortably. She had WordPerfect for DOS and would talk about how hard it was at her age to learn all the commands, you know, Shift, Alt, F1, F2, F3. She told me that she thought of them as "Fuck 1," "Fuck 2," and "Fuck 3," which from then on is how I thought of them too! She had her keyboard and computer screen set up on her desk in front of her, and she sat on a seat that swiveled like a piano stool but had a back. Just behind her was a table with an electric piano keyboard on it, so that she could swivel around whenever she wanted and play the piano and then swivel back around and write. She would give herself a break from writing to think things through at the piano keyboard, the way someone else might get up and walk around the block. She would twirl around and play some Bach or Brahms. She said that the music unlocked her, helped her to clarify her thoughts, and then it would bring her back to her writing. I was very struck by those two back-to-back keyboards. I had never seen anything quite like it. She would also love to swim naked in her pool, early in the morning, when no one else was around. That was the other thing she would do when she wanted to think about her writing.

Madeleine liked to talk about all the rejections of *A Wrinkle in Time*, and she told me once, perhaps apocryphally, that whenever she would be at a literary event, invariably some publisher would come up to her and say, "Oh, if only we had published *A Wrinkle in Time*. If only we'd had the chance!" And Madeleine would respond by saying, "Wait, wait a minute"—and she would open her pocketbook and riffle through the copies of all the rejection letters she had received. She claimed to carry them with her in her purse so that she could pull out the appropriate one from Harcourt or Doubleday or Random House or whatever and say, "See. Here you did have your chance and you rejected it!"

At Crosswicks, Madeleine was self-sufficient. She would make lunch—chicken salad out of leftover roast chicken was what she served me on two occasions—and it would all be very gracious and competent. The house was sort of messy, but in a really nice, lived-in way. Once we had a long chat about garbage. She had these enormous new garbage bins with wheels instead of the traditional kind that you have to drag out to the curb and back. She just loved them! When she showed me the famous stargazing rock, it felt very familiar to me, maybe just from my knowing her books so well. Or maybe it was something about her that made it seem familiar.

*Q: Did you see her in New York too?*

A: I saw her in the city only once. She didn't seem to be especially comfortable there, at least not when I saw her. It felt as if she had to gird up to be in the city. It may just have been that she was having a particularly frantic day, with lots of appointments. I don't know. But when she was at Crosswicks, she had more leisure, and she always seemed relaxed and at home there.

We went to the Hungarian Pastry Shop across from the cathedral. Her relationship with the cathedral . . . There must be some great big metaphor you can drag in relating to the fact that that's a building that is perpetually under construction. I feel as if she had some sort of kinship with that space. It stood apart from the city for her, as a sanctuary.

We didn't talk about the specifics of the book I was writing. But I found that it was an incredibly valuable thing to have someone who simply made you feel seen and recognized. She *expected* me to write novels. She had a way of respecting young people and taking them seriously. Now, when I'm doing thesis advising at Columbia, I often meet with students at the same pastry shop. I don't talk about Madeleine, but I always am aware when I walk in that *that*'s the table where we sat and that now here I am, the author of five novels and a memoir, and I am a mentor to this person sitting here with me.

*Q: How much of Madeleine do you see in her books?*

A: Fiction writing can be a thespian activity. For the most part, she didn't write novels about people just like Madeleine L'Engle. She is Meg in *A Wrinkle in Time* in the way that you could say Louisa May Alcott is Jo in *Little Women*—but not really. In many ways, she was also Mrs. Murry. Instead of a mad scientist's lab, Madeleine had the Tower, where she was cooking up her books. She was the same sort of absentee, absentminded mother to a houseful of children. I think that for her, writing fiction was more often a way of being outside herself.

Madeleine's kids and grandchildren certainly feel that she was not truthful in her memoirs, that she just glossed over things or spun stories. So, for instance, Hugh being virtually an alcoholic for decades is not in the story, though in reality it was a big part of the story, as well as his being unfaithful to her, which she did not acknowledge either. *Two-Part Invention* is a beautiful portrait of the marriage she wished she had.

*Q: She became a kind of beacon for people, and then that became a role that she felt she had to maintain.*

A: Yes, and then she played herself. There was the public face and the private face. But she didn't necessarily take off the mask when she looked at herself in the mirror. She became "Madeleine L'Engle." I don't make any claims for some extra-special in-sy relationship, but I feel that I had a kind of shortcut to a very frank intimacy because she'd known April so early in her life and because of my connection to her and my knowledge of the family history.

It was as if I had been there all along in a certain way. I had read all her books, and I was very knowledgeable about them. But I wasn't there as a sycophant looking for the way to Christ or the way to anything. So I think she almost acted with me as though she was "off duty." There were some people who were not especially interested in her books in a literary way but were devoted to her as a kind of Pema Chödrön or spiritual guide. She was a little nonplussed by that. She enjoyed having a following, but I don't think she meant to set herself up as a spiritual leader. She was very respectful of people, and she must have had an enormous mailing list. I don't know how many hundreds of people were on the list to receive her "Dear Ones" letters, which she sent out quarterly for years. It was a xeroxed letter, and if she wrote a few sentences in ink, you would feel special. I have a file thick with them. There was always a photo of her, and as time passed, of course she aged. One year she was in a wheelchair. And then finally the letter—or e-mail—would come from the family, not Madeleine herself, and there would be "news of Madeleine." If anyone could be sending you an e-mail announcing her death, it would be Madeleine. Madeleine would have been amused!

*Q: How do you understand Madeleine's tendency to adopt young people?*

A: She literally took in strays. She adopted Maria. She talked to me about how for a while she was an alien child, and then one day Madeleine found that Maria "smelled" like one of her own. The way she described it, it was almost like a biological process of becoming a member of the family.

*Q: But then there were others, some taken on as acolytes of one kind or another.*

A: It is a pattern I have seen in other people who are enormously accomplished and who have a great coterie of devotees but are not necessarily in such perfect shape in their intimate relationships with their family. There are these substitute relationships.

They're not as deep, though they may seem very profound. But they come and they go. I think she did get satisfaction from that. I don't mean to trivialize this by saying "flavor of the month," but there would be these people with whom she had intense relationships— for a time. I don't claim that we had a mother-daughter thing going, but it had that shape, that echo. She was of my mother's generation. I was of her children's generation. There was this familiarity, and I certainly didn't have fights with her the way her kids might. She also was guarded in certain ways, in the sense that I knew—and I don't even know how I knew—there were issues with Hugh Franklin. But I never would have heard about them from her. Acolytes don't talk back. Acolytes don't contradict you. It's very satisfying. And I think she had a lot to give people. But ultimately her children were a little frustrated with her because she could be an incredibly stubborn, pigheaded person who was very hard to argue with. She was just quite blinkered about certain things going on in the family. Bion's death was a hideous tragedy that pushed her further into old age and dementia as a way of not knowing about it or not feeling it as sharply.

*Q: Did your friendship change as you became more accomplished?*

A: I saw less of her. I had kids, family. She became less independent after a time. Whenever I got finished books, she was always one of the first people I would send a book to. She would sometimes write me a little note or phone on occasion, and I would be thrilled with her praise of my books. It was like the way you'd feel if you could go back in time and give something you are proud of to that English teacher who recognized you in fifth grade.

She was always a close reader. Even if she wrote just a few sentences, they weren't just from reading the flaps. She clearly would have read the book. You get so that you know the difference! Her praise was a wonderful thing. My third novel, *The Little Women*, is a kind of postmodern recapitulation of Louisa May

Alcott's novel, and she had some interesting things to say about it. I knew from her granddaughter Charlotte that she was not able to read *Triangle*, the last novel I sent her. She was one of those people whose enthusiasm and support meant a lot.

*Q: Did Madeleine have other guests at Crosswicks when you visited her there?*

A: Only the last time I saw her, when I think my husband and I were the only people there who weren't family. This was a giant family birthday celebration, and there might have been twenty people there. This would have been maybe in 2005 or 2006. She was in a wheelchair and was having good days and bad days. My husband has a wonderful ability to charm elderly ladies. Madeleine's daughters were saying to me, "Wow. She loves him!" He was getting her talking and focusing, and she was kind of flirting with him and just pulling every molecule of brain function together, and she had a really great chat with him. It was like someone playing tennis way over her game on a certain day. Nick had never met her before, and so he didn't realize what a particularly great moment she was having compared with how she was most of the time. We sat at these tables out in the barn and had a feast with her at the head of the table. It might have been her last birthday with meaning, her last big celebration with a group of people with whom she was completely present. I would notice that she was repeating herself, that she was not remembering a conversation from five minutes ago. But then, suddenly, she would be totally sharp. She and I talked about things that went back years, taking up threads from other, long-ago conversations. She had made a point of having my book *The Little Women* out on the coffee table, to show me that she had read it and that she knew it was mine. She would buttonhole a relative walking by and say, "Now, have you read this book? It's a wonderful book!" And the person would say, "Yes, Gran. Yes, you told me about it. Yes." I never saw her after that. I was going to see her again, but I put it off the way you can.

I was probably a little cowardly about it. You know, it's going to be work. It's going to be sad. Is it for me? Is it for her? I would have gone to the memorial service in Goshen but was out of the country.

*Q: Did Madeleine give you other presents besides her short story manuscript?*

A: She gave me copies of books and wrote in them. I never asked her for anything. I brought along with me, to sign for my kids, my own childhood copies of some of her books. She had a pro forma way of signing books. She always used a chunky marker, and she always would write, "Tesser well." When I think about the world she created in the Crosswicks novels as an appealing place for so many thousands of children to go to, and for adults to go to too, I can see that it was the same kind of literary oasis that had meant so much to her as a child when she read *Anne of Green Gables*. I think she succeeded in creating a real world that existed in the minds of so many people. It's a wonder to me that there isn't a path worn by avid readers coming to see that stargazing rock. It's a miracle she was not bothered by people incessantly knocking on her door. Sometimes a letter to her would be addressed to "Madeleine L'Engle, Crosswicks, Connecticut." Properly speaking, there's no such place. Crosswicks is the name of her house, but there's no town by that name. But the letter would get to her.

# WRITER

## JAMES CROSS GIBLIN

James Cross Giblin was an associate editor at Lothrop, Lee & Shepard from 1962 to 1967 before becoming editor in chief of Clarion Books. In recent years, he has focused primarily on his writing career as an author of nonfiction books for young readers.

When *A Wrinkle in Time* won the Newbery, I was working at Lothrop, Lee & Shepard as associate editor. My boss was Beatrice Creighton, Lothrop's longtime editor in chief and a children's book pioneer in her own quiet way.

She was the editor of Roger Duvoisin's Caldecott-winning picture book *White Snow, Bright Snow*, written by Alvin Tresselt, and Duvoisin's later Caldecott Honor, *Hide and Seek Fog*, also by Tresselt. Bea also published *One God: The Ways We Worship Him*, an innovative photo essay by Florence Fitch that compared religious practices of Protestants, Catholics, and Jews—a forward-looking approach back in 1944.

Miss Creighton was also the editor of Madeleine L'Engle's first book for young people, the teenage novel *And Both Were Young*, about Philippa's (Flip's) crush on another girl in a Swiss boarding school. According to Bea, L'Engle had intended it to be an adult novel, but her editor at Vanguard Press (which had published L'Engle's *The Small Rain*) felt the new manuscript would be better suited for publication as a novel for teenagers. He suggested L'Engle show it to his friend Beatrice Creighton at Lothrop, and Bea signed it up. While working on revisions of the story with L'Engle, Bea persuaded the reluctant author to change the object of Flip's affections from a girl to a boy. Bea was well aware that in those days even the slightest hint of homosexuality would have killed the book's chances in the children's book market. After all, the late 1940s were a conservative time when Hollywood censors decreed that even married couples sleep in twin beds.

Lothrop published *And Both Were Young* in early 1949. It got good reviews and was still in print in hardcover and selling nicely when I worked at Lothrop in the early 1960s. I've often wondered why L'Engle rarely if ever included it in discussions of her books for young people, since it was her first. Perhaps it was because Beatrice Creighton had demanded such extensive revisions, or because Bea was one of the twenty-eight or twenty-nine editors—the number frequently changed—who, Madeleine said, had turned down *A Wrinkle in Time*. Over a lunch one day, shortly after *Wrinkle* won the Newbery, a not-so-regretful Miss Creighton told me why she'd declined the story, which she said had a different title when she saw it: "Mrs Who, Mrs Whatsit, and Mrs Which." I remember quite clearly the gist of what she told me. It went like this: "Madeleine writes wonderfully well, but I just couldn't go along with all the religion business. I thought it got in the way of the story. But I knew Madeleine wouldn't consider revisions—so I said no." She was sipping a glass of wine as she spoke. "I'm sure I've cost Crown"—Lothrop's owner then—"a lot of money. But I'm really not sorry; I wouldn't have enjoyed working on that story." Interestingly, Beatrice Creighton was the daughter of a minister—I believe a Methodist minister.

# CARMEN GOMEZPLATA

Carmen Gomezplata headed Farrar, Straus and Giroux's legendary copyediting department for many years. Madeleine L'Engle dedicated *The Irrational Season* to her.

*Q: When did you join the staff of Farrar, Straus and Giroux?*

A: In 1965. I remember most precisely because Tom Wolfe had become a bestseller that year, and everyone received a terrific bonus.* I got fifty dollars! By the time I arrived, *A Wrinkle in Time* had been published and had had a big success. I worked on all of Madeleine's subsequent books.

Hal Vursell, who had edited *Wrinkle*, introduced me to Madeleine. He brought me by taxi from Union Square to the Upper West Side and escorted me to Madeleine's apartment. He stayed for a few minutes, just long enough to see that she and I had hit it off. He left me sitting with Madeleine at her long dining room table, where we went to work immediately.

Hal was a wonderful person and a fine editor. I admired him immensely. He was tall and thin and had a very good sense of humor. He could do everything. He oversaw production work. He was good with people. And he edited every kind of book: children's books, literary translations, strange, offbeat works of fiction. He

*In 1965, Farrar, Straus and Giroux published Wolfe's first essay collection, *The Kandy-Kolored Tangerine-Flake Streamline Baby*.

knew languages, and when he worked on a translation, he knew just how the phrase should turn. He understood the author's point of view. When he made changes to a manuscript or posed a question, it was as if he had *become* the author. There was a messenger who would often come to the office to deliver manuscripts. Then, one day, the messenger left a manuscript he had written himself. Hal read it and decided to publish it! In fact he published several more of this man's books, all weird, avant-garde novels. Hal was that kind of person.

There are various stories about who at the house had been the first to take an interest in *A Wrinkle in Time*. My theory—and a theory is all it is—is that the manuscript went to Hal and that he was the one who spotted it. In any case, he had that knack for seeing the possibilities in a book that others might pass over.

I don't know what the process was before a manuscript by Madeleine came to me: how many drafts she went through. I do know that she trusted Hal and she trusted her husband, Hugh, when it came to the bigger editorial issues that might arise, such as plot turns. By the time the manuscript reached me, any issues of that kind had been cleared up. I dealt, as do all copy editors, with the teensy-weensy details that no one notices—unless they are handled incorrectly. It was a pleasure to work with Madeleine because she was interested in everything down to the smallest detail.

Madeleine did not come to the office to work on a manuscript. We went to her. She was very regal in that way, though also very lovely and sweet. We went to Isaac Singer's apartment too. You would walk into the front hallway of her very big apartment on West End Avenue, and there would be a child's antique rocking chair. That's where you would put your coat—not in the closet. Spread out before you was a living room big enough to be a ballroom. At the far end, facing the Hudson River, was the dining table where we sat and worked. Madeleine had cats that would roam over the table. One time I brought her cookies. She set them out on a lovely plate, and while we were working, I could see the cats licking all the cookies! I sat there thinking, Suppose she offers me a cookie? What do I do?

The old-fashioned way of publishing would be for the manuscript to come to the copy editor after the editor finished with it. I would read the manuscript and then go to see Madeleine to discuss any questions I might have. She had a slight tendency to repeat a word. If she used the word "splendid" three times, I would point it out. She was very quick to make fixes. She would see right away what to do. The manuscript then went to the printer, and we pulled galleys. Madeleine would get a set, and I would get a set to give to a proofreader. I then returned to Madeleine's apartment, where we would collate the proofreader's changes and those that Madeleine had made. Next came the page-proof stage, when we would meet again. Then there would be one more round before we printed the book. It's all so different now with computers. Madeleine always wanted to be involved in every stage.

I'm not sure that she had been given the chance to do so for *Wrinkle*. When the names "Mrs Whatsit," "Mrs Who," and "Mrs Which" first appeared in print with periods, Madeleine had been furious. She had wanted no periods, as a way of signaling to the reader that these were not ordinary mortals but special creatures. This shows you the kind of care she took with her writing.

Madeleine could be a little stubborn at times. She might want a comma where it didn't belong. But she had a great facility for writing and she cared deeply about everything and she knew what she wanted. If I would say, "Would you prefer to do it this way or that way?" she would know.

It was always a delight to get a new manuscript by her because her very deep faith would be there in it, embedded in a great story with great characters. I gave my copies of all Madeleine's books to my niece, who was a teenager at the time I was working with

Madeleine and who made certain decisions in her life after reading her books. My niece told me once that she had decided to name her first daughter after Madeleine. When I told Madeleine this news, she laughed and said, "In that case she's sure to have only boys!"

# GEORGE M. NICHOLSON

George M. Nicholson is a senior agent at Sterling Lord Literistic. Earlier in his career, he founded Delacorte Press Books for Young Readers and Yearling Books and served as publisher of books for children and young people at the Viking Press and as publisher of Bantam Doubleday Dell Books for Children.

*Q: How did you meet Madeleine L'Engle?*

A: I became acutely aware of Madeleine after 1965, when we were putting together the paperback reprint list for Yearling Books at the Dell Publishing Company. We went through every publishing house's lists and frankly picked what we thought were the big bestsellers. Clearly, *A Wrinkle in Time* was one of the major titles. A few years earlier, I had included an excerpt from *A Wrinkle in Time* in an educational reading program that I helped create for Science Research Associates, a Chicago-based company. So I already knew bits and pieces of the novel. Rereading it at Dell, I found that I loved it.

I approached Farrar, Straus not through the person in charge of the juvenile department but rather through a man named Hal Vursell, who was one of the house's senior editors. I never fully understood his position there. He was a senior person and was handling Madeleine outside the juvenile department. The editor in charge of juvenile publishing at the time was Clare Costello, but I didn't deal with her, only with Hal. I remember going to lunch with Hal and making the case to him about why a paperback edition would not destroy the hardcover sales of the book, which had done so spectacularly well once it won the Newbery. We bought paperback rights not only to *A Wrinkle in Time* but to several of Madeleine's novels. I don't remember what we paid for the rights, but it was a lot of money. That is when I first met Madeleine.

From the very beginning, my relationship with her had almost more of a familial feeling about it than a professional feeling because, by sheer coincidence, my son was a schoolmate of her two granddaughters. St. Luke's School is a parochial grammar school in Greenwich Village. By the time I met Madeleine, I had already gotten to know Charlotte, Léna, and their parents—who were also our neighbors—through my son and the school. It was this contact, even more than my admiration of her writing, which was the basis for our connection, and it remained at the core of our friendship over all those years.

Even so, I wouldn't call our friendship particularly close. I never visited her in Connecticut, for example, and I knew her husband only slightly. I knew her daughter and then-son-in-law Alan Jones only through our school and neighborhood connection. Now and then I would take my son, Nicky, and the two girls, who were so bright and smart and funny, on an excursion, say, to Chinatown.

Hal understood what we were trying to do at Dell Yearling, and when he talked it over with Madeleine, I think he must have made the point that we were a respectable operation. My having a son at her granddaughters' school may even have figured in the pitch. Hardcover houses in those days saw themselves—and were widely seen—as the center of Literature, whereas paperback houses were vulgar reprinters riding on the back of the literary horse.

The other-side-of-the-tracks mentality persisted for a long time—until writers began to realize the financial benefits that only the paperback houses could bring them.

It was not unknown to Farrar, Straus and the other publishers in town that rather big money was being thrown around for the purpose of acquiring paperback rights to the most desirable books. This of course was in the pre-conglomerate days of independent ownership. Every house, but particularly smaller publishers like Farrar, Straus, kept a close watch on the flow of money, as you would immediately sense on a visit to Farrar's offices, which were very modest in an engaging—and I thought English—sort of way. You might see mice or other creatures scurrying about, but at least you knew the partners weren't squandering their money on glitz. In the 1970s and 1980s, Union Square, where Farrar, Straus's offices were located, was itself a pretty horrifying place, with drunks and drug dealers everywhere. It was not the high-rent district!

So to Hal Vursell, $150,000—or whatever it was that we paid for Madeleine's books—was a spectacular sum of money, of which the publisher got half. We negotiated a straightforward contract, which ran for a term of seven years, with a clause that provided for automatic renewal in perpetuity, or until such time as either party wished to terminate the agreement.

I didn't get to know Hal all that well, either. He was a solitary man, scholarly in his appearance—a rather dour character, I thought. I was a little in awe of him. I never felt that he was particularly passionate about children's books, but he was passionate about Madeleine's work, and he realized that it was a very valuable property.

I left Dell in 1970, and by the time I returned to the house in its much-expanded form about nine years later, Hal was semiretired, and *A Wrinkle in Time* had sold so well in both hardcover and paperback that there was no thought of termination on either side. Ironically, it was the great success of the book that led to the

one major "incident" I had with Madeleine, in which I found myself doing my best to protect her.

I had learned from my colleagues at Dell that the company
had underpaid Farrar, Straus in royalties for a period of years, to
the tune of several hundred thousand dollars. It was an appalling
moment for me, not least because of my role in having brought
Madeleine's books to Dell in the first place. I was so embarrassed,
and I couldn't see how this would have happened. It turned out to
have been a simple accounting error. I knew that Roger Straus,
who was a fierce protector both of his own interests and of the interests of his authors and who was a famously hot-tempered man,
was going to be in hysterics. His position had always been that
the paperback houses were the "bad guys." In any case, when I got
this news, I called Madeleine's agent, Bob Lescher, with whom I
was friendly, and told him the situation. I said that I was going to
call Farrar, Straus and that what I thought should happen was for
Madeleine to get *all* the back-payment money that was due—not
just half—in light of the fact that Farrar, Straus had overlooked
the accounting errors too, and therefore bore equal responsibility
with Dell. That in the end is how the matter was resolved, and
from then on Madeleine knew that I really was on her side.

We began to have occasional dinners together, during which
we would talk about what we were reading and about religion in
one's life—she as a practicing Episcopalian and I as a nonpractic-
ing Roman Catholic. She was amused by my stance that if you
didn't want to play by the rules of your religion—which in my
case would have meant going to confession, observing the sacraments—it was best to pull away from it altogether. She said she
found a good deal of comfort in religion. This was also the time in
her life when she was leading spiritual retreats, primarily for
women.

At Dell, we were in a position to publish paperback editions
of many of Madeleine's books that had gone out of print in hard-

cover, including religious books as well as fiction. We could be a "full-service publisher" for her as well as for a number of other authors. In those years, Walden and B. Dalton were the two national bookselling chains, and because they demanded "product" month in and month out, we were able to take a big career like Madeleine's and give focus to it by publishing paperbacks across the complete spectrum of her published work. Part of our strategy was to give all her titles a unified look, including even a specially designed "Madeleine L'Engle" logo. We released the books one per month, as if they were a series, even if the books weren't actually linked in terms of content. "There's a new Madeleine L'Engle book!" is what we wanted the people who shopped at those stores to be telling one another.

Madeleine had an amazing ability to surround herself with real-life characters. I didn't know Canon West well, but I did go with her to several parties at his apartment. He was what I would call a *very* High Church Anglican. He spoke with a British accent, although whether he was actually English I don't know. The diction of American theater at that time was English diction. Alfred Lunt spoke with an English accent because that is what theater people did. So to Madeleine with her own theater background, Canon West's inflated style of diction probably wouldn't have seemed all that outrageous. Curiously, this was one of the things that the church and the theater of the time had in common. I'm sure that Madeleine didn't patronize Canon West. But I'm sure she saw through him.

He had pictures all over his apartment of the queen mother and of the Russian imperial family (who of course were long gone!). Religious icons were everywhere. The place was full of stuff, and he himself was an ornate character: warm and friendly enough, but in an affected sort of way. He wore capes. Of course it could get windy and cold on the Upper West Side, so perhaps this was only sensible of him! Still, your first impression was apt to be: Who does this guy think he is? I always assumed that what fascinated Madeleine about Canon West was his extravagance as a character and that she must have taken him with a grain of salt. But she also would have had reason to understand his theatricality and how it could cloak—literally in this case—a personality that was well worth knowing.

I met Hugh only a few times. His fame as a television actor was enormous. Often when she spoke, Madeleine would be introduced as Hugh Franklin's wife, and a great collective sigh would rise up from the audience. He wasn't startlingly handsome, but he had a distinguished presence. He was always genial and supportive of Madeleine.

One of my most vivid memories of Madeleine is from two years after Hugh's death: her big seventieth birthday party, in November 1988, at St. John the Divine. Madeleine was dressed in a long gown and was wearing a chaplet or crown of ivy. She looked positively regal as she sat in a great wooden, thronelike chair and received her guests. It was her party, and she was going to have the time of her life. It was quite a performance!

Madeleine was strong and indefatigable. She took on financial responsibility for several members of her family, and I think she was really working for them as much as for herself. In general, the women who worked with her tended to become closer to her than the men. I always felt that I was one of Madeleine's courtiers, that my job was to look after her, make her life easier—not to be her best friend.

# SIDNEY OFFIT

Sidney Offit is the author of *Memoir of the Bookie's Son* and *Friends, Writers, and Other Countrymen*, among other books. He has served on the boards of the Authors Guild and PEN American Center and as curator of the George Polk Awards in journalism.

*Q: When did you meet Madeleine L'Engle?*

A: I first became aware of Madeleine when we were touring together during the 1960s as fellow authors on the annual fall children's book festival circuit. We would travel from city to city in the Northeast and Midwest, speaking to large groups of children, librarians, and parents. I had started as a novelist and had begun writing for kids only when I got stuck on my second novel. The next thing I knew, I was getting royalty checks for my children's novel that were bigger than the ones that my book for adults was bringing in. I was confused about how writing for children might relate to my being a "serious" novelist. I enjoyed writing the books, but I didn't want to be identified only as an author of sports fiction for young readers. I felt I had gotten off on a tangent, and I was a little self-conscious about the whole thing. Yet there I was.

I hate to be immodest about it, but what would frequently happen at these speaking events is that the "distinguished" writers would draw the crowd and then I would get up and tell the stories that wowed the kids. I had learned early on that when speaking to children, you had to be dramatic. So I would do voices for them and really ham it up, and I would always get a good response. I mention this because the first time I was on a program with Madeleine, at a huge gathering somewhere in Ohio, I noticed that the schedule called for me to speak first and for Madeleine to go second. I knew that Madeleine had written *A Wrinkle in Time*, but I had never met her before. And I knew that some of the best writers who went out on these tours were deadly dull as speakers. It might sound cocky, but I honestly thought that the response of the young audiences to me when I spoke was so strong that it simply was not fair to let me go first and then have somebody else come afterward. So I took the librarian in charge of the event aside, explained the situation to him, and said, "Out of fairness to Madeleine L'Engle, why don't you let her speak before me?" "Have you ever heard her speak?" he said. "No," I said, suddenly concerned that he might have taken my suggestion the wrong way. "I'm not being critical, you understand. She seems like a very fine lady. I'm just doing this to protect her." He looked at me and said, "I can tell that you've never heard her speak. Don't worry about Madeleine L'Engle."

We went ahead with the program as planned. I got up and I gave my talk. To say that it went over well would be a major understatement. Thunderous applause! Kids leaping out of their seats all over this giant auditorium! It was like rock-star stuff. Everyone wanted to get close to me! In other words, it all went just as I had said it would. Next would be Madeleine's turn, and once again I thought, Poor lady! Well, at least I tried.

So now Madeleine walks out onstage. She is a tall woman, but onstage she looks even taller, and she is carrying a big bag—not a paper bag, but more like a carryall. She tosses her head back with a regal flourish and looks directly at the audience. She hasn't said a word yet, but the auditorium has turned absolutely still. She has them in the palm of her hand. I'm sitting there at the edge of my seat, thinking, This is incredible! Now what is she going to do? She opens the bag, and she pulls something out of it—something, as I recall, which looks like a dead rabbit! It isn't a dead rabbit, and it may have been just a piece of cloth. Now a look of surprise crosses her face, and she says, "What could *this* be? And I wonder what else there might be in this bag." She pulls something else out of the bag, and she does this again and again—and as she does so, she begins to improvise a story involving each of the objects from her magical Scheherazade bag. I realize that what Madeleine is really doing is showing the audience the essential nature of story-telling: the fact that one can make a story from absolutely *anything*. It is a riveting performance. Afterward, I expressed my enthusiasm to her for what she had done. She responded in kind. From then on, we were always good friends.

Another year when we were on tour together, Maia Wojciechowska and Lloyd Alexander were part of our group. Maia was a rather difficult person, whereas Lloyd was a wonderfully pleasant and modest man. They'd both won the Newbery Medal by then, but in Lloyd's case you would never have guessed it from his manner. They were a fascinating threesome to be traveling with. At one point, we all piled into the same car, along with a librarian or two, to be driven to a dinner party. It was incredibly cramped, especially for Madeleine with her long legs, and as a kind of distraction I said out of the blue, in a baby voice, "You know, we're children's book writers and we like to sit together, don't we?" Then, to pass the time, I suggested, "Why don't we all do the part that people expect us to play—the part of the children's book writer." I went first, carrying on in that itsy-bitsy voice about "my doggy" and "my kitty cat" and so on. Then I said,

"Who wants to go next?" Lloyd was very witty in a subtle way, droning on and on like some kind of absentminded professor about the wives of Henry the Eighth. Then Maia spoke up in a haughty voice—which wasn't very hard for her!—and said something like, "Well, I write children's books and why not? The poor little things, what do they know? They can't tell the difference. And in any case one is not really writing for them. One writes for the librarians and for the parents. If they like the book, they buy the book. If not, who cares!"

Finally, it was Madeleine's turn, and could she ever act! She transformed herself into a completely different person, creating a complex character that somehow parodied each of our characters in turn. You could almost see her pulling it all out of that bag of hers. It was another amazing performance. We all laughed, and the experience brought the four of us closer together. A few years later, both Maia and Madeleine wrote blurbs for my book *Not All Girls Have Million Dollar Smiles* (1971). It blew my editor out of the box to have two blurbs by Newbery Medal winners. The following year Lloyd Alexander wrote a blurb for my next book, *Only a Girl like You.*

By then Madeleine had become a part of my life. Each time we saw each other, we would pick up where we had left off in our last conversation. There was always this warm, familiar feeling between us. On a couple of occasions she invited my wife and me to visit her and her husband, Hugh, in Connecticut. Once Eli Wallach and Anne Jackson were there. Madeleine played the piano for us all. I put Madeleine up for membership at a midtown social club—a club, it turned out, that her father had once belonged to. One day, when she and I were having lunch there together, she pinched both my cheeks and said, "My father, if he can see us now, must be rolling over in his grave!"

One of the members of that same club happened to remark one

day that Madeleine was the greatest preacher he had ever heard, that Madeleine's sermons were always captivating and original and yet informed by a powerful understanding of classic religion. Until then, I had known nothing of this whole other side of Madeleine's life! It was the first I heard of her association with St. John the Divine.

I never got to know Madeleine's other children, but I did meet her son, Bion, who, as you know, died young. I felt that Madeleine must have had to draw very deeply on her spiritual faith in order to come to terms with his horrendous death. Bion had been troubled even as a boy, I think, and Madeleine was so grateful to me for taking him once to a ball game.

What happened was this. At Madeleine's Connecticut home, Bion and I had gotten to talking about baseball. He told me what a big Yankees fan he was. Bion was about twelve at the time, and I had two young sons of my own, so I thought it might be fun for the four of us to take in a ball game together. I'd been a sportswriter during the 1950s and had covered the Yankees-Dodgers World Series rivalry. I had photographs of some of the great ballplayers, and I think I must have given one to Bion. The game I got tickets for was a matchup between the Yankees and the Baltimore Orioles. At first the three boys were all getting along just fine. Bion, as I said, was an absolutely passionate Yankees fan, whereas I was kind of schizy because while I loved the Yankees, I had grown up in Baltimore as an ardent Orioles fan. It somehow hadn't occurred to me that my sons might be planning to root for the Orioles. Bion was rooting at the top of his lungs for New York, but at a certain point his shyness overwhelmed him. He must have been saying to himself, you know, What am I doing among the enemy? I saw that I had to do something to put him at his ease, so I adopted his Yankee fandom. I put my arm around him and started rooting against the team that my own sons were cheering on. All in all, the four of us created quite a racket! As it turned out, the Orioles beat the Yankees that day, an outcome that no one would have predicted. Afterward, to console Bion, one of my sons turned to him and said, "Well, we just saw a wrinkle in time!"

People often assume that it is bliss to be the child of a great children's book author, that a child with such a parent starts out life holding every chip. But I think it must have been tough to be Madeleine L'Engle's child. How do you handle having a mother who was not just a celebrity but an institution? A mother who was constantly overwhelmed with offers to speak and perform? Madeleine used to sign every book, "Tesser well." On those two tours we went on together, I half noticed that when people approached her with books to sign, they would often have a look of awe in their eyes. I didn't quite recognize this yet for the sign it was of the special force of her impact on readers.

During the early 1970s I organized a program of workshops on behalf of the PEN American Center for the people of East Harlem, and I thought it would be great, as a kind of "noble experiment," to offer a writers' workshop for ghetto teens at St. John the Divine. I called Madeleine and proposed that she and I teach the workshop together, and she said she would love to do it. Other writers had expressed enthusiasm in principle for the idea but begged off when asked directly to take part. Madeleine, however, showed no such hesitation. She was in! It was then that I began to realize what a generous person she was. She could easily have said she was too busy.

She and I had fun collaborating as workshop teachers. The group met at the cathedral library. We continued to offer the workshop for quite a while. After each session Madeleine and I would have lunch at the library together, and so naturally I met Canon West. He was an impressive figure and a strong personality, and I noticed right away that he was very respectful of Madeleine. The canon seemed to be straight out of central casting, like an actor that Cecil B. DeMille might have hired to play the part. He had a marvelous manner, and there was nothing pompous in it. He would always ask me what I was doing.

Over lunch one day Madeleine and I were having one of those intimate exchanges between friends about one's growing-up and school years, when I said to her, "You know, even though my parents were always very supportive of me, I came away scarred with an inferiority complex because I could never do math at school." To which Madeleine replied, "Neither could I!" The only other person I had ever talked with about this was my mother, and she had had almost an identical response. So I told Madeleine, "The thing I never understood was the multiplication table. I understood that six times one equals six. I thought it should be more, but okay. Two fives equals ten—I got that one, too. Three fives equals fifteen—fine. But six times zero equals zero seemed just crazy to me! How could you have six of something and end up with nothing at all?" Madeleine said the answer to that was easy. "There's a very simple explanation," she assured me. "Zero is the devil! Anything multiplied by the devil is going to be zero." I loved that. My mother had had a far less colorful way of helping me to understand. "Zero," she said, as if this settled the matter once and for all, "is nothing. When you have nothing, you never have anything."

During the mid-1980s, as a member of the Authors Guild's nominating committee, I became interested in persuading Madeleine into serving a term as president of the guild. The guild was going through a period of transition, and it was difficult to find someone good who was willing to take the job. Our longtime executive director, Peter Heggie, had just died, and the publishing industry was in a state of turmoil. Bob Caro had recently completed a term, and Bob Massie, who had indicated his willingness to take on the presidency eventually, had too many commitments just then. In 1985, the time was right to ask Madeleine, and once again her answer was yes.

Madeleine made a very good president. She had the easy grace of a natural leader. She knew how to run a meeting. She not only conducted a meeting with great style but also made sure that other people had a chance to speak. She would turn to you and say, "What do *you* think of that?" She would engage everyone around her. This wasn't just an act on her part. It was rather that she possessed a quality of empathy that only certain people have. She also had a great sense of courtesy in the best sense, and she had exquisite manners.

During her two-year tenure, Madeleine worked successfully for changes in the tax code that benefited authors, and she organized a memorable seminar on the state of the book business. Among the issues that came up for discussion that day was the threat to the survival of the independent bookseller posed by the rise of the chains. Generally, panels such as this end in doom and gloom. I remember coming down the elevator afterward with Garson Kanin and Brendan Gill, both of whom had been on the program, and Garson saying, "I hope we weren't too discouraging," to which Brendan replied, "Oh, I don't think we gave anyone *any* excuse not to write."

The last time I saw Madeleine, she was in the nursing home where she died. Bob Giroux, who adored her, had told me she was there. I brought her chicken soup, which she thought was funny, and we talked. I recounted the car scene from our long-ago book tour, which she remembered well, and we talked about the other writers we'd been traveling with. When I mentioned Maia, Madeleine said, "I didn't like her. I couldn't *stand* her. You made her seem pleasant, but she was not!" I was struck by the fact that even then, that last time in the nursing home, when she was fading in and out, there was still a core of vitality to Madeleine. To me, the riddle of her life was how a person of such extraordinary imagination, a writer who could make the unreal seem so real on the page, could also be so incapable in her personal life of saying anything that she did not believe to be absolutely true. She and I discussed this a little. Then as I was leaving, she took my hand, and clutched it with that feeling that this was final and that it was okay. "I'll see you again," I said. She said, "Let's hope."

## PATRICIA LEE GAUCH

Patricia Lee Gauch is a former vice president and editorial director of Philomel Books, an imprint of Penguin, and the author of more than forty picture books and novels for young readers.

I first encountered Madeleine as a distant admirer, at an American Library Association luncheon attended by hundreds of her adoring fans. She had a classical presence that day, standing tall and straight at the podium, her short dark hair pixie-like, her gestures dramatic as she spoke. I had kept her philosophical memoir *A Circle of Quiet* at my bedside for months and found it an inspiration. Of course I had also read *A Wrinkle in Time*, which, of all the many fantasies I had read, stood out for being so remarkably human: full of wit, emotion, and intent. I remember thinking when I read it: *That's* what makes a great fantasy—not the bizarre characters or the otherworldly architecture and trappings, but the humanity of the story. Now here she was, this great writer and humanist, speaking before the audience of which I was a part.

The next contact of sorts that I had with Madeleine was over a manuscript. My agent, Dorothy Markinko of McIntosh & Otis, had spoken with Madeleine at a conference, and when Madeleine discovered a young man "who could write," she had sent the manuscript to Dorothy. It wasn't surprising that Dorothy would then send it along to me, her longtime author client, in my other role as an editor. I was just beginning my career in publishing and was looking for good manuscripts. I was a great admirer of fantasy—Lloyd Alexander's Chronicles of Prydain was high on my list—and I was intrigued with the manuscript that was sent to me. It was called *Heartlight*, and the author was T. A. Barron. In the end, I bought and published the book. That the manuscript came recommended by Madeleine L'Engle carried great weight with me.

Madeleine continued to be a mentor to T. A. Barron. She had met him, I think, at a Hudson River retreat; seen snatches of his writing and then finally the whole manuscript. She liked everything about Tom: not only his manuscript, but also his dedication to the natural world, his respect for family, and certainly his high regard for her. The two became not only writing friends but devoted friends.

I finally met Madeleine at her own Upper West Side apartment at a small party she gave in honor of Tom at the time of *Heartlight*'s publication. She had invited a few important critics, booksellers, and others. I recall being struck by how large her apartment was for New York. The grand piano in particular stood out, almost as if it too were one of the guests. The rest of the furnishings were comfortable and inviting and seemed to create something of a salon atmosphere. After a period of socializing, Madeleine formally introduced Tom and his new book. It was obvious how proud she was of him. On subsequent occasions when I saw them together, it almost felt as if he were a son of whom she was immensely proud, a son whom, at times, she also counted as a confidant.

Most dramatic for me about Madeleine's apartment were the walls with their elaborate displays of photographs of all the people she loved. Most of the photographs were black-and-white and were clustered in threes and fours to create striking abstract arrangements: here by the doorway, there behind the piano, and again next to a painting. What were they to her? Exclamation points?

Memorial altars? Reminders? Or did Madeleine, as I suspect she did, think of the many people pictured in those photographs as members of her sprawling, extended apartment family?

Tom, of course, was terribly proud of the honor that an introduction into the publishing world by Madeleine L'Engle implied. In all these years his gratitude and feelings of friendship for her have never diminished. Madeleine would give a quote for each of Tom's new books. As a result of this, I would have occasion to talk to her now and then over the phone. One time I visited her at the cathedral library of St. John the Divine with its ancient bookshelves stacked to the ceiling with huge—and to me indecipherable—volumes. The perfect place for a fantasy writer to set up shop, is what I remember thinking at the time.

The time I want to recall, though, was a personal visit to Madeleine's apartment. Her longtime publisher, Farrar, Straus and Giroux, was in some turmoil with administrative changes. In 1994 her editor of many years had left the firm.* Had he moved on to another publishing house? It is not uncommon for an editor, faced with the introduction of revised, more profit-oriented policies at a house, either to move to another company in search of nirvana or to strike out on his own. I had been editing for some seven or eight years by then and wondered—with my devotion to Madeleine and her writing being well-known to her—if she might consider, and need, a new editor and publisher.

It was a spring day when I came to see her at her apartment. Madeleine lived on the fifth floor, and her windows looked out over neighboring rooftops and the Columbia University campus. She had set up a little table with a fresh linen tablecloth in front of a wide window thrown open to let in the freshly washed spring

---

*Stephen Roxburgh left Farrar, Straus and Giroux in January 1994 to found Front Street Books, an independent publishing company. In 2009, he launched a second independent publishing venture, Namelos Books.

air. Once again I had the sense of Madeleine as a classic presence. Did she wear a cape that day? I picture her with a swirling woolen cape around her shoulders. She had made a simple lunch for the two of us—small sandwiches served on small plates, with small napkins. Everything looked to be a miniature of itself!

First, of course, we talked about Tom. By then he had written and published three novels. He was launching into a new Merlin series, based on Merlin's missing adolescent years. Madeleine and I were both delighted with its promise. We talked about Tom's relentlessness about hiking the mountains of Colorado. We talked about her affection for Crosswicks, her Connecticut weekend home. Both Tom and she clearly needed a freedom of space: it was one of the main things that had brought them together as friends. The afternoon wore on, and still I had not expressed to her my hope that she might consider working with a new editor—namely me. Perhaps there had been a pause in the conversation. And then music began to play.

It was the most extraordinary music. I had never heard anything like it: women's voices, a chorus of them singing in close harmony, sounding both eerie and joyful, and floating into the room. I shivered at the sheer beauty of the music. "Who are they?" I asked. In those days the Iron Curtain had not yet fallen. "They are the Mystère des Voix Bulgares, the Bulgarian State Television Female Vocal Choir," she said. I listened without speaking. The strange, lyrical music seemed the perfect accompaniment when we went back to chatting about books, and characters, and shared acquaintances, and in the process found ourselves becoming friends.

In the end, I never did ask Madeleine to consider me as an editor for one of her magnificent books. Oh, how I wanted to! But the time wasn't right. It would have been introducing a fox into a spring meadow to bring up business on that already perfect afternoon. So I left that day without what I had hoped to take away but completely satisfied nonetheless.

I know that Madeleine continued to write, and I am not certain who edited the books. But I know her editors at Farrar, Straus always and rightly counted her as their own. Perhaps everyone who came into contact with Madeleine felt that way about her.

# BRIDGET MARMION

Bridget Marmion has held senior-level positions in marketing and sales at Houghton Mifflin, Random House, and Farrar, Straus and Giroux and now heads her own marketing firm, Your Expert Nation.

*Q: How did you meet Madeleine L'Engle?*

A: I began working at Farrar, Straus, in publicity, in 1974. When I left the company eighteen years later, I was director of sales and marketing. *A Circle of Quiet* had been published not too long before my arrival and had been a bestseller. Part of my job from the beginning was to help authors plan and coordinate their speaking schedules. One of the things that one found out about Madeleine immediately upon meeting her was that she worked very hard and traveled continually. One also learned that she needed to have a bathtub in every hotel room in which she stayed. She was not a demanding person by any means—far from a diva— but the bathtub was nonnegotiable.

Madeleine didn't come to see us often in our offices, which was just as well. When Tom Wolfe visited, I always worried that he would soil his white suit simply by brushing up against the bookcases and walls!

On a few occasions, I not only made Madeleine's travel arrangements but also accompanied her to speaking events. Once, when we were in Chicago together and on our way to one of her lectures,

I suddenly found I was having a problem with my eye. I was in too much discomfort to ignore the problem, whatever it was, and from that first moment there was no question about where the cab was going. Madeleine instructed the driver to take us to the nearest hospital. "We have to make sure," she said, "that you haven't damaged your cornea." Madeleine's demeanor was not motherly, exactly, but she was very mothering in a brisk, matter-of-fact way. Looking back, I realize that she might have reacted quite differently, especially given her prominence. But while always professional, Madeleine was also always human.

She also taught me how to pack. With all her comings and goings, Madeleine had devised a packing strategy! She had it down to a science. "The secret," she said, was "to roll things." She thought about practical matters of this sort with a larger goal in mind. She wanted to be prepared, as she always said, to "land and perform." It is fun now to imagine how she might have used new media to satisfy all of the requests for appearances.

Over time I saw how devoted she was to her husband, Hugh. Madeleine would talk about Hugh almost as if she were still infatuated with him. He was of course a soap opera star, and she would always say at book signings how amused she was that so many people would turn out and happily wait in line—the children to meet the author of *A Wrinkle in Time* and the mothers to meet Dr. Tyler's wife.

Marcie Imberman is a partner with Kentshire Galleries Ltd., New York, and a former director of library promotion at Farrar, Straus and Giroux.

*Q: How did you meet Madeleine L'Engle, and when?*

A: I met Madeleine in 1975 when I went to work at Farrar, Straus and Giroux as director of library promotion. By the time I had arrived, we were publishing Natalie Babbitt, William Steig, Isaac Singer, Margot Zemach, Maurice Sendak: it was an illustrious list. Clare Costello was editor in chief of the children's department, which consisted of her and Michael di Capua. But as I recall, Madeleine was edited by Robert Giroux. Earlier on, I believe she had worked with another "adult" editor at Farrar, Straus and Giroux, Hal Vursell. But that was before my time.

*A Wrinkle in Time* had long since won the Newbery Medal, and Madeleine was famous. As the library promotions person, I was her "girl"—responsible for organizing her incredibly complex speaking schedule. On the one hand, I was supposed to be in charge of my very small department. But on the other hand, I often had the feeling that my real job was to serve as the administrative arm of the Madeleine L'Engle Speakers Bureau. It was as though I were *her* publicist.

We met for the first time over lunch. I was twenty-eight or twenty-nine, and Madeleine was in her late fifties. She struck me as a charming woman—and very much the actress, which of course is what she had once been. It seemed to me that she had her "persona" down pat. We had a cordial conversation during which it somehow came out that we shared a birthday. The only other thing I remember her saying that afternoon was that whenever I fielded a request for her to speak that would involve air travel, I was to make it clear to the host that she only flew first-class. Madeleine, as you know, was a tall woman, and she explained this requirement of hers by poking fun at her "giraffe-like" legs. By then she had been on the road tirelessly on behalf of her books for years, and she was going to go her way or not at all.

We spoke by phone six or eight times a week—sometimes twice a day. It was almost always about her schedule. Were her travel arrangements correct? Would her books arrive in time for an event? Would her hotel room have a bathtub? I don't recall traveling with her to conventions and the like, but perhaps that was because she didn't need a lot of the usual hand-holding.

She could also be a very motherly figure. I had recently married at the time we met, and even though we were not particularly close, I remember her offering me advice one day about married life. She was a natural talker, and she liked being the center of attention. She would tell me great stories of having owned the general store. She thought a lot of her skills at writing. She thought a lot of herself, and she was very devoted to her family.

Madeleine was generally very nice to me, but she could also be imperious and demanding and a hard taskmaster. There were times when she kind of drove me crazy. So there were those two sides to her. To some degree, she was entitled to be imperious because she was totally self-made, really, as a success. In those days, Farrar, Straus wasn't particularly good at promoting children's books. I would say that that was true of the other houses too. But Madeleine was a real champion at self-promotion. I soon came to admire her for the fact that she was the one responsible for the grassroots support she had for her books, which was quite unusual.

Partly this was a matter of the times. There were a number of authors in the children's book field by then who were "cash cows," but their publishers might not necessarily pay much attention to their promotion. In our case, Farrar, Straus's adult list was so august that Roger Straus pretty much looked after his stars and left the children's book department, of which he was certainly proud, to take care of itself. Michael di Capua was unusual in having one foot in both camps, as an editor of adult and juvenile authors. But in general the children's book department was a separate world.

## SANDRA JORDAN

Sandra Jordan is the co-author with Jan Greenberg of *Ballet for Martha*, *Action Jackson*, and other books about the arts for young readers and is a former editor in chief of children's books at Farrar, Straus and Giroux.

*Q: How did you meet Madeleine L'Engle?*

A: I was hired as editor in chief of the children's book department after Clare Costello left. It was a very small department, in part because Michael di Capua, who edited many of the great picture books of the period, including those by Maurice Sendak and Bill Steig, was in adult editorial. We certainly cooperated, but he was separate from us in day-to-day matters.

In 1969, when I came into publishing, I went to work for Ann Beneduce at T. Y. Crowell. I worked with Ann for seven years, and when I went to Farrar, Straus, I was relatively young for that job and had not been a senior editor, only an associate editor. But I had done some books that did well, and the reason I got the job is that it had been offered to Ann Beneduce first and she had laughed at the salary they offered her and said, "Who you want to talk to is Sandra." And so they did.

It was a great opportunity, but going in, I felt, Oh my God. Nervous doesn't even come close. The FSG children's book house authors included heavy hitters like the Nobel Prize winner Isaac Bashevis Singer, the Caldecott Medal winner Uri Shulevitz, and the Newbery winner Madeleine L'Engle. Madeleine in particular had been calling Roger Straus once a week, saying, "Where's my editor? I'm working on a book. Where's my editor?" As soon as I arrived, she came down to the office, and Roger brought her to meet me, and we went to lunch at the Dardanelles, which was our hangout. We could sign for meals there, and the bill went on the company tab. My memory of that first lunch is of relaxed and easy conversation about books and theater and things we loved.

My aunt Gay, who was an actress, had known Madeleine and Hugh back in the 1950s. When Gay first came to New York, she toured with the Lunts in *I Know My Love*, which Hugh was in. She'd been to parties at Hugh and Madeleine's house, feeling, she said, "like a very small mouse," because the two of them were both so glamorous. Madeleine wasn't conventionally pretty, but she could project a great aura of glamour.

All those many years later, the Madeleine I met was not the same one my aunt had known. She was a big presence but the Madeleine of the writing world, not of the theater. She ordered her clothes from catalogs. She was the first person I knew who did so. And she had a haircut that looked like Hugh's barber had given it to her. Her hair was very short, in part because she liked to swim every day when she could and didn't want to have to bother with her hair. Before she put the pool in at Crosswicks, she used to drag her guests off to the lake near the house every day to do some swimming. I would paddle around, and she would swim laps! She was exuberant but not stylish, a person you would notice in any room she entered. I liked her immediately in the way that you just meet someone and feel that you have always known them. I've been thinking about why that was, and part of the reason is that she was a great listener. She not only heard what you said but heard what you didn't say. She was curious about everyone and brilliant at subtext, which made her fun to talk to. I think she was my mother's age, but she didn't relate to me that way. In fact, at our first meeting, by way of welcoming me, Madeleine said to me, "I need an editor!"

In preparation for that first meeting, I had been taken to lunch by Hal Vursell, who had been her editor for *A Wrinkle in Time* and *A Wind in the Door*. Hal was retired but lived in the neighborhood, and he met me at the Dardanelles to brief me on what the house considered an important relationship. His words of advice to me were "Don't be intimidated!" He was an editor of the old school, from back in the days when editors were tweedy gents: very turned out in the manner of a distinguished academic. It was clear that he had been very fond of Madeleine.

Bob Giroux, who edited Madeleine's adult books at Farrar, Straus, also prepped me at lunch. Bob was one of the partners and had edited T. S. Eliot and E. M. Forster, among others. He socialized with Madeleine and Hugh in those days and with their mutual friends the Broadway theater critic Walter Kerr and his wife, Jean, who was also a writer. Bob was a really nice man, and he started the conversation by saying in his quiet, growly voice, "I just don't understand children's books at all!" Years later, he would describe Madeleine to me as "a writer right down to her bones."

Madeleine, unlike anyone else I had ever worked with, would show you the first forty pages of a book. That's what she did when we met for lunch that first time. It was a very rough draft. I wasn't quite sure what to do with it, except to stay out of her way because she obviously wrote very fluently. Writer's block was never a problem. What I discovered as we went along is that you had to be very careful what you said to Madeleine editorially. If you didn't pick your words right, you might end up with a whole new revision on your desk twenty-two minutes later; that is, with a manuscript that had been changed much more than you thought was necessary. So in the early stages of work on a book I tried to be little more than an encouraging presence, to act as a sounding board, and maybe say, "A little heavy on the history here"—things of that sort; and "But leave it for now, and we'll see how much you need when the first draft is finished."

Sometimes you'd get pages and pages of a character's back-story, material that Madeleine needed to know about the character but that the reader ultimately did not need to know. There would also be false starts. It was an interesting way to work, and I enjoyed getting to see so much of a writer's process. The only difficulty for me was that it was hard to bring a fresh eye to the final draft, because by then we had been through so many versions that I needed time lines to keep track of the progression.

The first year I was at Farrar, Straus was devoted to getting *A Swiftly Tilting Planet* finished and published. The book had a time-travel element and a lot of historical material, and it was a challenge to keep track of all the characters and discuss how much material was needed to link the characters of the past with those of the present. Even so, *A Swiftly Tilting Planet* was a very comfortable book for me to start out with her on because I had always been interested in pre-Columbian America and the elaborate theories about early explorers, Druid chambers in New Hampshire, things like that. So I was a good person to help her with the research aspects of her story. We talked about this at our first lunch, and it put us on the same wavelength right from the start. Once that book was completed, we then went directly into work on *A Ring of Endless Light*, which is a more linear story.

The editing was always in stages. We would work out the plot, then focus on the characters, and then look at the manuscript line by line. Madeleine didn't always agree with me, but she listened. Once, when I was up at Crosswicks, I knew I was going to have to tell her something she'd find difficult to hear. We were working on *A Ring of Endless Light*, and I thought that she had made the heroine, Vicky, so self-righteous that she came across to the reader as unsympathetic and smug. When I said this to Madeleine, she paused, thought about it for a long minute, and then said, "It's interesting how someone who loves you can say something like that and have it be okay, while someone who doesn't love you might say the same thing and it wouldn't be." She was right. I did love her enough to say it. Because with a successful bestselling writer there can be a temptation to let tough issues slide by. Madeleine never wanted that kind of pass. Not at all. It was a true pleasure to see how she took our conversation and transformed it into what the story needed.

Madeleine didn't come to our office on Union Square very often. I would talk to her a lot by phone. Because she and I both lived on the Upper West Side, she would sometimes stop by my apartment. Very often at the end of my day, I would go to the cathedral library and see her on my way home. Or I would go up there for lunch and then spend the afternoon working with her. I went up to Crosswicks for the weekend several times during each book. Those would be working weekends, but again we would set out across the fields with her eternal battle against bittersweet, which is a vine that strangles trees. The back hall of the house was a little unkempt but in a homey, comfortable 1950s way, with a random assortment of wraps and hats. I always said we looked like Mrs Who and Mrs Whatsit when we ventured out together in the cold months wearing hats, gloves, and anybody's old coat, so long as it was waterproof. Madeleine had these huge loppers—a long-handled pruning shear—and we would go off for a long walk across the fields, talking about the characters in her manuscript of the moment, talking about our families—all intermixed. Every once in a while she would stop and whack off a piece of bittersweet. As you took that walk, she would say, "There's the stargazing rock. There's the wall where the snake is. That's the vegetable garden where they see the angels." She had the property all around her house mapped out with her literary landmarks. At the end of the walk you came to a marsh, which is where she thought the ancient lake mentioned in *A Swiftly Tilting Planet* would have been. It was all there. So in a sense were her characters, including Calvin's toothless mother, Branwen O'Keefe, whom Madeleine told me she modeled on a real person—whether it was a neighbor in Goshen or someone she knew from the cathedral in New York, she did not say. Mrs. O'Keefe became very important in the third book, in a way that she hadn't been previously, and reveals herself to have the key. Madeleine talked about the significance of that character, which was meant as a caution to readers not to assume by a person's appearance who or what that person really was.

When Madeleine and I were at the library working together, we were always being interrupted because when she was there she was the acting librarian. Canon West's cavernous office was next door, and he would drop in now and then. When the three of us were together, he was a little proprietary toward Madeleine. He was gruff. He was sarcastic. He always made it clear that I was the junior member of the corporation. He was not a man who was going to be my friend just because Madeleine was my friend. It was a very formal relationship. During the work on *A Swiftly Tilting Planet*, Hugh read the manuscript editorially and so did Canon West. They both had strong opinions and weren't shy about expressing them. Canon West yelled at me for cutting some of the unicorn scene in *A Swiftly Tilting Planet*. What he didn't realize—or chose to ignore—is that while I made suggestions, occasionally strong suggestions, Madeleine had the final say. She did all the cutting and revising. Every single change, large or small, was her choice.

People who needed to use the cathedral library would wander in, as would people for whom Madeleine served as a spiritual adviser, who would come by to see if she was free to talk. She had a great many of those relationships, including with a number of people whose lives had been hard or complicated or who had suffered great losses and for whom Madeleine was a huge source of comfort. I think she felt a responsibility to people in need, as well as a responsibility to people who responded to her writings from some deep place in their lives. She was willing to engage them in dialogue. I asked her at a writers' conference once how she withstood all that intensity, the overwhelming tide of people wanting something from her, needing something beyond a book signed or a comment about their manuscript, needing a spiritual connection. She said, "I have a rule. At 9:00 p.m., I go to my room no matter what, and I'm done for the day." When we traveled together, she would excuse herself promptly at 9:00. Madeleine always traveled with a flask, the contents of which she referred to as "Ear Water"—it was brandy usually, for which you don't need ice—and about which she said, "A person needs a drink at the end of one of these days!" She also said, adopting the appropriate accent, "No southern girl ever travels without her Ear Water!" The two of us would go upstairs and have a drink, and then Madeleine would settle in for the night and write in her journal for an hour or two.

When *A Swiftly Tilting Planet* was just coming out, we thought it was going to be the last book in the Time sequence. So we decided to press-tour Madeleine, to make a big deal of the event. Madeleine was impatient about shopping, and being a full-service editor, I said, "You can't go out on tour in *that* dress! You're going to be on television. We've got to go shopping!"

I lined up a personal shopper at Bergdorf Goodman, and Madeleine said she would go and do that if I would go with her. We arrived at the store and made our way to a special room where we picked out a couple of outfits, including a then-top-of-the-line pink Ultrasuede suit. She wore that suit for years. It was a good outfit to travel with because—no pun intended—Ultrasuede doesn't wrinkle.

Madeleine would galvanize an ALA convention by her mere presence. (Judy Blume could do that too, although in a different way.) Very, very few authors had anything like Madeleine's impact. Somebody told me a story about her speaking at ALA once and announcing from the podium in the middle of her talk that there would now be a five-minute break while she used the loo, after which she would return! That's how comfortable Madeleine was as a public speaker.

One of the reasons it wasn't a problem at Farrar, Straus to hire relatively inexperienced library promotion people was that if you went to a convention with Madeleine, you immediately met everybody, and they all accepted your invitations to dinner. You did not have to know how to lure people in, only whom to invite. Madeleine genuinely liked the librarians, too, and she liked speaking. Not all writers do, you know. Both as a speaker and in private, she liked to tell jokes and had a horror of being what she called "pi"— too pious. She told me a very funny story about a religious friend of hers in Texas. This was before caller ID, and the woman was getting obscene phone calls in her motel room that would have scared the socks off of me. This woman would pick up the phone, the guy dirty-talked, and she would hang up. It happened repeatedly until finally Madeleine's friend said to the caller, "Son, I am worried about you. I'd like you to pray with me now." No more phone calls after that! Mostly, Madeleine's wit was in her wordplay, in a turn of phrase or an inflection in her voice. She was lighthearted and good company. In the years I knew her, she was on the road as much as she was at home, except for the summers, which she spent at Crosswicks.

Hugh liked having me at Crosswicks because it allowed him the chance to get his two cents in about whatever manuscript Madeleine and I were working on. Madeleine and I would work together in the Tower during the day. Then we'd be having a drink in front of the fire before dinner. That's when Hugh might take me aside and say, "Now, Sandra, about that passage that I think should be cut."

After our evening we would retire upstairs fairly early. Madeleine and Hugh slept at separate ends of the house. Hugh was very deaf by then, and the way a deaf person snores can shake the rafters and peel the paint off the walls. I could hear him halfway across the house. We would gather around Madeleine's four-poster bed, and she would hold court in her bed for twenty minutes or half an hour as we sipped our hot toddies from silver cups. Then we would go off to our own bedrooms.

I can't think of another author I have worked with about whom I would talk so freely, and that is because on several occasions Madeleine asked me to talk publicly about her. She asked me to be interviewed for the *New Yorker* profile of her by Cynthia Zarin, and on several occasions she asked me to talk about what it was like to work with her. Usually, as an editor, you feel that the author can talk about these matters but that you absolutely do not.

I really hated the *New Yorker* article. It didn't have anything to do with the woman I knew. I had no idea that Hugh had been unfaithful. Madeleine had never as much as lifted an eyebrow to suggest that. There's a certain kind of reviewer that you pray you never get. That's the one who's out to make his or her bones by dumping on a well-known author, by pulling down that sacred cow and exposing it for the sham that it is. I guess I should have known or at least suspected when Cynthia Zarin asked me if I thought there had been a romance between Madeleine and Canon West—in response to which I just laughed. I have no idea of Canon West's sexuality, but I couldn't imagine him doing anything so undignified.

I had such affection for Madeleine, and I somehow always felt protective of her. It isn't that she needed my protection particularly, but I sensed a certain vulnerability in her. Even though Madeleine could be kind of grand at times, I always sensed the presence of this other person, and so I never took the grandiosity seriously, and I thought that in any case it was sort of her due insofar as she had achieved so very much. She was very generous to other writers and very generous with herself. She had a very strong sense of reality, but she didn't have very firm edges. Flying saucers? Unicorns in upstate New York? Maybe! I liked that about her.

I thought the profile was a very mean-spirited piece of work about someone who didn't deserve mean-spirited treatment. But that being said, it is certainly true that when Madeleine wrote about her family, she was protective of them and presented a rosier picture than probably existed. I was not the editor on any of her memoirs; however, we had many general conversations about how much one wants to say in print about one's children and what it is fair to say about other people. I think she tried to be unvarnished about herself, about her darker impulses in certain situations. But I don't think it occurred to her to be frank about her children or Hugh. It was a memoir ethos drawn from another time. For her it was about the struggle to reach one's better self, not the airing of family laundry in public.

Charlotte would call me sometimes and ask if I was free to have dinner with her grandmother. We would go to Henry's. One Memorial Day toward the end of Madeleine's life, Charlotte called, and I said that I had a friend visiting from out of town. Charlotte said by all means bring her along. Madeleine, who was in a wheelchair by then, was very startled to see an unfamiliar person at our customary table, and about twenty minutes into the dinner I realized that the Madeleine I was used to talking to was not really there. Her responses were off. She wasn't remembering things. My friend didn't know what was going on as I began to be visibly upset by what I was observing. Afterward, I called Charlotte and said, "I have to tell you that maybe she's having a bad reaction to her medication." To which Charlotte replied, "No, it's much more serious than that." That was one of the last times we had dinner.

After a while Madeleine moved permanently to Connecticut. I didn't see her then, although I regularly heard news of her when I had lunch with her granddaughter the writer Léna Roy, who at that time also lived on the Upper West Side. One afternoon I received a phone call from her granddaughter Charlotte telling me that the end was close, and if I wanted to say goodbye to Madeleine I should plan to go to Connecticut in the next few days. They said she probably would be asleep and wouldn't know me. For a day I thought about going, but Madeleine was surrounded by the people closest to her, who loved her, and there was no need. I called the family and thanked them for inviting me. Then I walked over to St. Michael's with its glorious Tiffany windows shining in the late summer sun to say goodbye and wish a safe harbor for my friend.

Beverly Horowitz is vice president and publisher of Delacorte Press Books for Young Readers at Random House.

*Q: How did you meet Madeleine L'Engle?*

A: In 1978, I went to Farrar, Straus and Giroux as the company's school and library promotion and academic marketing sales director. It was my fourth job in publishing, and it happened that my first day on the job was the day that Madeleine L'Engle was going to the Catholic Library Association in Chicago. Part of my new job was to accompany her for such appearances. I came into the office early that first day, and from there I headed to the airport, where I had arranged to meet Madeleine, and off we went.

It all went smoothly, although one big surprise lay ahead for me. No one had told me we would be staying at a convent—the convent of the order of nuns who were hosting the convention. When we arrived, we each got our own little convent room, hard, narrow bed and all. Madeleine appreciated people who could adapt to circumstances and think on their feet, as she herself was so good at doing, and it was during that brief trip that our friendship began.

Madeleine proceeded to give her conference talk, which was wonderful and very well received. She spoke about having been a gawky, giraffe-like teenager. She told about her mother and father, how they had not exactly been the warmest parents. She described her experience of boarding school, how as a new arrival she had been caught chewing gum and how she had had to put the wad of gum in the headmistress's hand in front of all her fellow students. She described just how humiliating that had felt. It was thrilling to hear such an honest accounting, all of which served as her lead-in to a discussion of how her vision of herself and the world had developed over the years. She talked about having to make things happen for oneself and about her belief that there might be a higher power to help one along the way. All in all, I learned an awful lot about Madeleine L'Engle on my first day as FSG's library promotion director. Back in New York a few days later she called me and said, "Wow! That was your first day on the job? I had no idea!"

It was a good beginning, and it set the tone for a relationship that lasted long after we were no longer working together. This was the year that *A Swiftly Tilting Planet* was coming out, and in the months that followed, we planned a lot of activities to celebrate the event. Later that same year, I was walking the exhibition hall floor at another convention when I happened to hear one of two librarians just ahead of me speak Madeleine's name. My ears perked up, and the next thing I knew, this librarian was saying rather boastfully to his companion, "Yeah, I'm hoping I'll get to review *A Swiftly Tilting Planet*, because no matter what—if I trash it or I love it—I'll always be known as the reviewer of that book." I found that remark a bit startling. Even more, it impressed me as an indication of Madeleine's incredible power. Some time later, I found myself at another convention to promote Farrar, Straus's adult books for the academic market and overheard two academics having the identical conversation, only this time the "big name" that was being bandied about was that of the author of a new biography of Joseph Conrad.

One year after I arrived at FSG, I moved to Dell, which was Madeleine's paperback publisher, so we continued to work together. Dell had her books on the Dell Yearling middle-grade list, and while I was there, we put them on the Dell Laurel-Leaf list as well, formatted differently for teens. It was new at the time to package the same book in different formats and with different cover art in order to reach multiple readerships. Some people feared the two editions would compete with each other, but we knew that they would expand Madeleine's audience, and in fact that is precisely what happened.

Vicky Austin was the character closest to Madeleine, and at Dell I told her we would repackage all the Austin books. We did four of them while I was there. Madeleine felt very connected to Vicky—and to Camilla, another shy, lonely, family-oriented girl. Those two girls were the easiest characters for her to write about. Something good would always end up happening to them and they would do some good along the way. That was her unwritten formula; it was the way she thought—and lived.

Madeleine always had an extraordinarily full schedule. Everyone wanted her as a speaker, and it didn't seem to matter much that her fee was hardly a small one for the time. Once she explained to me why she insisted on flying first-class. "Beverly, I'm an awkward woman with bad knees. I'm a giant! I'm not going to sit all scrunched up in the back of a plane and then step out and perform. They expect me to give my all, and I'm happy to do it. But to do that, this is what I need." That need made her, in some ways, a creature of habit. She was always thinking about time and about maintaining her routine. She was determined not to let her time go to waste. Madeleine was well aware of how much people loved her and wanted a piece of her. She understood it and was willing to give of herself, and I came to think this was at least in part her response to the coldness of her own parents.

She maintained a vast correspondence, much of it with people who would want an emotional lift from her. Because the Dell paperback editions of her books had made such a big difference in her career, greatly expanding her audience, many of her fan letters came to our offices at Dell. Madeleine's fan mail was somewhat comparable to Judy Blume's in the degree to which the people who wrote were intensely emotional. People admired her for her personal commitment to God and faith, and they wanted it to rub off on them.

Today many writers want to be crossover authors with both an adult audience and an audience of young readers for their work. Madeleine was ahead of her time in that respect. I remember saying to her once how important her books were for all kinds of readers because there were so many strong adult characters as well as young heroes in her books. To which she replied, "I like you! You get it! I did not even have to tell you that." She may have said that to me on the plane that first day on the way to Chicago. I had read her books in anticipation of our first meeting, and that too had impressed her. In fact, as famous as she was, she seemed genuinely grateful.

Madeleine could be full of surprises. One day, having just returned from giving a speech somewhere, she called me with an unusual question: "Is there anybody in Whittier, California, who wants me?" I said, "Isn't that where President Nixon is from?" "Well, I don't care about that," Madeleine said. "But how about it—Whittier, California, or someplace close to there?" "I guess I could look into it for you," I said. Then she explained. "I met someone from the Golden Door"—a very famous and luxurious spa— "and she said that she'd love for me to come and stay at the spa. So I thought maybe I could give a speech while I'm there!"

Years and years after I first met her, Madeleine had a minor operation. When I stopped by the hospital after work to visit her, Hugh, her husband, was there too. We exchanged hellos and were chatting away when all at once the three of us noticed a stranger standing in the doorway. Madeleine and Hugh were a bit taken aback by this, but just then my library promotion skills kicked in and I turned to the stranger and said, "May I help you?" With a note of desperation in her voice, the woman in the doorway replied, "I know it's an imposition, but I'm here because I'm such a fan!" Madeleine assumed she meant a fan of hers. But then the woman, turning her gaze to Hugh, said, "Dr. Tyler? Would you please come see my mother?" Unfazed, Hugh replied, "Well, I am Dr. Tyler, but then again . . . I'm not." To which Madeleine responded, rather sympathetically, I thought, under the circumstances, "Oh, Hugh, go and be Dr. Tyler for five minutes. Just make sure you don't give out any medical advice!"—and off he went down the hall.

Neal Porter, editorial director of Neal Porter Books at Roaring Brook Press, has worked in publishing for more than thirty-five years.

*Q: How did you meet Madeleine L'Engle?*

A: I came to Farrar, Straus and Giroux, her publisher, in January 1979, having taken a job there without even realizing it was in the children's book department. Farrar, Straus was a company where I very much wanted to work.

In 1979, Union Square, where FSG had its offices, was a shambles: a well-known hangout for addicts and homeless people. There was a methadone clinic in our building. When I arrived in the morning, I was more likely than not going to be riding up the elevator with someone who had slept in it that night. The company's offices were themselves incredibly dingy in their way, crowded with desks and bookshelves. We all worked on top of each other. There was a kind of reverse-chic principle in operation, the message being that the money all went into the books we published. In fact, I felt it was a privilege to work at Farrar, Straus, and that *was* because of the books—and the authors we published. On a given day you might be running into Philip Roth or Bernard Malamud or Isaac Singer or Susan Sontag—or, from the children's book list, William Steig or Maurice Sendak or Natalie Babbitt. As was typical of publishers in general in that period, you got a very fancy title and very little money. My title was director of library services and academic sales, which essentially meant "children's book library marketing person."

Soon after my arrival, I had lunch with John Donovan, who was then head of the Children's Book Council. When the conversation turned to what I had to look forward to in my new job, John said, "Well, you'll get to work with Madeleine. Madeleine is a queen!" I wasn't quite sure what he meant by that, although it was obvious that he meant it affectionately. Looking back, I think he was preparing me for the formidable woman that Madeleine could be.

Not long after that I invited Madeleine to lunch for a get-acquainted session. Madeleine was of course very tall, and I am not. It was a cold winter day, and as we were leaving the restaurant, I asked for her coat and gallantly attempted to put it on her shoulders. Madeleine's shoulders were so high that I could barely reach them!

I was thrilled to meet the author of *A Wrinkle in Time*, which I had first read as an eight-year-old, soon after it won the Newbery Medal. I had been given a copy by a friend of my grandmother's, most likely *because* it had won the Newbery and was thus deemed a suitable present for a boy who loved to read. It instantly became my favorite book and remained so for many, many years. I loved the science fiction and fantasy elements in the story—the tessering and all that—and as an only child I could identify with Meg's sense of isolation and introverted personality. I was completely unaware of the religious underpinnings of Madeleine's writings or Madeleine's own spirituality. It wasn't until I got to Farrar, Straus all those years later that I realized what a significant part of her life that was.

At the time I joined the company, Madeleine and her editor, Sandra Jordan, were working on the final draft of *A Ring of Endless Light*, and we were all starting to prepare for its publication the following year. Anticipation within the house was running high. *A Wrinkle in Time* was one of Farrar, Straus's perennial bestsellers, as were the second and third books in the Time sequence, *A Wind in the Door* and *A Swiftly Tilting Planet*. *Ring* was her first novel about the Austin family since *The Young Unicorns* in 1968. We knew Madeleine's fans were eagerly awaiting her next book. Around that same time, we repackaged the hardcover editions of the Time books with new jackets that Sandra had asked Leo and Diane Dillon to design. So Madeleine had a lot going on.

I was responsible for advertising, promotion, and publicity on behalf of all the children's books we published. I organized and attended conferences on behalf of the house. In addition, I was responsible for marketing our adult books to colleges. Yet I'd say that Madeleine occupied about 40 percent of my time, in part because no other author received anything like the same number of speaking requests that she did, and it was my job to field those requests, negotiate her fees, and make her travel arrangements, the latter in collaboration with Madeleine's rather fearsome travel agent. I also forwarded her fan mail to her and sometimes answered it on her behalf. The range of her correspondents was unlike any other author's too: everyone from the latest eight-year-old to have fallen in love with *A Wrinkle in Time* to religious acolytes seeking spiritual guidance. Madeleine had a wicked sense of humor and could also be very casual about certain matters. To herald the repackaging effort for the Time books, we created a set of beautiful posters featuring the new cover art by the Dillons. When I asked Madeleine if she would sign a number of posters for booksellers, she said, "Oh, just sign my name, Neal!" I thought, My God—and for once I think I meant it literally, considering what a spiritual person Madeleine herself was!

Madeleine could be intimidating and she could be theatrical, but she often spoke in a quiet voice, and I suspect that buried within the public Madeleine L'Engle was a very shy person. She was always sweet to me. When we first met, she asked me about my previous jobs in publishing, about my family, and about my interests. We shared a love of the theater, and we often talked about that. We even went to the theater together a couple of times, which was fun because it would prompt stories of her touring days. Although I was at Farrar, Straus for only a bit more than a year, it was long enough for her to invite me to Crosswicks, where she made me feel completely at ease. I was her only guest that summer weekend, and I remember accompanying her on long walks and meeting Hugh, who was distinguished-looking and slightly arch and who struck me as very much a helpmate to Madeleine. On one of the two nights I spent there, we watched a spectacular lightning storm together. Madeleine, as the archetypal WASP, always seemed as if she should be fancy, but in reality she was something of an Earth Mother.

Still, she liked things to be done well, and there are certain things one did for her. The first time I ever rode in a limousine was when Madeleine and I were traveling together and I ordered one to take us to the airport. I remember feeling, Wow, I'm in a limo! But for her everything always came back to her work. She wrote continually and could write anywhere. When we were on the road together, she would agree to meet me in our hotel lobby at such and such hour. When I found her, she invariably had a notebook in hand and was scribbling away.

My most memorable trip with her was to Peoria, Illinois, for a regional International Reading Association meeting. It was in wintertime, and it was bitterly cold. A major snowstorm had blanketed the Northeast and the Midwest, complicating our plan to fly to Chicago and then take a puddle jumper to Peoria. All flights were delayed, and when we finally reached O'Hare, we had to run, dragging our bags from terminal to terminal, to make our connecting flight. We arrived in Peoria hours late, at something like two in the morning. What astonished me was Madeleine's reaction to all this: it was an annoyance, but one dealt with it. She was due to speak at nine o'clock the next morning, and when the time came, she took the podium, sharp as could be, and delivered a brilliant talk while giving the impression of being completely rested and relaxed. Coming back, we flew into LaGuardia, and Hugh came to the airport to pick her up. Hugh was well-known to soap opera fans as Dr. Charles Tyler on *All My Children*. The show had made him quite a celebrity. At the conference in Peoria, Madeleine had been a great star. Now, in LaGuardia, we were making our way through the corridor in the arrivals area, where essentially nobody had any idea who she was. When we reached Hugh, we found him surrounded by a massive crowd of adoring women, all calling out things like "Oh!"; "You're Dr. Charles Tyler!"; and "I love you so much!" Madeleine stood back, obviously used to scenes like this but still slightly bemused by it all. Eventually, we got out of there.

Madeleine was one of the Farrar, Straus authors I accompanied to the 1979 American Library Association conference, in Dallas. It was quite a heady meeting, with the temperature hovering around 105 degrees. As it happened, I was running a fever of 103 myself, but I had to be there because I was in charge of orchestrating a whole series of events for a cast of characters that, besides Madeleine, included Isaac Singer, Uri Shulevitz, and two or three other stars from our list. Madeleine, ever the lady, was sitting with me at dinner one evening when I became so feverish that I was practically sliding under the table. Each time I began to sink in my chair, Madeleine would prop me up again! It was so typical of her: having immediately grasped the situation, she carried the conversation for both of us, allowing me to save my breath as I quietly turned green! Isaac Singer had brought along his wife. I still can picture him in a cowboy hat as he stepped into the all-glass Hyatt atrium elevator and went up and down, up and down, because, as he said, he enjoyed the ride.

I kept my horribly mangled childhood copy of *A Wrinkle in Time*, in which, on receiving it as a gift, I had proudly written, "This book belongs to Neal Porter." Madeleine of course was delighted when I showed it to her, and writing above my name, she inscribed the book for me: "To Neal, companion on the way."

## STEPHEN ROXBURGH

Stephen Roxburgh is the founder of Namelos, an independent publishing company, and is a former senior vice president and publisher of books for young readers at Farrar, Straus and Giroux.

*Q: How did you meet Madeleine L'Engle?*

A: I started work at Farrar, Straus and Giroux on June 26, 1978. Sandra Jordan was the editor in chief of the children's book department. Her assistant was leaving, and I was hired to replace her. A little over a year later, our promotion director, Beverly Horowitz, left, and Neal Porter replaced her—briefly. When Neal left, I took that job with the result that for the next year or so I was responsible for Madeleine's speaking schedule. Madeleine kept up a grueling pace, spending a week or more on the road every month.

When Sandra left in 1981, I succeeded her as head of the editorial department. Our division grew substantially during the 1980s and 1990s. There were times when the income we generated supported the house. The Carl books by Alexandra Day were our biggest juvenile bestsellers. We began publishing Roald Dahl then, and his books were very successful, too. Madeleine's books always contributed substantially, and they had for years. Roger Straus often talked about the number of Nobel laureates on the FSG list, but few of those writers matched Madeleine's royalty income. It's interesting that with Madeleine, as with many established authors, we didn't have to worry much about what the reviewers said, because it didn't matter. Her fans would want her books anyway. All we had to do was let them know that a new book was coming.

Madeleine was a professional and a hard worker, and she was prolific. But she was undisciplined. She would write a lot, throw away a lot, and write a lot more. Sometimes that more was better, while other times it was worse.

Usually, when I would hear about a book that was still just an idea in her mind, she wouldn't talk about it in any detail. She assumed that I knew the extended families of her major characters intimately, and would simply say, "I'm going to write a book about so-and-so." We would not discuss the book further until I would get word one day to send over a messenger to pick up the manuscript.

She would send me a manuscript on a Friday, and I would work on it over the weekend. Then Monday morning would roll around, I would call her, and invariably she would say, "Oh, never mind, Stephen. I threw away that hundred pages!" This was frustrating, of course. Finally, I had to say, "Madeleine, please don't work on it after you send it to me." As I quickly learned, however, she couldn't help herself. The solution was to go and spend hours with her working through the manuscript page by page. It was a time-consuming process, but it was good, productive work.

Madeleine was wide open to editorial suggestions. If she felt strongly about something, of course she would defend it. And, as I said, she would freely chuck any number of pages that did not work. What I always try to do as an editor is to find what the author wants to say. Madeleine did not always know and would offer multiple solutions. She was extremely good at devising alternative plot variations. In fact, she was arguably too good at it because what she would do is abandon something that wasn't quite working and introduce an entirely new plotline. Often a radical change in plot was more than was required, and in this way she needed to be reeled back in.

Madeleine would refer to the censorship challenges to her books, but I don't remember censorship being a major issue with the books we worked on together.* The one book we anticipated some people taking issue with was *A House like a Lotus*, in which she gave a sympathetic portrayal of a lesbian relationship, a subject not common in young adult books at that time. Madeleine was determined to portray the relationship in a positive light. It is true that she took a mischievous pleasure in thinking that she was going to agitate people. She reveled in controversy. She delighted in debate and was good at it. Also, Madeleine was a highly sought-after lay preacher in the Episcopal Church. In a way, Madeleine was always preaching: in her books, in conversation. She had a mission, and a part of the editorial work was trying to pare some of that down in her fiction.

In the years that I worked with her, she reveled in her popularity. Fame fit her like a glove. When we worked together, we simply focused on the manuscript. But when I would be with her in public, which happened fairly often, whether it was on the road or at some New York publishing event, she became something of a grande dame. She was used to having flocks of adoring people around her. She knew how to engage them, and it was amazing to watch her do it.

---

*In 2007, the Office for Intellectual Freedom of the American Library Association issued a report titled "The 100 Most Frequently Challenged Books of 1990–2000." *A Wrinkle in Time* ranked twenty-second on the list, just ahead of *Go Ask Alice*.

She was an extraordinary writer and a remarkable person, and I learned a lot from her. One thing I learned from Madeleine was how to work with a writer who was more creative than disciplined. A new writer needs an old editor, and a new editor needs an old writer. I was lucky enough when I went to Farrar, Straus and Giroux as a young editor to work with a writer of Madeleine's complexity, generosity, and stature.

Catherine Hand is a former creative executive in the office of Norman Lear, vice president of Embassy Pictures, and director of development at American Zoetrope. In 2004, she served as executive producer of the Miramax/ABC film adaptation of *A Wrinkle in Time*.

*Q: How did you meet Madeleine L'Engle?*

A: In 1979, I was working for the writer/producer Norman Lear as his assistant and was tasked with reviewing material for him to produce. Mostly, I read scripts submitted by agents, Norman's colleagues, or friends. A friend of mine asked me, What would you like to produce? I know it sounds odd, but I was always thinking about what Norman might like to produce, never thinking about what I would like to produce. But with the question came my answer—a book I had read in fifth grade called *A Wrinkle in Time*.

I asked my friend to read it, and he loved it, which gave me the courage to ask Norman to read it, and he loved it, too. He suggested I check to see if the rights were available. I sent a letter to Madeleine, she followed up with a phone call, and three days later we met in New York at Windows on the World, the restaurant at the top of the World Trade Center.

*Q: The film was not produced until 2004. Why did it take so long?*

A: Norman knew it needed a writer or director who had the right vision to bring it to the screen, but we never imagined that it would be a difficult book to adapt. We started with one of the best, Sir Robert Bolt, screenwriter for *A Man for All Seasons*, *Doctor Zhivago*, and *Lawrence of Arabia*. He was someone who knew how to tell big stories with great characters—which is how we saw *Wrinkle*. When his screenplay didn't work, Madeleine asked to try her hand at writing the script. It was a very exciting time sitting around Norman's conference table with Madeleine trying to map out the adaptation. Unfortunately, Madeleine was just too close to the material to see it differently as a film, and we realized we would have to bring in someone else.

At a critical point in the process, Norman's company, Embassy Pictures, was sold to Coca-Cola/Columbia, and he kept *Wrinkle* out of the deal. That decision made it possible for me to continue my quest to bring the book to the screen. At a certain point, Norman's option ran out, and Madeleine graciously gave me time to try to set it up elsewhere. I met with a number of folks at various studios who all wanted the rights, but just as I was about to give birth to my youngest daughter, I got a call from Bob Weinstein at Miramax. He was so insistent that he "had to make this movie" that I agreed to meet with him a week after the baby was born. I didn't understand how a small independent company like Miramax could afford to make *Wrinkle*, but he assured me he would find a way. We signed a deal, and two months later Disney bought Miramax.

*Q: What made it so very hard for such talented writers to come up with a satisfactory screenplay?*

A: In her preface to one of the later editions of *A Wrinkle in Time*, Madeleine wrote that the book has meant different things to different readers, and that it has even meant different things to the same reader at different times in his or her life. I have sat with many, many people who were absolutely sure they knew how *A Wrinkle in Time* should be made into a film, and each one had a different idea.

It was difficult to find agreement on how to change the characters and plot for a screen adaptation. I even had one executive say to me, "It has to be about something other than 'love triumphs over all.' People have said that for two thousand years, and we know it just doesn't work." I read a book called *The Making of "The Wizard of Oz,"* by Aljean Harmetz, from which I learned that the talent behind that movie had similar issues. There were dozens of screenplays written. Reading the book gave me hope and insight into our process.

*Q: Were you still living in California?*

A: Yes, first in Los Angeles when I worked with Norman, then in San Francisco when I worked at Zoetrope, for Francis Coppola, who at one point was interested in executive-producing the film.

*Q: How often would you see Madeleine?*

A: I would visit her periodically in New York, at her apartment or at the cathedral library. We would talk on the phone from time to time. I always sought her guidance about any major development. She was my touchstone. I would talk to her about the various people I was meeting with and about different directions the film might take.

*Q: With Madeleine having a theater background, did the two of you enjoy exchanging stories about the entertainment business?*

A: Yes, and that was a lot of fun, especially because Madeleine had been an assistant to the great actress Eva Le Gallienne. She told me that as she wrote *A Wrinkle in Time*, she had been imagining Eva Le Gallienne as one of the ladies.

*Q: What about Madeleine herself? Was she ever considered for an acting part in the film?*

A: No, but what I eventually realized was that she was the inspiration for all her characters and no one could ever play Meg as well as she could.

*Q: She was fond of quoting from literature.*

A: Yes, and that of course was Mrs Who. And she had such a great sense of joy—very much like Mrs Whatsit. She "trusted in us," and that kept me going many times when I wanted to give up. She could also be like Mrs Which—very exacting and intimidating!

*Q: Tell me about Thomas Banchoff.*

A: In the early 1980s, I read anything I could get my hands on about higher dimensions, theories of time, things like that— topics that are much more widely discussed today. But back then it was all new thinking. One day I came across a *Scientific American* article about the work of Tom and his colleagues on fourth-dimension imaging. I called Tom and asked to meet with him. He showed me a Möbius strip and a tesseract he had built out of cardboard. It was all so fascinating. I wanted whatever changes we would need to make to the book to include the current thinking about multiple dimensions. I introduced Tom to Madeleine, and we had interesting conversations about the tesseract—what it would look like, et cetera.

*Q: Why was a television movie finally made instead of a feature film?*

A: Everything in the entertainment business comes down to timing and money. Disney had decided not to make it as a big-budget picture, but Disney owned ABC, where there was interest in making it as a film for television. The problem was that it now had to be a four-hour miniseries, which was tough for the material to support. We were working under several other major constraints as well: an impending actors' strike, the decision to make the film in Canada, and very little time for preproduction.

*Q: Was Madeleine, who was not in good health by the time the film aired on television in May 2004, able to see it?*

A: We had a reading of the first act for her, and she said she thought it was well written. But I think she was always concerned that the film was never going to live up to the book.

*Q: Tell me more about what you learned from Madeleine.*

A: She was my mentor in every way that a mentor can be. She supported me when I needed her support as a producer, which was very generous of her. She gave me important advice about life. She was there for me when my husband died. And I think I learned so much in talking with her about *A Wrinkle in Time*. Early on, Madeleine said to me that she understood the book was going to have to change for the screen, but she made me promise that one line would always be in it: "Like and equal are not the same thing." To be honest, I didn't quite understand why that was so important to her, but as my thinking evolved, my understanding of her request evolved, too. It's really the essence of the story. Most readers will tell you it's about love, because love does triumph over all. However, Meg's development arc is connected to her ability to understand that like and equal are not the same thing, and it is out of that understanding that she realizes that she loves her brother in a way that the dark forces cannot. In the beginning of the story, she feels badly that she isn't like everyone else—that she's an oddball, a biological mistake. But when she meets Aunt Beast, she discovers that who you are as a person isn't defined by what can be "seen," but rather by what is "unseen"—the eternal truth of you. It's really at the heart of anyone fighting for equality—I don't look like you, I have a different religion, color of skin, gender . . . fill in the blank, but I'm a human being and want to be heard. Fundamentalists or absolutists are essentially people trying to make others like them. Tolerance, openness, new thinking, are about accepting our differences and "trusting" that differences might be more difficult, but also more rewarding in the end. Mrs. Murry says something to Meg that captures this really well: "Just because we don't understand doesn't mean that the explanation doesn't exist." Madeleine wanted us always to be brave enough to ask questions. There is so much yet undiscovered. And at the same time we need also to be willing to trust, to have faith, and to love.

Q: *At the core of the book is a girl's search for her father.*

A: Meg is searching for her father—because she wants her father to make everything better for her. Then she finds her father, and he isn't able to make everything better; in fact, he makes things worse. Almost fifty years ago, Madeleine was wrestling with such fundamental questions about growing up: What happens when no one can save you? What is my place in the world? Are there others in the universe besides us? Are like and equal the same thing? What does trust mean? What does faith mean? What is love?

Q: *Did she ever act out a scene from* A Wrinkle in Time *for you?*

A: Yes. She and her husband, Hugh, would do readings of the book, and nobody read Meg like Madeleine. You couldn't help but fall in love with Meg when Madeleine read her out loud. She would read with such intensity and earnestness. Meg was just like Madeleine—sometimes fiercely insecure and at other times fiercely determined, always with a passion about life. That is adolescence, isn't it? Madeleine captured the essence of the young adolescent girl, and I think that for a great many girls that is why Meg has been such an incredibly important character.

# JUDY BLUME

Judy Blume is a novelist for children, teens, and adults and has served on the boards of the Authors Guild and the National Coalition Against Censorship, among other organizations. In 2000, the Library of Congress honored her as a "Living Legend."

*Q: How did you meet Madeleine L'Engle?*

A: We must have met through the Authors Guild Council, possibly in the early 1980s. We would go to meetings together. Madeleine would often talk to me about her granddaughters. It may have been that her granddaughters were reading my books. I always felt that I knew them and loved the idea of their closeness to her.

But Madeleine and I *really* bonded over the issue of book banning. Her books were being challenged all over the country. They were being challenged—and I love this and have used it in every speech about book banning that I've ever given—for teaching "New Age–ism" to children. I always say that I can guarantee you that when Madeleine wrote her books, she had never heard of New Age–ism. The attacks on her books made her absolutely furious. She was beside herself, not just because her books were being attacked, but because *any* books were being targeted in that way. We would go out and do TV shows together in defense of banned books. An evening news show might have a segment on the censorship of children's books. This was during the 1980s. She was so elegant and so down-to-earth, and some of her answers were so funny, as much as to say, Why are you guys so stupid? Why would you be asking questions like this? She never actually said those things, but it was absolutely clear what she meant. I just loved her.

After the novelist Norma Klein died in 1989, an award was created in her memory to be given out through PEN, and Madeleine and I were on the committee to choose the first winner. One day she came to my apartment for a meeting. My husband, George, was there too, and I remember her telling us a very funny story about her dog. She had a very large dog, she said, that she would take for walks along Riverside Drive, high above Riverside Park, at night. She told us that she had decided that when the dog pooped, she would clean up after it and then hold on to the poop so that in case she was attacked by a mugger, she could really let the person have it! Then one night she *was* attacked, and she did let the guy have it, and in his haste to get away, the attacker threw himself over what he thought was a low stone wall, not realizing how big the drop was on the other side, down into the park below.

After she left the meeting, I found that she had forgotten her calendar, and I looked at it, and I was just overwhelmed at all the places that she was going. Madeleine was already in her seventies then, and I remember thinking, Oh my God. She's still doing this! She was going all over the country, and I just couldn't believe it! She must have had a tremendous amount of energy, and she must have loved to do it.

I don't think that I actually met Madeleine's granddaughters until her eightieth birthday party [in 1998]. That was quite a party. Madeleine wrote for *Victoria* magazine, and the magazine gave a huge birthday lunch in her honor in New York. She invited a few people from the Authors Guild to sit at her table. Jim Gleick, the science writer, was one of her guests, and I was seated next to him. Herbert Mitgang, from *The New York Times* and the Authors Guild Council, was also at our table. I didn't really know Jim, and at one point he and I asked each other how we had come to be invited. He said that all he knew was that it was well-known that he had loved *A Wrinkle in Time* when he was growing up. If you think about what he does now, it makes a lot of sense. Later, we were each asked to stand up and say a few words about Madeleine, and so that is what Jim talked about. When it was my turn to speak, I must have said something about book banning because, as I said before, that was how Madeleine and I really connected. It was extremely important to her that people were saying, "We want these books removed. We don't want children to read these books"—whether they were her books, or my books, or anybody's books.

Q: *Considering what a public figure Madeleine was, does it surprise you that she saw herself as gawky-looking, sometimes even comparing herself to a giraffe?*

A: That's interesting because to me she was pure beauty and elegance. She was so tall and straight. And those long skirts, the flat shoes . . . I was a great admirer of everything about her. And she was so enormously friendly and generous to me and, you see, I didn't even know her well.

I have a very strong memory of being invited to go to the Four Seasons for lunch with Norman Lear. I didn't know Norman Lear, and I thought, Why is Norman Lear inviting me to lunch? I'm not sure I ever found out! But at that lunch what he talked about was having a film option on *A Wrinkle in Time*. Now I'm wondering, Was he trying to figure out if I could write the screenplay for it? Or did he just like meeting with writers? Maybe . . .

I even remember what I ordered, because it was all so unusual! I wasn't one of those sophisticated New Yorkers, and yet there I was having lunch at the Four Seasons and talking about *A Wrinkle in Time*.

## HELEN STEPHENSON

Helen Stephenson is a former executive director of the Authors Guild.

*Q: How did you meet Madeleine L'Engle?*

A: I was from Vermont and had been in New York for a year when, in late 1980, the longtime executive director of the Authors Guild, Peter Heggie, hired me as one of two assistant directors. One of my first assignments was to work with the Children's Book Committee. Madeleine L'Engle and Isabelle Holland were the committee's co-chairs. Suddenly to all my friends and relatives with children in the middle grades I was a celebrity because *I knew Madeleine L'Engle.* Judy Blume was on the committee too, which made me a double celebrity.

The Children's Book Committee was a very active part of the guild. We had meetings and events at which the craft and business of writing children's books were discussed. We talked about new technologies—for example, personal computers! Children's book authors, including Madeleine, were among the earliest adapters.

When I got to the guild, publishing was being corporatized, and the guild committed itself to fighting, as best it could, the mergers and acquisitions that were becoming increasingly prevalent. Our main concern at the time was that publishers not fall into the hands of owners who were themselves not publishers and who therefore did not understand publishing's role in the larger culture, such as when a Canadian railroad company tried to buy Houghton Mifflin.

The Children's Book Committee was well respected within the guild, especially considering how many subcultures we had. There were the nonfiction writers. There were the fiction writers. The writers who did not live in New York always assumed they were missing out on something special by not living in the city and were sure that if they did live here, they would become bestselling authors. We had the *New Yorker* group and the *New York Times* group. There was always a lot going on. Madeleine was the first children's book author to serve as an officer—first as vice president and then, beginning in the spring of 1985, as president of the guild, succeeding Anne Edwards. She held the latter position for two years. She was a very effective president in part because she was a workhorse and a pragmatic person and in part because she knew so many people and was herself so well-known. Everybody knew who Madeleine was.

All the factions of the guild would come together in support of freedom of expression. When Brezhnev was in power in the Soviet Union, we were always trying to get some Soviet author out of jail. We would circulate petitions, and Madeleine would always be among the signers.

Not long after I got to the guild, Madeleine and I were sitting around with Judy Blume, Norma Klein, and the rest of the committee to discuss the fact that one of Judy's books was in trouble once again. Madeleine talked about how she had been in shock when *Wrinkle* was declared anti-Christian and there were attempts to ban it at various schools. That experience had been an eye-opener for her. The question for us was: Do we or don't we put up a big fight any time a book was banned? There were different views on that. Madeleine favored taking a case-by-case approach, whereas Judy, because of the more broadly controversial nature of her books, had come to the idea that she did not want to venture into a small southern town, say, and cause more trouble for the local librarians who were trying to combat censorship. Usually, the librarians themselves wanted to go to the barricades. Madeleine didn't want to be hostile, but she wanted to be firm. Sometimes we would sit at the enormous dining room table in her West End Avenue apartment, which I always felt could be expanded even more, like the loaves and the fishes in the New Testament parable, to invite in ten more. I always felt there was that side to her.

Madeleine was fantastic at chairing a meeting. She insisted that progress be made, and while she tolerated a certain amount of dissent, she didn't allow things to get nasty. If a situation arose in which she thought there could be no resolution, she had the sly habit of taking whoever she thought responsible for the impasse and appointing him or her to chair a new committee. She would then make sure to appoint one or two other people to the committee who she knew would serve as moderating influences. As a final touch, she would instruct the group to report back to her on their progress in a month's time.

I had been at the guild for four years when I decided to leave to pursue graduate studies at the University of Chicago. A year later I returned to New York and was on the Broadway bus one day—this was in late 1985—and I ran into Madeleine, who was now the guild president. We exchanged pleasantries, and I didn't think much about it. Then, in March 1986, I got a phone call from the guild saying that the director, Peter Heggie, was very ill, and would I come back and run the guild until he got better? I said, "Sure." Then Peter died, and the guild asked me to stay on permanently as the new director.

This was an exciting time for the guild. Robert K. Massie, J. Anthony Lukas, David Halberstam, and other nonfiction writers had taken over the organization's reins, and because they were freelancers, and did not have day jobs or pensions, they were deeply concerned about the difficulties faced by writers trying to make it on their own. Under their leadership, the economics of publishing became a major focus of the guild's activities—just as publishing was becoming big business.

Previously, under Anne Edwards's presidency, the guild had commissioned Columbia University to conduct a major study of authors' incomes. We were fighting at the time for public lending rights—for royalties paid to authors when their books were borrowed from the library, as was the practice in England. Columbia used our membership as a database and sent everyone questionnaires. Madeleine was in favor of public lending rights but only if it was set up in such a way that the payments would not take away from the librarians' budgets. She did not want the libraries to suffer for the authors' sake!

Not long after the Columbia study was completed, Congress enacted the Tax Reform Act of 1986, which upended authors by barring them from deducting their expenses unless they could match them against revenues. By the time the Tax Reform Act was passed, Madeleine was president and Bob Massie was vice president and was working closely with her. We decided to fight the new tax provision on Capitol Hill. Robert Caro was also involved in this decision. We soon realized that we were combating the caricature of the author as someone who made heaps of money by sitting at home and doing a little bit of work once in a while. The IRS in particular held this view. It was up to us to prove to the government that most authors were in fact poor and not living the high life like Jacqueline Susann! Thanks to the Columbia study, we were able to show just how low the typical author's wages were. Even so, the battle dragged on for about two years.

Madeleine's own books sold very well, but on one occasion it was discovered that Dell had forgotten to pay her four years' worth of her paperback royalties—a very substantial sum. Because this was not an unusual situation at that time, the guild became

interested in auditing publishers. Madeleine was certainly in favor
of that. It wasn't just her own situation that disturbed her. Some
of the romance writers *never* saw their royalties. We would sometimes cite Madeleine's case to show that it wasn't only romance
writers who were being shortchanged.

Madeleine was president of the guild while Hugh was dying.
Bob Massie would sometimes cover for her, and he was astounded
to see how strong Madeleine was, how she was able to spend long
hours at the hospital and still do the guild's work and do her own
writing as well. We weren't sure how she put that all together, but
of course it had to do with her extraordinary sense of discipline.
Once we were together at a meeting, and I overheard her talking
with a science writer about mitochondria. I thought, Wait a
minute, she's not doing guild business! A moment later, she was
right back with me. I was amazed by her ability to refocus at will.

By the time the Authors Guild went to Washington to lobby
against the Tax Reform Act, Hugh had died, and Bob Massie had
succeeded Madeleine as president. Madeleine remained on the
board and continued to do a lot for us. There came a time when a
certain senator, a member of the Senate Finance Committee and
an ardent supporter of the arts who was on our side, suddenly let
it be known that he had changed his mind. One of the Hill staffers
said to me, "I have no idea why, and the only way you're going to
find out is if you know somebody who knows the White House
ophthalmologist." I said, "Huh? Why?" "Because," he replied, "the
White House ophthalmologist is this senator's friend and they'll
be seeing each other at a White House dinner very soon." Soon
afterward, I happened to be on the phone with Madeleine—this
was in 1987 or early 1988—and I said to her, "Oh, Madeleine, I've
got to try to track down somebody who knows the White House
ophthalmologist." I said this with a little laugh because I never in
a million years thought that I was going to be able to do that.
Which is why Madeleine's next words floored me. "Well, *I* know

him!" she said. "Really?" We were both laughing now. "Yes, I do," she said. "He and I are both members of the Order of St. John of Jerusalem."* I was acquainted with that group's history. "Madeleine, is that the same group as the Knights of Malta?"†—which has a very controversial past. "Not exactly," she said. "We're just involved with the hospital in Jerusalem, the eye clinics, and all of that. I would be happy to call him if you'd like." That is how we found out that the senator had a problem with dueling constituencies and that he was trying to sort out the situation as best he could. Without Madeleine, we never would have known why our ally was suddenly wavering. In the end, the senator abstained—and the guild managed to win the day without him.

Some time after Hugh died, my husband, Larry, and I drove up to see Madeleine at Crosswicks. David Levine, director of the Dramatists Guild and a colleague of mine, had also been invited up for the weekend. This was the first time I heard Madeleine reminisce about the theater side of her life. Larry and I went for a swim in her indoor pool. On the way there, Madeleine said, "These would be my paperback royalties. Let me show you!" She had paid for the construction of the pool when Dell finally made good on her royalties.

Around 1991, when my son Ben was two or three, I brought him up to Madeleine's apartment to meet her. I had said jokingly

*The Order of St. John of Jerusalem traces its origins to the year 1048. The very first chivalric order of knighthood, the Order of St. John established itself in Jerusalem prior to the First Crusade, offering medical treatment, food, and lodging to pilgrims of all religions. In modern times, the order administers the St. John of Jerusalem Eye Hospital, providing medical care throughout Israel and in the Gaza Strip.
†The Knights of Malta grew out of the original Order of St. John. Sent into exile from Jerusalem following the fall of the last Christian outposts in the Holy Land in 1291, the knights developed a formidable military arm and won renown as fierce defenders of Christendom.

that Ben needed to be blessed. Madeleine did not bless Ben, but she gave him a signed copy of her book of Bible stories, *Ladder of Angels*. By then Canon West had died, and she had his two Irish setters. At one point the dogs began circling us as Ben sat on my lap in growing terror! Ben was little and the dogs were big, and for a long time after that visit he was afraid of dogs.

The Madeleine L'Engle I read about in the *New Yorker* profile wasn't the person I knew. There was that story about the alligator. I thought, I can imagine Madeleine *kidding* about that. But I never saw her living in a fantasy world. Not *ever*, and I knew her off and on over a period of fifteen years. Madeleine herself didn't want to hear people saying gossipy, nasty things about people she knew. It seemed as if there was a conscious effort in that article to meld what Madeleine did in her fiction with her life. I no longer was in touch with her in 2004, but I cannot believe she changed that much! She knew how to be pragmatic, and I don't think that side of her life came out at all in the profile.

I went with Sandra Jordan to Madeleine's memorial service at St. John the Divine. I sat behind Marian Seldes, whom I had met through Garson Kanin at the guild. She and Madeleine were old friends. The cathedral organ had recently been repaired following a major fire, but the rear portion of the sanctuary was partly blocked off where reconstruction work was still under way. I remember thinking, This is so typical: the cathedral is *still* "under construction." They got the organ fixed, but it still isn't perfect. It occurred to me that Madeleine always knew how to deal with "it isn't perfect." Then I looked all around, and I said to myself, Oh my goodness. Where's Madeleine? Where *is* she?

## MARY POPE OSBORNE

Mary Pope Osborne is the author of the Magic Tree House series and other books for young readers. She is a past president of the Authors Guild.

*Q: How did you meet Madeleine L'Engle?*

A: I first met Madeleine when I began serving on the board of the Authors Guild. Though she had completed her term as president, she still attended board meetings now and then. As one of the few children's book authors on the board, I was shy when I first started attending these luncheon meetings. But when Madeleine was present, she would reach out to me and ask me to sit next to her. I remember a contentious meeting in which a controversial issue was being hotly debated. As the temperature in the room rose higher, I noticed Madeleine energetically writing in a notebook beside me. Assuming she was taking notes on the subject at hand, I glanced down and was startled to see that Madeleine was composing a prayer. I looked away quickly, feeling like an intruder. I've long since forgotten what issue was being discussed that day but have never forgotten that private moment of discovery.

# THOMAS BANCHOFF

Thomas Banchoff is a geometer and has been a professor of mathematics at Brown University since 1967.

*Q: When did you meet Madeleine L'Engle?*

A: I have a pretty good bead on that because I found my *Wrinkle in Time* folder and I have in it a letter I wrote to my daughter on February 19, 1984, just after meeting Madeleine L'Engle in person for the first time.

I was in touch with Madeleine after having first been contacted by the film producer Catherine Hand. Catherine had read a *Scientific American* cover story about there being eleven dimensions and our work on that subject at Brown University. We were working on areas that were related to the question of visualizing higher dimensions, and Catherine was interested in the images of higher dimensions because she was planning a movie or video or some adaptation of *A Wrinkle in Time*. Catherine came to see us in Providence, and she was excited about the project, and she was very interested in the kinds of images we were creating with computer graphics.

By way of background, I'm a mathematician at Brown University. I got my Ph.D. in 1964. I've often told the story that shortly after I got here, I was introduced to Charles Strauss, a fellow my age who had just gotten his Ph.D. in computer graphics—the first computer science doctorate here at Brown. Charles's mentor,

Andy van Dam, was the first or second person in the country to have gotten such a degree. Charles had a remarkable computer program that allowed him to visualize higher dimensions.

By the early 1970s we were getting some publicity. In 1975 an article in *The Washington Post* led to an invitation from Salvador Dalí to collaborate with him.* In 1978, I gave a big presentation to the International Congress of Mathematicians in Helsinki. It might have been as early as 1981 that I started to work with Catherine Hand on images and ideas for her project. So, I was doing that before I was introduced to Madeleine, and she had already seen some of the images when she invited me to stop by her home on the West Side of Manhattan. And that's when this letter I wrote to one of my two daughters takes over. Do you want me to read some of it?

*Q: Sure.*

A: This is from a letter:

> . . . *In the meantime, I want to organize my impressions of yesterday and in particular my dinner* [on February 18, 1984] *with Madeleine L'Engle and Hugh Franklin last night. It went well, the sort of good time that makes people look forward to seeing each other again . . . I showed up just at 6:30 p.m. after an aggressive sixty-block taxi ride, and I easily found the elegant entrance to their apartment building between Broadway and West End Avenue. I was announced by the doorman, so Madeleine was waiting at the open door when I got off the elevator at the fifth floor. She is tall, and the first thing you notice is that her hair is thin and combed down so that it is almost as if her eyes are slightly higher on her face than you'd expect. You notice her eyes also because they're always alert, always taking in things, never looking dreamy or distant. I gave her the flowers I had bought*

---

*In 1954, Dalí had painted *Corpus Hypercubus*, a depiction of the Crucifixion that revealed his interest in the representation of higher dimensions.

*outside Grand Central Station, six small roses—three yellow and three yellow-orange, which . . . she handed . . . over to her husband, Hugh, as she introduced him. You or your friends might know him as Dr. Tyler from one of the soap operas—*All My Children. *His eyes are prominent, but they aren't always looking at you, like his wife's. He seems to be thinking about something else every once in a while . . . We had drinks from glasses decorated with images from unicorn tapestries. Their living room is large, "the kind you only find on the Upper West Side," Madeleine said, with a Steinway grand piano that she can play any hour of the day or night because noise doesn't travel to their bedroom, let alone to the next apartment. There were a lot of great old pictures on the wall beside the sofa, including a portrait of her father in some orchard in Brittany. We talked about math, and she said that she had been discouraged in the fourth grade because, although she could easily understand why $3 \times 0$ should be $0$, she couldn't be convinced that $0 \times 3$ should be $0$. "What makes those three oranges go away?" I said those were two separate questions, all right, and that the way that always made the most sense to me was to think of the area of a rectangle. If either the vertical or the horizontal dimension is zero, the area is going to be zero. Nobody had ever suggested a geometric interpretation to her when she was in school, she said. I realized that somehow I have always thought of multiplication in terms of a picture. She also said that her high school teacher couldn't understand how someone so good in geometry could be so bad in algebra. I told her I had just said in my talk at IBM that afternoon that I was much better at geometric thinking than at algebraic thinking. Madeleine mentioned that their son had written a paper on polarity and hyper-polarity of molecules, and at that point I asked if people became left-right exchanged when they tessered as their molecules went from left-handed to right-handed and conversely. Then she said something that I found discouraging, that somehow all the molecules turned into energy as they moved into the fourth dimension, and that that was why they moved in time. That was so far from my own view that I* *thought there probably wasn't anything I would have to contribute, if that was the interpretation she felt committed to maintaining in any film version of her book.*

*Q: Are you saying that she didn't really understand the science?*

A: No, not at all. It was just that she had an alternative view of the science. Hers was more like *Star Trek*, you know: "Beam me up, Scotty!" That kind of thing. According to this view, the molecules somehow go into a different state and then re-form, whereas for me it's just going into the fourth dimension, as an alternate spatial thing.

Let's see [going back to reading from the letter]:

*We didn't pursue that any further at the time. We did talk about timing. I was assured that the 6:30 appointment was what it sounded [to be; that is, that she had not expected me to arrive fashionably late]. It was early, she said, so I would leave early. She had . . . [known] that she would be tired after a session at the Authors Guild in the afternoon and [that] she was still somewhat tired because of a combination of a cold and a case of shingles! "It doesn't go away, but at least it doesn't kill you." She [had] said on the phone that I could help her with the dishes, an invitation for an informal supper, and indeed I was able to bring out the Crock-Pots too and the rice. We didn't say grace, although even by that time we had talked a lot about religion. She's very theological, she said, and we then discussed the fact that the three ladies [in* A Wrinkle in Time*] are angels in spite of the fact that some people want to purge such references from books in children's libraries along with any witches or ghosts. "That rules out the Bible," she said, with its witch of Endor and its accounts of Christ's appearance after the Resurrection. She expressed the opinion that Michael and Lucifer had been best friends and denied that* Wrinkle *was based on some sort of Gnostic dualism with the forces of evil as powerful as the good, although she admitted that that symbolism was there. At* *dinner we talked about giving talks at different places. She gets fifteen hundred dollars for a talk, and I was actually surprised that she wouldn't be getting more. It turns out she has talked twice at Barrington College [near Providence], although she is more Anglo-Catholic than Unitarian or fundamentalist. We talked about the Danforth Foundation and the American Scientific Affiliation—these different places where scientists and teachers try to reconcile views of religion and science, something Madeleine considers an important part of her work. She said she had a lot of trouble getting a publisher to do* Wrinkle *because of all the theology in it. Later on she told me that she had tried any number of publishers before Farrar decided to publish it. They all wanted to cut out a lot of the stuff in it, and she refused to do any cuts. During all the conversation Hugh too was involved, although it was clear he wasn't very deeply into the religious aspect. He was from Tulsa, Oklahoma, so he did know about the context of midwestern Protestantism. Madeleine said she could never really be a Protestant. "They have to have the answers," she said—I think a comment that people used to make about Catholics. It turns out that Hugh is somewhat deaf, which became apparent when he answered a completely different question than one I had asked. ("You have to shout in his ear, right here," Madeleine said.) He told about how he'd suggested deafness as a theme to the soap opera director, but he said there seems to be a resistance to treating the problems of aging, so he was fitted with a hearing aid . . . He and his wife had met when they were both acting in* The Cherry Orchard, *in a production with Joseph Schildkraut and Eva Le Gallienne, and they got married during their next play together because it was going to be in Chicago for a long time, and in those days "people just didn't shack up together." That was thirty-eight years ago, and she had stopped acting. She had only had bit parts, while he had gone on to star in several Broadway roles. I had seen a large political-type poster in the kitchen with "Russell" written under a younger picture of Hugh looking very dashing. I had asked him if it was from* Of Thee I Sing, *forgetting that it would have been "Wintergreen" in that case. And he said it was from Gore Vidal's* Best Man, *which I had seen as a film some twenty years ago.\* It must have been shortly after that that he quit acting, a decision that had lasted nine years. Both of them agreed that it had been a good move for him to come out of retirement for his present acting [ job], although it seems that the Dr. Tyler role is over now.*

*Madeleine loves to travel and she does a lot, just a little bit more than Hugh, who comes with her when his schedule permits. They have sailed around the Horn, for example. They've been to Russia together. I observed that she must love languages, and she said that she did, although she had to admit that she doesn't speak all of the languages she used in* Wrinkle. *We talked off and on about the project to turn the book into a movie, and she mentioned that Catherine Hand is under the gun, because that option that Embassy [Pictures] has will run out in August. Madeleine has signed with them because she liked Catherine, because she liked Norman Lear's work and understood that it would be the first film venture for him, and because she had been able to maintain control over the plot and the characters, a provision that had not been offered by any of the other producers who've been interested in doing the book over the years. The screenplays that have been generated were not acceptable. Robert Bolt's attempt had made Meg into a ten-year-old, and the version by two other writers had made her into someone practically hysterical. Then Madeleine had done the screenplay herself, doing the whole thing in two weeks while she had shut herself up in a convent. That bothered the Hollywood people, she said, because it was supposed to take six months or something like that. So, she thinks there's a pretty good screenplay to operate from, and the job Catherine has right now is to find a director. Hugh agrees with all this, though both of them claim no real familiar-*

*Hugh Franklin replaced Melvyn Douglas in the starring role as President William Russell in Gore Vidal's political drama* The Best Man, *which had a successful run in Broadway's Morosco Theatre from March 31, 1960, to July 8, 1961.*

*ity with this business. They do counsel together with a lawyer as well as with an agent before doing any major dealings in that work. They're happy with the advice they're getting from Madeleine's agent . . . In any case, she got the potential producer to double the original offer, so now she has something like 10 percent as part of her agreement, but if the option is not renewed, she's not at all sure if she will go for another producer. She doesn't feel it's necessary that the book be made into a film, although she agreed that a lot of people would like to see it. But they don't want to see the basic things changed . . . I think the both of them have serious doubts that a movie could be made that would be satisfactory. They don't know who would be a good director. They don't seem to like Francis Ford Coppola. And I didn't see much optimism about something developing within the crucial next few months. Madeleine clearly hopes that Catherine will be able to pull it off, though.*

By the way, Madeleine told me that one of the writers who wrote a screenplay had made the main character into a little boy. "Can you imagine that?" she said. "Missed the entire point!"

*At one point I raised the question of what part in the process I might play. Hugh seemed to react negatively: "I thought we were just meeting each other." Madeleine didn't seem to have any problem with exploring this, and we all agreed that there could be some value in looking over the mathematical and scientific images. They didn't have a slide projector there, so we couldn't look at any of the best things. But I said we could look at a couple of the models anyway, and at the end of the evening Hugh said that he wanted me to show "the pictures." Around 8:30 they said that three hours was the optimum length for an evening, so we all leaped up when we realized it was already 9:40. Madeleine had offered coffee if I didn't mind instant. So I took her up on that, while Hugh showed me a wall full of photos of their three children and their families and the two of them at earlier stages of their lives, including pictures of Hugh as President Russell shaking hands with President Kennedy and Vice President Johnson when they came to see the play. I asked Hugh where he fit in to all the discussion of a possible film, and he said he honestly didn't know, that no one had put that question to him in just that way. Madeleine came with the coffee. I opened my case to give some copies of the magazines with my work in them, and I pulled out the cross, the unfolding cubical cross— hypercube cross.*

The article in *The Washington Post* had shown me holding this model . . . And that's why Salvador Dalí had contacted me.

*I pulled out the hypercube model. I set up the mousetrap model of a cube. I had this idea that you could take an ordinary cube and fold it out into a cross shape and if you did it with rubber bands, and left it in tension, then what would happen is that if a mouse got onto the middle of the cube, the tension would be released and all the sides would collapse into a cube and the mouse would be trapped in the mid-dle. The four sides spread out into a plane under tension from a rubber band, so that it snaps up into 3-space when the mouse disturbs the equilibrium. They both seemed delighted by the image. I was sitting there on the floor explaining how the models worked, and they seemed much more receptive than earlier. As Madeleine said, "There've been a lot of developments in the last twenty years." I asked Madeleine if she would sign my* Wrinkle in Time *and she did, "For Tom, with best wishes for successful tessering." I signed a copy of* Computer Graphics and Applications, *"To Madeleine and Hugh, the best to you, Tom." I asked Hugh if he would sign too. He said that he didn't really have a part in the book, but Madeleine said, "That isn't really true. You're my Calvin." He said, "You've never said that to me before," and put his arms around her. It was really touching. They stood there with arms around each other and looking very happy. I went over to them, and we had a three-way hug and all laughed. So I asked Hugh again if he would write something, and he did . . . Earlier in the conversation, Madeleine said she had been booked up [for talks] through 1985. I asked her if she would ever like to talk at Brown, and she said yes. I said it was too bad about the heavy booking because a good time to speak would be this October. Madeleine asked why October was so important . . . I told her about our party for* Flatland's *one hundredth birthday.\* She [said she] wants to come! [She wasn't able to.] After I left, I looked at what Hugh had written in my* Wrinkle. *"In search of my dimension. Hugh Franklin." It's a good story, right? Love, Dad*

In a letter to me dated April 6, 1984, Madeleine wrote:

*What a delightful letter to find waiting for [Hugh and me] when we got back from Egypt. It was a special treat in . . . the mail. Yes, Alex Murry [Meg's father] was a teacher by nature, but by the time of* Wrinkle *he was involved with research. But I think of him very much the way I see you, as a teacher full of enthusiasm. I love the dialogue you wrote between Meg and her father. How was it the world got along so many centuries without zeros? I agree with Meg that sometimes they can be confusing. You almost convinced me that zero times three equals zero, but not quite. However, when I was in Egypt, one night I explained L'Engle's Law, which, if you remember it, is that the square of any number is one more than the multiple of the numbers on either side of it [a well-known thing that she had somehow figured out by herself]. Now, if you multiply two numbers which are separated by one number, the answer will be two more than the multiple of the numbers on either side. If you multiply two num-*

---

\**Flatland: A Romance of Many Dimensions* (1884), by the English schoolmaster and theologian Edwin Abbott Abbott, is a satirical novella that considers the consequences of inhabiting a two-dimensional world. In 1984, Thomas Banchoff organized a three-day conference at Brown University to celebrate the centenary of Abbott's thought-provoking story and the scientific work on the visualization of multidimensionality that it helped inspire.

*bers which are separated by two numbers the answer will be three more, et cetera, et cetera. That goes on forever in a beautiful pattern. Hugh and I hope to see you soon and meet the rest of the family. Love, Madeleine*

*Q: It sounds as if Madeleine did have an understanding of mathematics.*

A: Yes, she did. Most of it was from the popular literature. She liked playing with numbers.

*Q: Can you talk about tessering and the validity of what Madeleine says about it in* Wrinkle*?*

A: Tessering is going into the fourth dimension to get from one position in the three-dimensional universe to another one. In the book there's a place where Mrs Whatsit has an apron on and she shows how you can bring one portion of the apron close to another portion, which would then enable somebody on it to jump instantaneously from one place to another. Tessering essentially means going into a higher dimension where things can fold together, even though the people living in this folded universe aren't aware of the fold. For them it just represents something kind of impossible. We can't instantaneously go from earth to another planet unless there happens to be some such fold. Other science fiction writers talk about wormholes, which means that there are tunnels going from one place to another. But this is almost the same kind of thing. Tessering is moving out of the third dimension as we know it into another part of the universe or into a bigger universe. At one point when they're tessering around on their way to Camazotz, they actually spend a brief time on a two-dimensional universe, which is very, very stifling because it's like living on a planet with a huge gravitational field, and then they have to get off it. They can't live in two dimensions. So I guess the idea is that the created universe consists of pieces that are two-dimensional pieces, and that there are also three-dimensional pieces and also pieces that are in the fourth dimension. Camazotz itself is rather three-dimensional. You just have to get there by going through the fourth dimension. As a matter of fact, Madeleine talks about going through the fifth dimension. That's because she already thinks of the physical world as consisting of the three dimensions of space and the one dimension of time. So she needs an additional spatial dimension. Now, I would count it differently and say we have four spatial dimensions and time. Time is a fourth dimension; it's not *the* fourth dimension. In order to have a tessering, there has to be at least one more spatial dimension than the three we're familiar with. It's not time travel; it's space travel. And she understood that.

*Q: So, from a scientific point of view, what she describes is hypothetically possible?*

A: If the universe is curved back on itself . . . but I don't know that anyone has ever had any evidence of anything like that. The unexplained things in the universe are things like black holes and white holes and various things that you can't escape from, that are so dense that light can't escape from them, so you can't get a message back at all. Who knows where they lead? That sort of thing . . . In science fiction, some characters travel at warp speed, others find shortcuts, and hers is more of a shortcut universe than a warp-speed universe.

*Q: Is what she says on* the *subject rooted in the work of any particular scientist?*

A: No. I never got that impression from her. She was familiar with science fiction. She said she wrote the manuscript on a cross-country trip. She and her family were driving across country, and she was writing as they were going along, sometime in the 1950s. She said she wasn't spending a lot of time ferreting things out of libraries.

*Q: Did you know* A Wrinkle in Time *from before you met Madeleine?*

A: Yes. From the time I was at Brown, I was teaching a course on the fourth dimension. Most of my female students would have read *A Wrinkle in Time* when they were in junior high school, and a lot of the male students had read it too. A couple of students even did projects based on *A Wrinkle in Time*, including a couple who tried to write a screenplay. We discussed the mathematics behind the book.

In 1998, I was a visiting professor at Yale for one semester, teaching a course on the fourth dimension. One group of students did their final project on various aspects of *A Wrinkle in Time*, including the religious dimensions and use in classrooms. One first-year student, Jessica Weare, made a complete analysis of all the mathematical aspects of the book, a very impressive project.

*Q: Would you say that the science that Madeleine was drawing on in* Wrinkle *was fairly current, or had the ideas she was playing with been around for decades by then?*

A: I would say that she didn't have to go very far. She didn't need anything very deep. She just needed the ability to move in space.

*Q: Or to ask the question differently, would someone who was steeped in science fiction have found anything that was particularly new or cutting-edge in her book?*

A: I think that it is science fiction in some sense, but I don't know which science fiction writers I would compare her to. It was more of an adventure story. A girl's father disappears mysteriously. It's really adolescent literature: How can the kid save her old man?

*Q: Is there an underlying consistency to the math and science in the book?*

A: I can make sense of just about everything that is in it. I believe that Dr. Murry was imprisoned in a hypercube in Camazotz. There are different models of the four-dimensional cube projected into 3-space, the most common one being a cube within a cube. Do you know that image? If you think about looking down a long hallway, at the end of it you'd have a rectangle, another rectangle inside, and the corresponding corners connected, going off to a vanishing point. You can do the same thing in one higher dimension: have a cube inside a smaller cube, with corresponding corners connected. All those lines that connect corresponding corners from outside to inside would all meet at the center. That's called a tesseract. That's where the word "tessering" comes from. I don't know who invented the word, but it was definitely used by C. Howard Hinton, who was a contemporary of Edwin Abbott, the author of *Flatland*.* They knew each other's work. They diverged, though, because Hinton was primarily a scientist, whereas Abbott was more interested in using the exploration of dimensionality as a metaphor for social commentary and for the physiology of sense experience and for investigating epistemology—how we know things, especially those things that transcend our ability to gather sense data about them. Abbott was much more philosophical, more theological in fact—and much more in the spirit of Madeleine L'Engle. Madeleine really was interested in theological import. Her ladies were angels, and she was quite aware of the dualism built into Camazotz, the fact that the cold and the warm universes are interlaced, if you will. Those are the images that I was pushing. The central image that I use in my own work is a torus, the surface of a doughnut or an inner tube that turns inside out in the fourth dimension, so that you get the impression that you have a doughnut that is wrapped around another doughnut. One is the world of warm and the other is the world of cold, and they somehow both envelop our existence. So we're very, very close to both worlds at all times. I always thought of cold and

*Charles Howard Hinton was a late-nineteenth-century British scientist, science fiction writer, and follower of Theosophy who devised methods of visualizing higher dimensions.

warm as being the essential duality rather than dark and light, which is problematic for other reasons. I have some images that I really thought were absolute naturals for the beginning and the ending of the film.

Salvador Dalí was probably the most fascinating person I've ever met—and the strangest person I ever met, including mathematicians! Madeleine was a very impressive person, but I wouldn't consider her a strange person at all. In fact, she was very approachable. In 1993, I was there for her seventy-fifth birthday celebration at St. John the Divine. That was the last time I saw her. It was an open-air kind of event, and she was surrounded by people who loved and admired her.

In my file there's an e-mail message, dated November 19, 1993, from me to my editor and good friend Jerry Lyons:

> I did do a bit of reading of A Wrinkle in Time, impressed once again at how skillfully Madeleine L'Engle handled the displacement her heroine feels. She's really out of her time and that has to be addressed.

# MATRIARCH

## GRETCHEN GUBELMAN

Gretchen Gubelman grew up in Goshen, Connecticut, where her parents were founders of the Goshen Players. She is a singer-songwriter and has toured with her son's band, Beau Borrero and His Mom.

*Q: How did you meet Madeleine L'Engle and her family?*

A: My dad and Hugh were friends in New York in the 1930s. Hugh was acting, and my dad sang German lieder on the concert circuit and occasionally appeared on Broadway too. My mother was trying to make it on Broadway when she met Dad. After they married, Hugh decided he'd better settle down too, and so my parents would introduce him to women. Hugh would always say, "Oh, she's not like Martha"—meaning not as good a woman as my mother. But then, quite suddenly, he found Madeleine, and that was it! He realized she was the one. After that, there was no going back for him.

When my parents abandoned the New York theater scene and moved up to Goshen, Hugh and Madeleine would come to visit. With some urging from my parents, they finally moved to Goshen as well. That is when I first came to know Madeleine, at the time when I was a young girl. She and Hugh lived a few miles from us, and we all spent a lot of time together.

In fact, my dad found Hugh and Madeleine the house that came to be known as Crosswicks, which was a rather typical colonial-era house for Goshen. And it was he who did the carpentry and interior decoration work that was needed to get the house in order. Later, he built the addition that became Madeleine's writing studio, the Tower.

That was just one of the ways that our families were linked. Madeleine was my piano teacher. She was a good teacher, and I loved my piano lessons. Madeleine could be hard on her own kids, but she was never that way with me. She let me learn music that I was excited about, as opposed to just doing scales and exercises. She always sat there next to me and would write little notes on whatever piece I was learning.

Because Hugh and Madeleine's oldest child, Josephine, was a couple of years younger than me, I babysat for her as well as for Maria and Bion. Our two families also spent a lot of time together socially, in church, for example. In 1954, the year I was ten, we even went on vacation together and drove all the way to Florida to see Madeleine's family. We drove down in our family cars, and the image I have is of all that hanging Spanish moss and of the water smelling of sulfur.

In many ways Goshen was a typical New England farmer town. We had a good public school, and all the parents were involved in the PTA. On an average Sunday, a couple of hundred people came to the Congregational church, which was one of the two churches in town, the other being Catholic. Hugh would preach at our church from time to time. Madeleine directed the choir, in which both my mom and my dad sang. The church organist—Grandma Vaill—was ninety when I was a child and the tiniest little woman. Madeleine adored "Grandma." At Christmastime, we reenacted the Nativity, and—this was so wonderful!—each kid received a beautiful big Florida orange as a special gift.

All of us kids saved all year long for the Goshen Fair, which was held over the long Labor Day weekend. We lived for it. We would exhibit in the hobby competition and the baked goods competition, and as we got older, we would get jobs there. It was all very old-timey and we loved it. The livestock, the pie making, the horse and the oxen pull! Madeleine's house was within walking distance of the fairgrounds.

There was a small circle of five or six Goshen families who got together every Sunday after church. Included in this group were the minister and his wife and their five children. There were also the Hannas and the Moores, sometimes the Wallachs—who were Jewish—the Franklins, and ourselves. Each Sunday we would decide on the spur of the moment whose house we were going to go to after church for dinner. There was always a great gang of kids around on those occasions.

The minister was an extraordinary man. He had come from the South and studied at Yale. It's very possible that he influenced Madeleine religiously in some way. The Moores were a local family with roots in town that went back for generations. The Wallachs were German Jews who had escaped the Nazis. My parents and the Wallachs were involved in World Federalism, which was considered very pink at the time, and I think that Madeleine and Hugh were, too. There was also a British family. We thought of Cornwall, just down the hill, as more of an intellectual center than Goshen, the place where the artists and writers tended to live. Even so, I would say that my parents, and Madeleine and Hugh, had a very interesting group of friends.

When Hugh moved to town, he had decided he was done with acting and that he wanted to try something completely different. He had had some success on the stage but not enough success for a stable, satisfying career, and the continual uncertainty about when the next part would come along was awful. The grocery store that he and Madeleine bought was in the center of town, directly across from our church, and I think he loved it—at least at first. It had everything that the local people needed. We never went anywhere else for groceries, for example. As kids, we were given a nickel for the collection plate and a nickel to buy a candy bar at the store after church. You climbed these big steps up to a front porch. Inside, it seemed big and dark. The cash register was right by the door.

Hugh got the acting bug again eventually, and that was because my mother lured him back through the Goshen Players! When I was growing up, the Goshen Players theater group, which my parents founded, was a big part of our lives. The group performed for three weekends in May. We always talked about the "spring musical," and every year from January onward the world revolved around the next production. Both my parents acted. My dad designed and built the sets, and my mother directed. Hugh often took a leading role. Madeleine acted and sang, and once, when we went to Europe for a year and a half in the mid-1950s, Madeleine took over for my mother and wrote and directed a musical comedy called *Come to the Ball.* One of the lyrics went, "It's time to change the diapers! The diapers! The diapers!" It was really wonderful and very funny.

One year, the Goshen Players put on the Victor Herbert operetta *The Red Mill,* and Hugh had a scene in which he had to fall down a ladder. It was pure slapstick. He was absolutely hysterical. Our bellies hurt from laughing so hard. He was such a wonderful performer! The quality of the productions was always high.

Madeleine enjoyed being part of it all. Even so, she was bound to stand out in a place like Goshen. My mother came from a tiny town in Washington state and was much more comfortable with small-town life than Madeleine. Madeleine was so out-there. Once, when she was nursing Bion, she carried him onstage during rehearsal, and suddenly Madeleine whipped out her big, floppy breast and began to nurse him in front of everybody. That was just shocking to the people of a place like Goshen. But that was Madeleine. Before she had the Tower to work in, she had a tiny room just off the kitchen where she wrote. When I was a kid, Madeleine was the only woman I knew who was trying to do anything other than be a full-time mother. It seemed to me that she was always writing. In the summer, the moms and the kids would go to some pond or lake every day, but Madeleine would not be on those excursions. Even when she put in time at the store, she would be sitting there writing and keeping up her journal during downtime.

Madeleine and Hugh both had big, powerful voices. In a way, it was as though they were always onstage. As a child, I would go over to their house, and they would be shouting at each other. My dad and Madeleine would get into arguments too—about politics or whatever. Life at the Franklins' house always seemed so dramatic! And if Madeleine or Hugh told one of their kids to do something and the child didn't obey, they would both start counting at the top of their lungs. Madeleine and Hugh were different with their children than the other parents we knew. They were of the old school that believed that children should be "seen and not heard."

The studio that Dad built for Madeleine was a lovely place. It was away from all the noise and drama of the main house. I recall coveting it! There were beautiful old rugs on the floor. The walls were lined with books, and Madeleine had a pleasing view out the window. She had a little stove to keep her warm.

The house itself felt special to me too. The high ceiling of the Franklins' living room made the place feel grand. Everything about that room was grand: the old family portraits, the antique silver, and the many other beautiful old things that were there. Add Hugh and Madeleine to that scene—two tall people with big personalities—and it all kind of blended together. On the stairway going up to the bedrooms were wonderful framed publicity shots and head shots of Hugh and Madeleine and the famous theater people they knew. I had never seen anything like it.

In 1964, I lived with Hugh and Madeleine and their children in their apartment on West End Avenue for a year. This was a few years after their move back to the city. I was in college and had just transferred to Columbia University as a junior from Oberlin. It was during that year that I came to see for myself what a terrible life the actor's life was for Hugh. He would always be waiting for the phone to ring. He would go to an audition, and they'd call him back, and then he'd stay home all day and the next day and the day after that, until he heard back about whether or not he had gotten the part.

I majored in Western religious thought in college, and Madeleine became important to me in terms of my own religious life as well. I had started college at Oberlin, where so many of the students were agnostics and professed atheists, and had felt uncomfortable there, so I transferred to Columbia. Columbia students were not necessarily all that different from those at Oberlin, but it was such a relief to be around Madeleine most evenings: to spend time with somebody who was intelligent and worldly and also a believer.

I was also deeply involved in the civil rights movement, Vietnam War protests, the Student Nonviolent Coordinating Committee, and SDS, and Hugh and Madeleine were more conservative politically than I was.* When we argued and debated at dinnertime, it would feel as if we were starting from two completely different sets of facts. Hugh read *The New York Times* every morning and accepted everything he read there as gospel, whereas I was listening to student radicals like Mark Rudd.† Even so, our nightly political arguments never got in the way of our liking each other. To take the edge off—I think Madeleine instigated it—we had a game that we would always play at the dinner table. Before sitting

---

*During the 1960s, Students for a Democratic Society organized political protests on college campuses throughout the United States.
†Mark Rudd led the Columbia University chapter of SDS and was later a cofounder of the more militant Weather Underground.

down at the table, we each had to pick a card with a vocabulary word on it from a little container and then use that word in conversation at some point during the course of the meal. If nobody was able to guess which word was the one you had drawn, you scored a point. If on the other hand someone called you out as you tried to insert your word into the conversation, then *that* person got a point. Sometimes you would be stuck with a word that the others all knew you would never in a million years come out with on your own. That game guaranteed that dinner would be a lot of fun.

Both Hugh and Madeleine made time for long talks with me. They were very nurturing. The one and only time in my entire life that I got stinking drunk and had a vicious hangover, Madeleine was completely accepting and treated me as someone in need of care. She never wagged her finger at me. I went through a breakup, and she was there for me for that, too. Madeleine was always taking in stray people and befriending them, too. That year, a girl of about twelve who lived in the building and was always very unhappy kept showing up at the apartment. Madeleine would invite her in, fix tea, and spend hours listening to her and talking to her.

By that time Madeleine had had a major success with *A Wrinkle in Time*. Having come into her own, she was all the more concerned for Hugh's happiness. She would fuss over him and wait up for him to come home and cook him nice dinners. She was great to him, and I know he was crazy about her.

There was a great upheaval in the Franklin family during the year I was living with them in New York. It had to do with Maria, their adopted daughter, who was very beautiful and popular with the boys, and Josephine, who was not so popular. During the year I was living with them, Maria had all these boyfriends, and Josephine had none until finally someone asked Josephine out, and the next thing anyone knew, Maria had scooped him up right out from under Josephine! That caused a great deal of upset over "bad

Maria." Later, Josephine came into her own magnificent beauty but not so during her teenage years, and it was hard for her, to say the least, to have a sister who was such a ravishing beauty.

The adoption of Maria in 1956 had changed everything in the Franklin family. I remember that most clearly. Here was this incredibly gorgeous child, a dream of a child, and both Madeleine and Hugh thought she was spoiled rotten, that she had been over-indulged, and that that was why she wasn't fitting in as well as she should have. I think that Hugh and Madeleine felt they had no choice but to adopt Maria but that they resented having had to do so from day one. It made for a pretty toxic mix for all concerned, and I don't think it ever resolved itself to everyone's satisfaction. Maria had to have been suffering from post-traumatic stress following the death of both her parents—her father of a heart attack, her mother a few months later of an aneurysm. The car crash simplification showed up in *Meet the Austins*. I don't think Hugh and Madeleine ever fully appreciated the impact of that tragedy on her. As parents with such strict views about childhood, they somehow couldn't give her the benefit of the doubt.

Bion was twelve that year. I had sometimes changed his diapers when he was little. Now he and I would hang out together. After dinner, we would do the dishes and clean up the kitchen. I loved that kid. He was all into hockey, and I remember going to watch him play down in Riverside Park. It certainly wasn't easy for him to have two parents who were so intelligent and so eccentric and so domineering. Madeleine and Hugh were hard on him, as they were on all their children. Then, when Madeleine—and later Hugh too—got to be so famous: it's crazy making to have everyone in the world think your parents are wonderful when that is not your experience at all! I think that Bion did the best he could with what was there.

When we were all kids in Goshen, my older brother, who later became an architect, and one of his friends built an amazing tree house that wrapped around the trunk of a beautiful maple tree in the front yard of Crosswicks. It was not your average tree house, and it was very cool. We would all get together up there and write plays and piece together our costumes, and after the big Sunday meal we would give a show for the grown-ups. Josephine, wanting to impress her parents, would get all caught up in the writing and the performance itself. One Sunday after our play was done, Hugh or Madeleine—I forget which one of them it was—turned to her and said, "Well, Josephine. You had better not try to be an actress!" It was not what she had been hoping for.

## FREDERICA BRENNEMAN

Frederica Brenneman is a retired attorney.

*Q: How did you meet Madeleine L'Engle?*

A: We had been living in Washington, D.C., and had just moved to Goshen. This was in the fall of 1956. Goshen was a pretty small town: fifteen hundred people and fifteen hundred cows. We went into the Goshen General Store, and sitting behind the counter was this tall lady who was reading a book. I peeked over to see what book it was, and it was Proust. So I thought, Aha! There is more here than meets the eye. And of course that was Madeleine, the grocer's wife.

She and her husband, Hugh, very quickly invited us to a party where we could meet the rest of the "New York crowd," which meant anybody who wasn't born and raised in Goshen. That was very nice of them, and so we soon met the other people who had come from the big city, maybe a couple of dozen in all.

The next thing Madeleine did was to say, "You have to sing in the Goshen Players." I said, "But I can't sing." She said, "It doesn't matter!" The Goshen Players had been founded in 1941 to give you something to do after the excitement of Christmas and before the planting season began. So in January, February, and March, you'd rehearse a musical. The year we came to Goshen, Madeleine had written words to famous music by various composers for a show called *Come to the Ball,* which was a musical version of *Lady Windermere's Fan.*\*

Then the next thing Madeleine said was "You have to sing in the church choir." She was the choir director at the time. Again I said, "But I can't sing." And she said, "That doesn't matter either." There's very little to do in Goshen, so I sang in the choir—and discovered I loved it, sitting with all the silent altos. There were a lot of us.

*Q: What had brought you to Goshen?*

A: My husband and I are both lawyers. He had been in the JAG Corps of the U.S. Army, and we had this idyllic idea of practicing law in a small town in New England.† We found a 1790 farmhouse to rent, and that was our introduction to Connecticut. We've been here ever since.

The rich people lived in Litchfield. My husband's law office was in Torrington. His secretary was this wonderful, peppery old lady, who said to him, "Well, where did you find to live?" "A farmhouse in Goshen," he said. And she said, "That dump!" But we loved it. At the Goshen Fair, it was wonderfully relaxing to sit in the bleachers in the sun and watch the ox pull, which is probably the slowest thing you can do besides watching grass grow. Each May after the last performance of the Goshen Players show, there would be an all-night party, and at dawn we'd all go and help Gordy Vaill milk the cows. At least that was the plan.

---

\*Oscar Wilde's comedy *Lady Windermere's Fan: A Play About a Good Woman* premiered in London in 1892.
†The Judge Advocate General's Corps (JAG Corps) is the legal arm of the U.S. military.

Josephine Jones is a psychotherapist and the eldest of Madeleine L'Engle and Hugh Franklin's three children.

*Q: Are your first memories of living in Goshen?*

A: I have a few even earlier, snapshot-like memories from New York. Standing by the bathroom sink, watching my father shave and him putting shaving cream on my face too. We had a poodle called Touché, which my mother wrote about in *The Other Dog*. I remember taking Touché down to the corner to pick up the news-paper for my father, with both my parents leaning out the window to watch. I was not quite three then. We were living in a ground-floor apartment at 32 West Tenth Street, in Greenwich Village. Leonard Bernstein was our upstairs neighbor.

*Q: Why did your family move to Goshen soon afterward?*

A: For a few different reasons. One was that my parents thought that New York City was not a good place to raise children. Also, my father had a really good friend named Herb Gubelman who lived in Goshen. My parents would drive up to Connecticut for a visit, and one day Herb and his wife, Martha, said to them, "You're moving up here!" They found my parents the house that became Crosswicks. Dad was feeling a little disenchanted with the the-ater at that point, so he was ready to leave New York for that reason too.

*Q: Did your mother see Goshen as a good place to write?*

A: I was too young to know what she thought then, but certainly there would be fewer distractions in a place like Goshen.

*Q: Was it during those years that she first became deeply interested in religion?*

A: I don't know whether it was for the first time or not. But by the mid-1950s she had become close to the local Congregationalist minister, and their friendship may well have been what sparked her interest. At that same time, my dad became a preacher. He did quite a bit of preaching at local churches, filling in when a minister was on vacation or ill. Later, he completely lost his faith.

*Q: Did she set up the Tower early on as a place to write?*

A: My recollection is that it was always there, though that may not be right. It was Herb Gubelman, who did carpentry work on the side, who converted it from a chicken coop over the garage into a space for Mother.

*Q: Your mother wrote about a cross-country road trip that your family took shortly before moving back to New York City.*

A: I have vivid memories of that trip, during which I turned twelve. Some of what she wrote about it in *The Moon by Night* actually happened, while other incidents were completely made up. On the second day of the trip, we stopped in the Smoky Mountains. In the middle of the night, I had to go to the outhouse. On my way, I was sure I saw a bear. When I told my parents, they both pooh-poohed it, but later that night we heard a big crash, and when we investigated, we found that our big cooler had been overturned. By then I was more sure than ever about that bear. Still my parents insisted, "That's impossible! It's just your imagination running wild." Then a ranger came along, and Dad said to him, "Tell me, what kind of animal might have overturned our cooler?" Without any hesitation the ranger replied in his strong accent, "*Baaar.*"

We would camp for two or three nights and then spend the next night in a motel. This was surprising because my dad hated eating outdoors. He even hated picnics. Mother loved picnics and we would go up to Mohawk Mountain several times each summer and have picnics there, and Dad never came with us. My parents' friends were all astounded when Dad announced that we were taking a cross-country camping trip. I think they expected us back within two days. It must have surprised them that we lasted a whole two months.

We headed west along the southern route and made our way down to Oklahoma, where we stayed with Dad's parents. Then we continued on to California, stopping to see friends of my parents' at Laguna Beach and Santa Monica. We celebrated my twelfth birthday in San Francisco. We were in San Francisco the previous night, when we went to the movies to see *The Inn of the Sixth Happiness*.* I remember my parents being emphatic with the person at the ticket window—"No, no. She's not twelve yet," which was technically true—so that I could get into the movie on a children's ticket. We drove up the coast to Victoria and then swung back east along the northern route. We stopped for a rodeo, where Mother had one of the few beers I ever saw her drink.

It was on that trip that Mother started writing *A Wrinkle in Time*. I think of her as always writing. I don't remember if she did any of the driving or not. I remember her reading aloud to us, but not from *A Wrinkle in Time*. And I can believe the story she later told about having suddenly come up with the names Mrs Who, Mrs Which, and Mrs Whatsit while we were traveling cross-country together. But I don't recall the moment when it happened, if it did happen.

Home was still Goshen. After the trip, Dad went to work as an actor for the first time in years, playing Mr. Frank in *The Diary*

---

*A feature film released in 1958 by 20th Century Fox, in which Ingrid Bergman stars as an English maid who against all odds realizes her dream of going to live in China.

*of Anne Frank* in summer stock. Then he moved, ahead of us, to New York City, where he was opening in another play. He rented a wonderful apartment in the Hotel Dauphin, on Sixty-seventh and Broadway, where Lincoln Center is now. We would go down on weekends. When it became clear that Dad's play was going to have a long run, we moved to the city—on February 1, 1960.

*Q: Were your father's parents reconciled by then to the fact of his being an actor?*

A: His dad was. But his mother was a strict Southern Baptist, and it was a lot harder for her. Later, when I was in high school, Dad played a gangster on one of the soaps, and one day his character said, "You know who you gotta respect? You gotta respect women! Your mother? The greatest woman who ever lived. You gotta love 'em!" After that, my grandmother's friends all telephoned her and told her, "Your son said the most wonderful things about you on television." From then on she was fine with him being an actor too!

*Q: Do you remember the events surrounding your mother's winning of the Newbery Medal?*

A: It was all very exciting. I was fifteen or sixteen, and we were in New York when Mother received the news. I remember that she had to go and buy a long dress because she did not have one. We all thought it was made out of curtain material!

*Q: Do you recall the pre–*Wrinkle in Time *years, when your mother was receiving lots of rejection slips from publishers?*

A: Oh yes! She told the story—and now I don't know if I really remember it or if I just remember her telling it—that she went through a period when she thought she would give up writing for good. She had put the cover on the typewriter and declared, "No more!" After four days of that, I begged her to start writing again because, as I told her, "You're being so horrible!" When she wasn't writing, and especially when she wasn't being published, she was very depressed. I remember that as a very difficult time when I spent a lot of time out of the house.

*Q: Did your mother let you read her books in manuscript?*

A: There is one book in particular that I remember her reading aloud to my friends and me. It is a book that has never been published. The working title was "Brigitta," and it was a boarding school story, a light and sunny story, and I loved it. She made several copies, and my friends and I would all take parts and read it aloud together. I would always be Brigitta.

*Q: Was there a moment when you realized your mother was just a human being like everyone else?*

A: Yes, actually. It's a rather sweet and yet sad memory. It was when we were visiting my grandmother in Florida. I was about ten. Things must have been going pretty well for my mother at that point because she was in such a wonderful mood. We were playing outside in the park, and Mother was playing with us. I can remember stopping what I was doing and looking at her and thinking, I wonder if this is the last time I'm going to see her young? I wonder if I'll ever see her like this again?

In Florida, my mother would just be Madeleine again—not *Madeleine L'Engle*. In fact, she was always "Little Madeleine" to the members of her family there. She wasn't crazy about that! Around the time that I was married, my father's sister came from Oklahoma to stay with us at Crosswicks. Mother had just sold a book for ten thousand dollars, and my aunt's reaction was "And just think. Some people have to work *hard* for that kind of money." In Florida, my mother felt the same lack of understanding of who she was. She always expected to be treated in a certain way. When as children my brother and sister and I misbehaved, she would quote Jesus to us: "A prophet is not without honor except in his own country." She was the prophet we weren't honoring.

*Q: At Smith College were you treated differently as her daughter?*

A: Yes. Great expectations were placed upon me, and I was absolutely miserable there. I had just turned seventeen when I arrived as a freshman. Two years later I left to get married.

*Q: Did you know your mother's childhood nanny, Mrs. O.?*

A: I adored Mrs. O. She was from Liverpool, and she was very loving and warm. She would come and visit us, though when we lived in Crosswicks she wouldn't stay for very long, because she found so little to do there. Once she said, "In Connecticut, there's nothing but cows and clouds!" Whereas in New York she liked looking out the window at the passing scene. She always fixed dessert for us. I got a lot of my nurturing from her.

*Q: You must have gotten to know Canon West.*

A: He was quite a formidable character. My girls called him "Uncle Father." He and Mother were very close. I think he shaped her theology and her way of thinking.

*Q: When did your father turn away from religion, and why?*

A: That was after we moved to New York. Here in Connecticut they had been Congregationalists. But as I said, my father had been brought up as a Southern Baptist. My mother was an Episcopalian. When they moved back to New York, Mother wanted to go to an Episcopal church, so they began attending services at St. Michael's, which is on Ninety-ninth Street and Amsterdam Avenue. They got to be friends with the curate and his wife, who came over for dinner one night. Dad had quite a moralistic streak. Things for him were often black-and-white, and he believed that people should adhere to certain moral standards, period. At dinner that night, the curate proceeded to get drunk—and for my dad, that was it: not just for the curate, but for churchgoing. I don't think he ever set foot inside a church again, except for my wedding. That, anyway, is how it seemed to me then as a fourteen-year-old.

*Q: Would you say that Canon West filled a void for your mother after your father lost his faith?*

A: Absolutely. She met him some time after this happened.

*Q: Did you ever hear your mother preach?*

A: I hated her doing it. I used to call her a religious maniac.

She would kind of blackmail me into going to church. So it was very ironic that I ended up marrying a priest.

*Q: Your mother took many young people under her wing. How do you understand her tendency to do that?*

A: She really needed to be needed and loved. I guess she didn't feel she got enough of it from her family.

*Q: Her own father was very distant. Would you say she was more her mother's daughter?*

A: No, I would identify her much more as a daddy's girl, although she adored her mother and her mother adored her. Of course her father died when she was seventeen. *Certain Women* is really about him. I couldn't stand that book, because it made no sense psychologically. She would tell deeply conflicting stories about her father, and in all likelihood both sides of those stories were true. On the one hand, he could be stern and withholding. At one time, for example, Grandmother wanted my mother to attend a particular private school in New York. Then, when Mother was unhappy there, my grandmother wanted to take her out, but Charles said, "No! You enrolled her there. Now she's got to stay the full year." He wouldn't let her leave. On the other hand, he would take my mother to the opera. When he returned from a trip, he would come home loaded down with presents for her. And he would have hugs and kisses for his daughter.

*Q: There is some question as to whether or not he really was gassed during World War I.*

A: Yes, there definitely is some reason to doubt that. I would say that Francis Mason, who questioned the story in the 2004 *New Yorker* article about my mother, was a reliable source.*

---

*Francis Mason was the longtime editor of *Ballet Review* and a dance commentator for the *New York Times* radio station WQXR-FM. Mason was born and raised in Jacksonville, Florida. His mother, Hattie Camp Mason, was one of

*Q: Why would your mother have made up a story like that one?*

A: She did it because, despite what she says again and again in her books, she liked having answers.

*Q: And to get an answer, she would turn speculation into fact?*

A: Yes, even if there was nothing at all upon which to base her speculation. She would make up a narrative to confirm what she thought should have been. I'll give you another example that my daughter Léna and I were talking about the other day. When Léna was nine, she was hit by a truck and severely injured. It happened up here in Connecticut. Mother, I think, was in New York at the time. She was nowhere near. Yet Mother built a whole scenario as to why Léna was hit by the truck, and the other day Léna was giving it forth to me as *fact*. So I said, "Léna, that was Gran's *interpretation*. That's not what happened. At least, we don't know that it is." Mother was convinced that she did know. She did that kind of thing all the time.

Why would she have made up that story about my grandfather? What purpose might it have served? My feeling, based on something my grandmother once said to me, is that it was because my grandfather was an alcoholic and my mother could not face that in him. She did not want it to be true that her beloved father was an alcoholic. So here was another plausible explanation for his frequent headaches and need to lie down. It was not that he was hung over but rather that he was suffering the effects of having been gassed in the war.

*Q: Do you think your mother actually believed the story?*

A: Yes, I do. She would make sense of a thing to her own satisfaction. Then for her that story was reality.

---

Charles Wadsworth Camp's older sisters, thus making Francis and Madeleine first cousins. Their shared distaste for Jacksonville society was enough to make them friends for life.

*Q: What was it like being a "character" in the Crosswicks books?*

A: The Josephine my mother wrote about was somebody else. That was not me. People would come up to me and say, "I read all about you. I feel I know you so well." I would always reply, "You have to remember that my mother is a fiction writer." "No, no," they would say as if I had somehow misunderstood them. "I'm talking about her nonfiction." So I would repeat, as patiently as I could, "You have to remember that she is a fiction writer."

A typical exchange might go something like this:

"I loved it when you did such and such."

"I never did that."

"Yes, you did! Your mother wrote it in her book!"

I found this kind of thing difficult at times, although it was mainly just an annoyance. But once my mother wrote about a miscarriage I had had—and from *her* point of view. To her credit, she showed me what she had written in manuscript, and she agreed not to publish it when I asked her not to do so.

*Q: How did your parents cope with each other's fame? Did the fame of one tend to overshadow the other's?*

A: My feeling is that my mother's fame overshadowed my father's and that while he was always very proud of her, and he loved her very much, it still was hard for him. She would try to make it up to him by putting him forward, by having him go on her reading tours with her. But I think it must have been really hard on him. That is just my impression of course. He might have disagreed.

*Q: Your mother was a complex person. Did having her as a mother influence your decision to become a psychotherapist?*

A: Definitely! I used to say that I became a therapist so that I could figure out my crazy family.

*Q: Did it work?*

A: Well, yes, in a way.

*Q: What were your mother's great strengths? What were her great struggles?*

A: She was charismatic, and she was an extremely hard worker. She gave an awful lot to people. But she also could be self-absorbed, and at times she didn't have a clear enough sense of boundaries. Oftentimes, it was not her but the people who admired her who lacked a sense of boundaries, as with those fans who insisted they knew more about my life than I did.

*Q: Would you say that your mother created a character called Madeleine L'Engle?*

A: Oh, definitely. I used to divide her into Madeleine Franklin and Madeleine L'Engle. People would say, "What's it like having Madeleine L'Engle for a mother?" and I would say, "But I don't. My mother is Madeleine Franklin." I'm not sure now what purpose that served. If I would get mad at one Madeleine, I was inevitably mad at the other as well.

## ALAN JONES

Alan Jones is dean emeritus of Grace Cathedral in San Francisco. From 1972 to 1982, he served as the Stephen F. Bayne Professor of Ascetical Theology at the General Theological Seminary, New York. He and his former wife, Josephine Jones, had three children together.

*Q: How did you meet Madeleine L'Engle?*

A: I came to New York in 1964 as a graduate student at the General Theological Seminary down in Chelsea, and a year later, after I was ordained a deacon in 1965, I was chaplain at St. Hilda's & St. Hugh's school up on 114th Street and Broadway.* St. Hilda's & St. Hugh's was run by a fierce nun named Mother Ruth. She was an amazing woman and had founded the order and got this school built. One day she summoned me to her office and said, and this is a quote, "Father, I hear you are interested in histrionics. I have made an appointment for you to see Mrs. Franklin, and you're to have dinner with her this evening. I want you to direct the school pageant this Christmas." This must have been September 1965.

Madeleine's husband was in a play, *The Devils*, by John Whiting, which was having a preliminary run in Boston just then. Hugh and Madeleine used to direct the school pageant in the Cathedral

*St. Hilda's & St. Hugh's is an independent Episcopal day school.

of St. John the Divine, which is why I was sent to meet her. So off I went to see Mrs. Franklin in this big apartment—Madeleine and her son, Bion, and another young man who was staying there because he was going to school at St. Hilda's & St. Hugh's. Her daughter Josephine, whom I would later marry, was at college. One of the first things I said to Madeleine was "I've never directed a pageant." She just laughed and gave me the script. It was a wonderful first meeting.

*Q: What were your first impressions of her?*

A: I'd come from a working-class background in England, and it all seemed very romantic to me: the novelist, the Upper West Side apartment, lots of books, a grand piano. Spaghetti on the stove, Brahms on the stereo—and this intellectual brightness of conversation and willingness to explore ideas. My first impressions were very, very positive.

*Q: Why did you want to study in the United States?*

A: I was in seminary in England, studying to be a priest at Theological College in the north of England, and the Church of England offered scholarships for four of us to finish our studies in the United States. I was twenty-three or twenty-four, and I thought, Well, why not? And so I applied for a scholarship and came over on a student ship—they don't have those anymore—in 1964. It was an adventure.

*Q: Did you and Madeleine become friends?*

A: We took to each other very strongly. Hugh came back down from Boston for his play to open on Broadway, and I remember seeing him in that show and thinking he was a very good actor. Then Josephine came back down to New York from Smith for Thanksgiving, and I was invited for that. One thing led to another, and, very strangely, thinking back, we were married within six months. She wasn't quite nineteen. It was a kind of whirlwind. I think I had this vision of this American family—the mother a novelist, the father an actor, good food, and good conversation—

and I wanted to be part of that. It was all very seductive and very attractive, and they were all very kind to me.

*Q: When did you first visit Crosswicks?*

A: I think we went up to Crosswicks in the spring of 1966. That house too was so amazing.

*Q: Madeleine's early life wasn't so much steeped in the church. Do you know when religion first became important to her?*

A: The irony of Anglicanism in the South especially was that that was the church you *didn't* go to. If you died, you went there. People mainly went for funerals and weddings. I get the impression that church for Madeleine began in Goshen, in the Congregational church. They bought Crosswicks around 1946. Whether she was lonely then or not, I don't know. She wrote in her journal that on her fortieth birthday she got a rejection letter from some publisher. It was about then that she started reading theology— Niebuhr and so on. And she talked theology with the local Congregational minister. But her cultural background was Episcopalian. When she and Hugh and their children moved back to New York City from Crosswicks, she went to the Church of the Resurrection [on East Seventy-fourth Street], which is an Episcopal church.

*Q: Did she approach you as a student speaking to a teacher?*

A: Not at all. We talked a lot about religion, but it was very much as sparring partners. Hugh was part of the religious community in Connecticut, but he left that behind and didn't go to church in New York. I think that isolated Madeleine a bit from any sort of home conversation. It may be because she came from that Congregational side and I came from the Anglo-Catholic side—I was trained by Anglican monks—that we had so much to talk about. And we were both seduced by language and loved to argue and discuss. I think it was hard on everyone else because we would go off on these theological tangents. It must have been hard on Josephine and irritating to Hugh.

*Q: When did she become associated with St. John the Divine?*

A: They had nine years in Crosswicks, and when they came back from Goshen, she became very close to Canon West. He was a perfect foil for her. And then she got involved with St. Hilda's & St. Hugh's, the Community of the Holy Spirit, and I think that absorbed an awful lot of her energy and an awful lot of her time.

*Q: How was Canon West "a perfect foil" for her?*

A: Well, he was a character, and he was very learned. And he loved dogs. If you were writing Trollope for the mid-twentieth century, you know *Barchester Towers*, there would Edward West be. A lot of clergy found him laughable and eccentric, and that hurt him and that made him more so. But I heard him preach and heard him speak at meetings, and I got close to him. So I can say that he may have been eccentric and he may have been a bit pompous, but he was also brilliant. And I think that he valued Madeleine and her own particular genius.

*Q: He seems to have played a unique role in her life.*

A: Yes, he did. He was her spiritual guide—her spiritual director and confessor. He had a kind of wisdom—and I think that, like her, he probably had a wounded soul. He was a great friend of Bishop Donegan, who came from a wealthy family and had been rector of St. James' Church, on Madison Avenue, in the grander days of the church.* These men were like ecclesiastical noblemen who might almost have stepped out of the court of Louis the Fourteenth. It was a different era. Bishop Donegan being friendly with the queen mother. His Christmas card one year adorned with a photograph of him dressed in a kilt and full Highland outfit and looking adoringly at a corgi. It was all very odd. Still, I would want to say to people who might think to caricature Canon West, Look deeper. He was a very good man who liked to play a role.

---

*Horace Donegan was bishop of the Episcopal Diocese of New York, 1950–72.

*Q: It seems to me that both Madeleine and he saw some connection between religion and theatricality.*

A: I think that's exactly right. He was a liturgist, and in the best sense he liked to put on a good show at St. John the Divine. He would walk around with a little baton, a stick, and point to people to march this way or that way. It was all very regimented but also very beautiful—and good for its time. He was also a consultant for church architecture. When people wanted to build a church or change the interior of a church, he would advise them on what to do with liturgical space. Yes. Theatricality in the best sense—or maybe the word is "drama," the dramatic shape of life.

*Q: Madeleine shunned pomp and pretense, yet she found the grandeur of the cathedral appealing.*

A: I think she was torn. The bigness of vision of St. John the Divine appealed to her, the wanting always a more generous and bigger world. I can remember one funny argument that she and I used to have. We would argue about which one of us had the poorer background. "I am more poor than thou." She said, "You know, once when we lived in France, we had rabbit and Daddy could have only one martini." She said it jokingly, but yet there was a kind of seriousness in it too. Well, she had a good sense of humor.

She liked style. But when it came to clothes, she couldn't dress well. For one thing, she was awkward physically, and she was very tall, with large limbs. She could look handsome and strong, but she didn't have an eye for clothes. She wore lots of dangly jewelry.

*Q: When did she go to All Angels' Church, and why?*

A: That was puzzling. She had an interesting relationship to fundamentalists, when you think of Wheaton College. All Angels' was an evangelical church. The American evangelicals fell in love with C. S. Lewis and made him their Thomas Aquinas. And so evangelicals who didn't want to be fundamentalist were attracted to art and novels and narratives. So, for example, Madeleine had a strong relationship with Beatrice Batson, who was head of the

English department of Wheaton College. Madeleine was connected to Wheaton through the English department rather than the religion department. When I went and lectured there years ago, it was also through an invitation from the English department.

I suspect there were evangelicals who were her fans and she responded to people who liked her books. There were other evangelicals who would want to ban her books, the way they would want to ban Harry Potter. So the evangelical picture isn't monochrome. The fundamentalist evangelicals would go crazy over any reference to witches, but the literary evangelicals would see it as metaphor, as a richness of the imagination. The real division is between those who see religion as a work of the imagination and those who don't.

*Q: Did Madeleine ever discuss the attacks on her books?*

A: Yes, she did. She was both amused and horrified. That certainly didn't stop her writing, though, I think because she had enough of a following, enough of a fan base, to keep her encouraged.

*Q: She had such a highly developed public persona. It makes one wonder what was going on behind the version of herself that most people saw.*

A: She had a very passionate life. She could be very hurt. I think of Madeleine, born in 1918, as that lonely little girl in the Swiss boarding school, writing in her journals, doing her amazing writing, and having this interior life, and then in the 1940s going into the theater. It all made for a very complicated and interesting woman.

Early on, writing had become a way for her to control the narrative of life. Later, I think it was very hard on her children when they'd say something about a personal experience and she'd say, "No. It didn't happen that way. I have it in my journal." That was a way of somehow denying other people's experience. That was a source of tension within the family. I remember someone bouncing up to Josephine at a conference I was attending and saying to her, "Oh, I love your mother. I love her books!"—talking about the Crosswicks Journal—and Josephine said very clearly, "Just remember. My mother writes fiction." Madeleine was such a good writer, and she would work things out in her journal and idealize reality, and I think she sometimes thought of it as objective truth. We all do that to some extent, inventing our lives as we go along. Madeleine was a storyteller looking for a story.

*Q: Did the parties at the West End Avenue apartment have a salon-like atmosphere?*

A: Occasionally, they did. I would bring in stray bishops from England. There would also be theater people and writers. Lincoln Kirstein, the founder of the City Ballet, was sometimes one of the guests. There was a strange friendship we all had for a while with Lincoln Kirstein. He took a shine to me, and we used to have lunch once a month. He said to me over lunch one day, "Alan, my dear"—and he didn't mean this to be the least insulting— "Madeleine has no intellect." He meant by that that for her it was all about metaphor and imagination as opposed to her having a philosophical mind. I found that interesting. And then one day he abruptly got up from lunch and walked out and I never saw him again. I heard later that I wasn't the only person to have had this experience. He was a very eccentric but also a very great man.

*Q: When would that have been?*

A: Early 1970s.

*Q: Did Madeleine ever ask your advice about her writing?*

A: She would occasionally share a poem. But more often the boot was on the other foot. When I was writing my master's thesis, she went through it with me line by line, and she said things like "Tell me that paragraph in your own words." I did as she asked, and then she said, "Now look what you've written." She was a very good teacher, and I think she certainly had an influence on my writing and she was very generous about it. There was a new edition of a novel about St. Thomas à Becket, *My Life for My Sheep*, and the editors of this new edition said to Madeleine, "Would you write a new introduction?" and she said, "Only if I can write it with my son-in-law." And we wrote this little piece about Becket and his personality. It was a very sweet thing that she did. And of course she was an enormous correspondent and touched a lot of lives that way.

*Q: How do you understand her need to take so many young people under her wing?*

A: My amateur psychologist's mind thinks of her childhood, her own isolation, her strong interior life, and her need for people around her to give her reality and authenticity. You may know the story about when she and her parents were in Switzerland and one day they said, "We're going off for a ride in the car," and they took her to a boarding school and left her there. Pretty hard stuff, and it was through writing that she held her life together. Having young people around gave her a sense of real fulfillment, though often her own children would feel a bit neglected or out of the picture.

*Q: When you think of Madeleine, what do you think of as some of her great strengths?*

A: Discipline is the big thing. A daily writing out of things. A tremendous will to do that. Her bashing out Bach on the piano when she was upset. She had a way of negotiating her craziness. Of moving through things. What I think is wonderful about good writing is that it shows you there is another world out there besides the little world of your own psyche, and she would insist that what was going on inside her was not the only reality. She would do it through music, through writing, through argument. At her best, she was trying to enlarge people's worlds—including her own. She could be painful, narcissistic, difficult as well. But the overwhelming thing was that she was an artist.

*Q: Was she a good preacher?*

A: I think she was okay. Remember I'm a preacher and a theologian, so what would thrill others I didn't find so thrilling. But she certainly had a presence, and I could see that she was effective and that she touched a lot of lives.

Q: *What do you think she most struggled with in her life?*

A: What immediately comes to mind is struggling with relationships. Her marriage to Hugh—Midwest Baptist coming to New York to become an actor; Madeleine coming from the South—was really a clash of values and of different worlds. Coming from the South with a very liberal mind-set and being an only child and having absolutely no training as a woman or as a mother. I don't know how to put it. She was awkward. And I think she overvalued the power of writing as a way of making things all right. There was a therapeutic side to writing for her, and it didn't always work. But I think she struggled a lot with her relationship with her mother, with her children, and with her husband. In the Crosswicks Journal, she idealized her relationship with her mother enormously. And while I don't think her marriage was at all disastrous, it was complicated, and *Two-Part Invention* was a tremendously idealized picture of the marriage. I always thought the title was suitably ironical.

Madeleine was not always good at understanding boundaries. While Josephine and I were in England when I was teaching there, from 1968 to 1971, Madeleine and I had an intense correspondence. It was quite appropriate, but still: for her to be writing intense letters to her son-in-law, and not to her own daughter. Letters would arrive in Lincoln, England, addressed to me. It was not inappropriate in the usual sense, but it was inappropriate. I didn't know any better, and she obviously didn't know any better, either. I think that was probably hurtful to Josephine. Madeleine didn't know boundaries sometimes, and she idealized people.

Q: *Did you continue to be in touch with her after you and Josephine were no longer married?*

A: No. What was very sad for me was that the summer before Madeleine died, my daughter Charlotte and I were on a long walk, and she said, "Gran spoke very warmly of you and would have loved to have seen you." That made me feel pretty sad. It was very good for me to go to the memorial service for Madeleine at St. John the Divine, where the dean and the others there were very gracious to me. It was a kind of reconciliation. I had always a great admiration for her as a writer and as a person, acknowledging her complicated character.

*Q: How did her life change after Hugh died? Charlotte said that in part it had freed her to travel more and enjoy herself more.*

A: Madeleine was much more generous. Hugh could be quite difficult. She wanted to be more gregarious. She wanted to write intensively and then burst out and do something for fun. He was much more reclusive. She used to get mad at him for not phoning his agent more often to see if there was work out there. She would say, "He won't call his agent." She couldn't understand why he would spend hours doing crossword puzzles and playing solitaire. Later on he never put on a suit. He'd always be wearing sneakers. I can remember clearing out his closet when he died and finding shirts that had come back on hangers from the laundry that had stayed on the hangers so long that the hangers had rusted through. So I think there was a kind of freedom that came with his death. At a certain point I think Hugh just gave up on life, and I think that was hard on Madeleine because she wanted to idealize their relationship.

Madeleine used to say, "Everything they say about Mother Ruth is true." In other words, Mother Ruth was horrendous *and* Mother Ruth was wonderful. I would almost say that everything you hear about Madeleine L'Engle is true, too: she was a rich, complex, marvelous personality, and it was a great privilege for me to have known her.

# LÉNA ROY

Léna Roy is the author of *Edges*, a novel for teens, and is the older of Madeleine L'Engle's two granddaughters.

*Q: Tell me when and where you were born.*

A: I was born on June 20, 1968, in New York City. My parents were living with my grandparents at the time. Then, when I was six weeks old, we moved to Lincoln, England. We came back after a couple of years and lived on 102nd Street, three blocks away from my grandmother. My dad was the chaplain at St. Hilda's & St. Hugh's, which is how he met my grandmother. Then my grandmother introduced my mother to him.

*Q: What are your earliest memories of your grandmother?*

A: We saw each other all the time. I have memories of being in the cathedral library with her. My sister and I would play quietly while she worked. She adored me, and my sister too. We had dogs, and we would all walk our dogs together. She always had big dogs, except when my mom was little, when she had Touché, who was a stage dog, a toy poodle. This was a magical grandmother! This was someone who knew what it was like to be a child and who could be with us in our imaginative play. She could be on our level and feel like one of us. At the same time she was this incredibly creative, magnetic, successful woman. She would metamorphose, and we would see her first this way, then that way. I think she got a tremendous lot out of it, too. She always said that we kept her young.

*Q: Do you remember when you first became aware that your grandmother was a writer—and a famous one at that?*

A: Yes, I do. My grandfather, as you know, was an actor, and he was famous too. When I was nine, I was hit by a car and I got a concussion and two broken legs, and I was in a coma for nine days. The story my grandmother loved to tell was that one day after I had just come out of the coma, and they were keeping the television on for me, I was watching *All My Children*—which was my grandfather's show—when the nurse came in and said, "Oh, what are you doing, dear?" To which I replied, "I'm watching my grandfather on TV." When I said that, the nurse got all excited and ran out of the room calling, "We've got to get the doctor! She's having hallucinations! She thinks she's seeing her grandfather on TV!"

My grandmother loved telling that story. She came to visit me every day while I was in the hospital, and she read me *A Wrinkle in Time*. She wrote somewhere that she had been in a plane when the accident occurred and she had somehow known—she had gotten a psychic vibe—that something terrible had happened to me. We had a very strong connection.

Once I was aware of her being famous, I became jealous of all the attention she would pay to other people. She would be so kind and so magnanimous to so many other people! I would think, She is not *everyone's* grandmother. She's *my* grandmother! I had to work through that. Because of her work at the cathedral and her having contact with so many students from the writers' groups she led for teenagers and kids, she was always around other young people. I think both my sister and I could get jealous. Now of course I realize that that was such a huge part of who she was and that it was such a service to other people: being present for them, drawing their creativity out of them.

*Q: What would you and your grandmother like to do together in New York?*

A: She and my sister and I would often go to the Hayden Planetarium. We would go to the Frick Museum and the Metropolitan Museum. When my grandmother was growing up in New York, she would go to the Metropolitan Museum, and her character Camilla goes there. She did not take us to the Museum of Modern Art! We would go to the opera and to the ballet. She would take us to *The Nutcracker* every year. We'd go to the Russian Tea Room. She would have tea parties with us. We would sing together from *The Fireside Book of Folk Songs*. We would climb up onto her big bed with our hot chocolates and read Shakespeare together out loud. She made Shakespeare accessible. She never talked down to children. She met us at our level, and she really enriched our lives.

*Q: Did you spend much time as a child at Crosswicks?*

A: Yes, and those were great times too. My grandmother had her Tower, over the garage, where she went to write, and we would sit on the floor there and play while she worked. We would go with her on walks in the woods, to the brook, and discover things. She would see fairies in the trees. She was always right there with us in our play. We'd go out at night and look at the stars. We'd look at the fireflies. It felt that she was guiding us through a world of possibilities. Crosswicks was Meg Murry's house. It was the Austins' house. All those characters were alive there, and they were alive in my grandmother.

My grandmother gave me my first journal as a birthday present when I was nine years old. I have been writing in a journal ever since. She always gave me beautiful leather-bound journals. She said that journaling was the best way to get things out of your system and also to remember who you are.

*Q: Did you let her read your journals?*

A: I did until I was twelve or thirteen. She was the only one I showed them to. You know, I would write when I was angry with my parents, that kind of thing. It was good! You have to do that, and I've told my son to do that too. Sometimes my grandmother and I would sit together and write in our journals, or I would do homework while she wrote in hers. In the beginning, we would sometimes write stories together too. First I would write a little bit of the story, then she would write a little bit. The first one was about two frogs who were friends. She also thought that being quiet together was important.

As we got older, my sister and I would read some of our grand-mother's manuscripts. I remember feeling that that was quite an honor. *The Joys of Love* was one that we read in manuscript. It felt like our delicious secret. By then my sister and I were feeling very protective of our relationship with her, so to have that experience meant a lot to us.

My grandmother could be vulnerable at times. She wasn't a stranger to insecurity, or pain and suffering—what all artists strug-gle with—and that was one of the beautiful things about her. That also, of course, is what made it possible for her to connect with people. But it was a double-edged sword. I have that same quality, and she would tell me that I would get through a problem because I was like her. She would always talk about what we had in common. She would say that I would "come through." I remem-ber her telling me several times about having been an understudy in a play and having worked with a famous actress who became her role model. This actress always wore a locket, and inside that locket were the words "Everyone is lonely." She would tell me this story countless times because, as a teenager especially, I felt so alienated and lonely. This was her way of saying both that I would get through it and that she could be lonely too.

*Q: Did you act in school plays?*

A: Yes! That was what gave me a sense of community at school. My grandmother was so supportive. In second grade we did *Many Moons*, a musical adaptation of a James Thurber book. I had a solo, and my grandmother just gushed about me. Then in high school I did a lot of plays, and I remember her and my grandfather coming to see me and my grandmother beaming and my grandfather giving me a compliment under his breath, and my grandmother beaming at that too, saying, "He never gives a compliment!" She wanted to see me become some kind of artist. For a while we all thought it was going to be acting. It gave me a sense of belonging, and I think that that is also why I got involved in drama therapy.

*Q: Tell me about your grandfather.*

A: He was a lovely, taciturn man and a very classy actor, but he was not a very huggy kind of person. My grandmother was very touchy-feely. She said once, "Oh, he *loved* you!" My grandfather thought that being an actor was an awful life, that it was such a hard road, and he would never encourage anybody to go into the theater. My grandmother, on the other hand, was supportive of anyone pursuing their artistic dreams and talents.

*Q: Would she bring you roses when you were in a play?*

A: Once, when I was performing in a play in San Francisco and she was unable to come out to see me, she sent me her fur coat! I had been lusting after that fur coat for years. She said, "You have finally earned it!" She hadn't been able to come out for the play, so she sent the fur coat instead of herself. It arrived, out of the blue, on opening night. This would have been about 1992. My grandmother, you see, was really good at grand gestures!

After my grandfather died, my sister and I moved in with her in her West End Avenue apartment. I think it was really helpful to her to have us there. She was still traveling a lot then, but when she was home, we had a great time.

*Q: Did you meet her friends?*

A: Constantly. She had friends who were mathematicians and scientists, musicians, all different kinds of people from all walks of life. She had dinner parties at least once a week for fifteen or twenty people. She had an informal way with people. She wasn't hoity-toity! But she liked to be the matriarch, the grande dame, to sit at the head of the table and be the center of attention and tell the stories. She also loved to go out to dinner with friends, and in her later years she lived in Henry's, the restaurant downstairs from her apartment. She was treated like a star there, and she would always see people she knew.

As she got older, she tended to have fewer friends who were her peers and more friends who needed her. I think she liked to be needed. And she did a lot of service for the church. In addition to her work at the cathedral library, she would preach at the cathedral. And she became a member of All Angels' Church, which is an evangelical parish. I think that that was where she thought she could make a difference, because she herself was not an evangelical.

She always walked the dogs past the statue of the Japanese Buddhist monk Shinran Shonin on Riverside Drive, between 105th and 106th streets. She loved that statue. Her theology is so fascinating to me. She always kept a Buddha on her desk to remind her that there are all different kinds of philosophies and that we are all one.

*Q: During the time you lived with her, was she usually working on a book?*

A: Always.

*Q: Did your grandmother base any of her characters on you?*

A: I don't think so. I always identified with Vicky because she was a writer, and I liked it that Gran said that she was Vicky too. I'm sure she made use of some of my experiences. And I'm sure that being close to both Charlotte and me helped her to write young adult literature.

Q: *What did your grandmother like to read?*

A: Well, for fun she loved reading mysteries, including some that were pure schlock. But she read everything. She was incredibly well-read. She would read scientific journals. She had memorized passages from Schopenhauer and Plato and Shakespeare and Chekhov and could quote from these and many other writers. She had "quotitis," as she liked to say. My sister, my mother, my grandmother, and I all read the same books together. We had our own little book club.

Q: *Was your grandmother writing at the end of her life?*

A: No. That was a really, really hard time. Bion died at the end of 1999, and I think it was around the time of his death that my grandmother became depressed and started deteriorating rapidly. It could be that she was good at covering up her condition from us and that her decline was not really as rapid as it seemed. Bion's death must have broken her heart. She was putting vodka in her tomato soup, and the doctor said she couldn't drink alcohol with her meds. Some of her friends who would go out to dinner with her couldn't say no to her, and they would let her have a glass of wine with dinner, which would just make it harder for her. The problem was that her friends didn't see her as debilitated. They only saw her when she was "on" for those two hours that they were having dinner together, and she was able to be Madeleine L'Engle for them. So that was rough. She became a different person. She didn't read. I would try to read out loud to her. She wasn't writing. She would tell people she was writing. She would sleep more and more. She would watch *Judge Judy*! I became close to her home health aide, who loved her and did a wonderful job. Finally, my grandmother needed to be in a nursing home. The people at the nursing home loved her too. I picked up crocheting, and I crocheted a blanket while sitting there with her. And my mom took such good care of her. It was so sad, because if you read in *The Summer of the Great-Grandmother* about what she went through with her mother, it had all happened in one month's time. We went through seven years, and my grandmother never would have wanted that.

## CHARLOTTE JONES VOIKLIS

Charlotte Jones Voiklis is a nonprofit consultant. She is the younger of Madeleine L'Engle's two granddaughters and is responsible for her grandmother's literary affairs.

*Q: Where did you live as a child?*

A: I was born in 1969 in Lincoln, England, where my father was getting his Ph.D. We stayed there for about two and a half years and then came to live in New York. My grandparents lived at 105th Street, and we lived at 102nd Street for two years, and then we moved downtown to Chelsea.

*Q: Do you have a first memory of your grandmother?*

A: I have strong memories of lying under the grand piano in her apartment while my grandmother practiced. She always said she didn't play well, that playing the piano was good discipline for her. But of course she could pick up any piece of music and read it and play it.

*Q: What would you and she do together in the city?*

A: I would see her at her office at the cathedral library. I would be dropped off there after school, and she would have a stack of coloring books and a tin of cookies from the Hungarian Pastry Shop. Every year she would take my sister and me to *The Nutcracker.* Later, when I was in college and graduate school, she would get season tickets, and we'd go to the ballet together.

Most of my memories from my early childhood are of domestic activities: singing songs, being read to and reading aloud to her, sitting in the kitchen while she cooked dinner. She was an erratic cook, but she certainly enjoyed being in the kitchen. She made awesome salad dressing and spaghetti sauce and hot fudge sauce. But once, at a dinner party, the children's meal was Spanish rice and it was cold and not very good, and she caught us flushing it down the toilet! She didn't scold us or yell at us, but her face fell and she just walked away. She didn't like conflict, but I think it deeply wounded her.

*Q: Did you read her books as a child?*

A: Oh yes. I don't remember the first time I read *A Wrinkle in Time*. The first book I do remember reading was either *The Joys of Love*, which I read in manuscript, or *A Swiftly Tilting Planet*, which I read when I was eight or nine.

*Q: Did you know other family members of your grandmother's generation?*

A: My grandfather was around, and two of my grandmother's first cousins from Florida. We didn't have a large extended family. My grandmother was an only child. My grandfather was not an only child, but his siblings were in Oklahoma, and I've actually never met any of them. We would see our cousins once or twice a year.

*Q: Why did your grandmother call herself Madeleine L'Engle, taking her mother's maternal family name rather than her father's name, Camp? Did she see herself more as her mother's daughter than her father's?*

A: What she always said about that was that her father was a published writer and she didn't want to be seen as trading on his name. But there is definitely a strong streak of matriarchy in our family. All the family history is matriarchal, even down to my generation.

*Q: How well-known a writer was her father?*

A: I don't think he was terrifically well-known. He was a theater critic, and he had published six thriller-like novels, which I've never read.*

*Q: She talks about her choice of a writing name in* The Summer of the Great-Grandmother, *but I somehow wasn't totally convinced by her explanation.*†

A: Me neither. It's also true that "L'Engle" sounds so much better than "Camp."

*Q: Was your grandfather's family of less interest to you and other members of your generation?*

A: Well, my grandfather didn't share a whole lot. I'm quite interested in his family now because I know less about them and I want to have that balance.

*Q: Did he come from humble origins?*

A: I'd say humbler origins. His father was a lawyer for the Bureau of Indian Affairs. I did a little research about that but did not get very far. I was always trying to figure out: Was he on the side of justice, or what? I'm still curious. They lived in Tulsa, Oklahoma, and they were Baptists, which meant that alcohol and acting and card playing were not all right as far as they were concerned. So my grandfather's parents were not thrilled that he decided to be an actor.

*Q: You lived with your grandmother around the time that your grandfather was dying.*

---

*Published under the name Wadsworth Camp, the novels are *Sinister Island* (Dodd, Mead, 1915), *The House of Fear* (Doubleday, Page, 1916), *The Abandoned Room* (W. R. Caldwell, 1917), *The Hidden Road* (Doubleday, Doran, 1922), *The Communicating Door* (Doubleday, Page, 1923), and *The Forbidden Years* (Doubleday, Doran, 1930).

†L'Engle, as she wrote in that book, may well have wanted not to trade on her father's name and professional reputation. But she may also have had it in mind to surpass Charles Wadsworth Camp as a writer and to do so entirely on her own terms.

A: He got sick in May 1986. My sister and I both graduated from high school that June, and then we both moved into our grandparents' apartment for the summer. We were sixteen and seventeen. They were in Connecticut when we first moved to New York. It wasn't a long illness. My grandfather died in September.

Our parents had moved to San Francisco, and the plan had been for the two of us to stay at the West End Avenue apartment just for the summer, and that fall my sister did move into the Barnard dorm. But I had decided to study at a college—the New School—that didn't provide dorms, so I stayed on, and I lived with my grandmother for the next seven years.

I think the time that I spent with my grandmother then was an amazing period for both of us. She was trying to figure out what life looked like without my grandfather. She had a grueling travel schedule—speaking and teaching and all that. But we had a dog, and when Gran was home we had multigenerational dinner parties and really enjoyed the time we had together. Then she would go off again, and I would go back to enjoying my adolescent freedom. I think I kept her young. That's what she always said. She valued the relationships she had with people of all different ages. She really was a twelve-year-old and a sixteen-year-old and a thirty-year-old. She had access to all of that. She could remember. Not everybody can.

Q: *Was she writing much during the time that you lived with her?*

A: She was very disciplined about her writing routine. She would arrive at the cathedral library at ten, but she could write anywhere. She wrote on airplanes. When she was home, she would retire at nine and take a bath. She had shutters in her bedroom. Every morning she would open all of the shutters, and every night she would close them all, and she'd get into bed and read. She always had a mystery—say by Anne Perry or Tony Hillerman—on her night table, and the Bible. She would read and go to bed.

*Q: At one point you became one of her trusted readers.*

A: While I was living with her, yes, I would read her manuscripts. We had conversations about voice. I studied literature in college and graduate school, so I thought I knew a whole lot about narrative. We would have good conversations about her books. She always said that my grandfather was her best editor. When he died, she missed that. She wanted and needed that.

*Q: What was it like to be her editor?*

A: She could be sensitive, but she also could listen. She might think about something for a while, and if it was right, she would change it. She always "served the work." If she felt the advice also served the work, she was totally ready to take it. Otherwise, she would stick to her guns. I think she was fortunate to have such a strong sense of what the work was, early on. In *Meet the Austins*, which has a death in it, people were saying to take that out. She was a workhorse. She was not afraid of rewriting. But certain things she would not change, because if she did, it would not have been the book she was writing.

*Q: Did your grandmother's apartment change much during the time she lived there?*

A: It was the same for years and years: same green carpet, same marble coffee table. But after my grandfather died, in 1986, she redecorated, and it changed considerably.

*Q: Was there a pattern to the choices she made?*

A: Not really. She had a decorator friend who said, "Let me do this for you." He didn't do it for free! She agreed and let him go to town. She didn't have time or patience for those kinds of details, really. She didn't have a strong aesthetic sense when it came to things.

*Q: Was her idea to "start over"?*

A: I don't think so. The apartment had been neglected for a long time. My grandfather had been raised in Oklahoma during the Depression. He never wanted to spend money on anything.

She loved to go out to dinner, and he hated that. She was an extrovert, and he was not. She loved to travel. He wasn't into attending church, either. I don't think that my grandmother attended church regularly until after he died, although her travel schedule often interfered with that, too. So when he died, she had a lot more freedom. It was a very big adjustment for her. Some adjustments were more welcome than others. She enjoyed being able to go out more, but missed him terribly.

Q: *Did your grandmother give you memorable gifts?*

A: I've got a large cast-iron nutcracker in the shape of a dog that belonged to her. She had a bunch of different nutcrackers that were fun for my sister and me to play with when we were at her house.

Q: *Did she collect them?*

A: No. She wasn't a collector. She was more interested in experiences than in things. Often people would give her giraffes and dolphins and penguins and unicorns because they associated those animals with her and her books.

Q: *She sometimes compared herself to a giraffe, didn't she?*

A. Yes, because of her long legs and her long, skinny neck. As for the other animals: she wrote about dolphins in *A Ring of Endless Light* and penguins in *Troubling a Star*, the book about Antarctica, and of course she wrote about unicorns.

Once, when I was in college, her gift to me was a trip to Jacksonville, Florida, where her family was from. That was about 1988, most likely during my spring break. In Florida we saw her best friend from there, Pat Cowdery, whom she had met in Jacksonville when they were teenagers and who had become the first woman chief medical officer for the county. My grandmother was always very proud of her for that. We stayed with Pat, who lived on the St. Johns River, and I remember being warned against the alligators. Later, when my grandmother was deteriorating, she would imagine alligators, but they would be friendly alligators.

Some would be friendly and others not. By the time I visited Florida with her, her grandmother's house was gone. It had been from that house, as Gran remembered it, that she had been taken out of the crib and shown the stars.

*Q: Did your grandmother like celebrating her birthday?*

A: Oh yes! She wrote a funny piece about that, about people making fun of her for reminding them of her birthday, and then one year deciding not to do so, and then regretting *that* decision, and finally vowing that the following year she would be sure to remind everyone well in advance. She loved being feted.

*Q: One visitor, Patricia Lee Gauch, recalled that your grandmother had a great many photographs on the walls of her New York apartment.*

A: The hallway was a portrait gallery. The designer had expensively framed a bunch of family pictures and other pictures and put them on the wall. Often, particularly if someone had gotten divorced, my grandmother would take their picture down and put up another one in its place. The gallery was always changing.

*Q: Did your grandmother think of herself primarily as a writer or as a religious person who happened to write?*

A: She was a writer. She was also a committed Christian, and she wrote books about the relationship between her faith and her art. But for her, writing was itself an incarnational act—an expression of God in the world. She had such a fluid mind that she didn't have to prioritize by saying, I'm this first and these other things are secondary. She was always a "both/and" thinker, not an "either/or" thinker. It was the same with her frustration and bafflement with people who would get so tied up in the debate about religion versus science. The two weren't incompatible for her.

*Q: Why did your grandmother become interested in All Angels', a parish church in New York, when she was already so involved with St. John the Divine?*

A: The cathedral remained important to her because of her

connection to the library and because she would go for the noon-day Eucharist. But I think she found the Sunday services to be not the kind of intimate worship, and social experience, that she wanted on a Sunday. So, yes, she became involved in All Angels', which was nominally Episcopalian but heavily evangelical and fundamentalist. I think she felt she had a real mission with what she called the "fundalits"—fundamentalist literalist interpreters of the Bible. She felt she had something to say to them. She said that to me. She developed great individual friendships with many of the people there. They were good friends to her, and that was important to her. She felt that she was part of their community and that she didn't have to agree with them about everything.

*Q: Did your grandmother see herself as "political"? Did she have strong political views?*

A: She would say, "Good Lord, no!" and she would never want to get sucked into a political argument. But in some ways she was political: in terms of insisting on the writer's freedom of expression. There was an intense period during the mid-1980s when the fundamentalists went after her particularly hard.

*Q: That was because of the supposed references to witches in* Wrinkle?

A: That's an element of it. That's why *A Wrinkle in Time* would be challenged. A lot of what she wrote in *Walking on Water* and in some of her nonfiction books is challenging to those folks.

*Q: She writes in the Crosswicks books about being a part-time believer. She talks about going in and out of faith. Would that have set them off?*

A: That would have given them a reason to say, "You're not a real Christian." But I think what they objected to had more to do with doctrinal issues: whether it was about the Trinity, or about taking Communion, or about the way God operates in our lives, us not knowing who's saved and who's not. As in, Of course if you don't believe what we believe, you're going to hell!

As a twenty-year-old college student, I was going to reproductive rights conferences. Knowing that the crowd that my grandmother was running with was heavily antichoice, she and I would have lots of conversations about that. She would insist that she supported abortion rights. But she wouldn't stand up for that publicly, because that would have pulled her in a totally different direction, and that was not where she wanted to go. When it came to the debates about gay clergy or ordination of women or gay marriage, she would say that she was just baffled by the rigidity of people's thinking on these issues and bewail our fixation on genitalia and plumbing. Her way into the discussion was always to talk about the dangers of fundamentalism. I think she was very wise.

*Q: Your grandmother enjoyed teaching classes at St. John the Divine during Lent. Why did Lent have special meaning for her?*

A: The discipline of the liturgical year is a sort of tool. Lent is a time to go inward and be contemplative in order to prepare for a celebration. So, yes, she loved Lent. Those kinds of external disciplines help you focus, and that's what Lent did for her.

*Q: Going back to what we were saying about different kinds of political engagement. Your grandmother was a schoolmate of Betty Friedan's at Smith. Did they remain in touch over the years?*

A: I believe they had run the school literary magazine together. Betty was the business manager, and Gran was the editor. They were very different, but they definitely interacted. My grandmother didn't let anything stop her, but her class background meant that she didn't have to face some of the same choices that other women faced. I remember the first year I was in college, my grandfather had just died, and my grandmother was writing about their marriage. I was studying at the New School, taking a class on narrating gender, and it was a very political environment, and we were reading Tillie Olsen's "I Stand Here Ironing," which is an early feminist working-class manifesto in the "I want to write, but I have to work to feed my family" vein. I remember discussing it with my grandmother. She was just so unsympathetic to all that. Her idea was that if you need to write, you write.

Q: *Some of that could have been a generational response.*

A: Oh, most definitely. But issues of class are tied into it too, and she didn't feel that imperative.

Q: *What was it like for you as a schoolchild to have such a famous grandmother?*

A: It was great at first, but my feelings about it changed a lot over the years. When I was very young—five, six, and seven—I'd say when I introduced her, "My grandmother wrote such and such," and then it would be: Get ready for the shock and awe! Time to bask in her reflected glory. But then, as I got to be a teenager, when you become more self-conscious, I did not want anyone to know who my grandmother was, because I was afraid her light would expose my own deficiencies. My freshman year at boarding school, which was my ninth-grade year, she and my grandfather came to visit on grandparents' weekend. They came to my classes with me, and unbeknownst to me one of my teachers had gone to Wheaton College, and so he recognized Gran. He was great about it, actually. They chatted before class. Then, at the beginning of class, when we were all going to introduce our grandparents, he asked me if I wanted to say anything special. I gritted my teeth and said, "These are my grandparents." That was all! Later, my religion teacher recognized her too, and it was all so embarrassing. And because my grandfather was on a soap opera, kids would stare at him as we walked through campus. It was just awful! My grandparents didn't come back the next year.

Q: *Did you feel you could never write well enough?*

A: No, I never felt that. Writing wasn't a big issue for me. It was more about personality and wisdom. Maybe it was not so much that it would expose my own deficiencies as that I was just not ready to live my life in that public a way. People look at you differently. It creates an imaginative narrative in people's minds about you. In her young adult fiction and her nonfiction and her religious writings, my grandmother really touched people's nerves, and many of them felt very close to her who hadn't known her. Often there'd be these weird undercurrents of competition, and jealousy, from folks. I felt that. That was and still is difficult.

*Q: Jane Yolen talked about the Smith students who wanted literally to touch the hem of your grandmother's dress.*

A: Oh, totally! But my grandmother was a performer. A lot of performers love and need that acknowledgment and feedback. Overall, I don't think it made her uncomfortable. She was in charge! She understood that she moved and touched people deeply and that that was a huge responsibility.

*Q: She must have been very self-confident to seek out and cultivate such a public role for herself.*

A: She would deny that she had done that, but I do think it is true. Her need for connection and for attention was instinctual. There didn't need to be an ego on top, managing it. Her id did it all—perhaps.

*Q: Are you aware of being the model for any of the characters in her books?*

A: No. The only people she admitted to being models were my uncle Bion for Rob Austin and Canon West for Canon Tallis. And she would always say that she was Vicky and she was Meg.

*Q: Do you think your grandmother ever regretted that she hadn't continued to act?*

A: No, because being a writer was always the most important thing to her. And she didn't have many regrets.

She was a great public speaker and a very skilled performer. She would write her lectures out, but then she wouldn't necessarily read from the text. Her lectures always had a structure, whether it was a series of quotations that built an argument or an overarching metaphor. They are quite impressive. My grandmother would rework them and rework them. They fall into groups. "Oh, this one is the Amoeba lecture . . ."

*Q: Can you tell me about her friendship with the actress Anne Jackson?*

A: I don't know a whole lot about it, but they were often in touring companies together. Annie would play the ingenue, and my grandmother was an understudy.

*Q: Did they remain friends?*

A: Yes, although they probably didn't see each other often. I remember her and her husband, Eli Wallach, coming over to dinner at my grandmother's apartment when I was about five. Not that I had a sense that they were famous people, but I did think, Here are some fun new grown-ups. I was showing off for them a little bit when I did a somersault and hit my head. It was so embarrassing that I had hurt myself trying to impress these people!

*Q: When we talked before about* Meet the Austins, *you called it a "revenge fantasy." Would you care to elaborate on that?*

A: Let's see. I think the Austin books were the most uncomfortable books for us because they always felt like a kind of carnival-mirror version of our own family. It was not as difficult for my sister and me as it was for my mom and her siblings. As kids, you pick up on things like that. It is really my aunt Maria's story to tell. I don't want to put words in her mouth. I think she's always felt silenced and invisible. I want to make as much room for her as possible.

*Q: Because she felt that she wasn't completely included in the family?*

A: Yes. She was adopted when she was seven. Her biological parents were friends of my grandparents' from New York, and they died six months apart from each other.

*Q: There are some famous cases of the children of writers— Christopher Milne and the son of Frances Hodgson Burnett—who in later life made a public thing of having been "fictionalized" in that same way. It created a reality that wasn't real for them.*

A: It's tough. It can be internalized too. How do you live up to that legacy? How do you make yourself real to your own mother?

*Q: Did your grandmother have a model for herself as a journal writer?*

A: That's interesting. No one I can recall. She kept journals from when she was small. That was part of her discipline. And it was always part of her advice to writers to use your journal both as a chance to practice your craft from a technical point of view and as an emotional tool to sort of dump things out and see what's there—as therapy. She'd always say, "My journals were never meant to be published." Then she published them anyway! So it was a little bit disingenuous. I think that the lines for her were so blurry between fiction and nonfiction, and I think often they were hard for her to keep straight.

*Q: Would you tell me about your uncle Bion?*

A: Sure. He was her youngest. He was a model for Rob Austin, and in her nonfiction she would use his childlike dialogue and malapropisms as a springboard for some of her talks. He may have felt oppressed by her fame, but I think he would have developed into an unhappy adult even if my grandmother had never become famous as the author of *A Wrinkle in Time.* You know he died of end-stage alcoholism. That was very painful for her and for the whole family. As a writer, she used her work to construct her reality, to make sense of painful experience, to rescript difficult relationships. He was very resentful of her.

*Q: I read in one of the journals that your grandmother thought of praying as being like practicing her scales on the piano.*

A: She talked about writing in terms of always serving the work and somehow being an instrument for something coming through you. She would also say that in order to play the music well, your instrument has to be tuned. So you have to practice your scales every day. I think that for her this was similar to being open to grace.

*Q: She also associated playing the piano with swimming—and writing. She said that those were the two things she would do when she was stuck as a writer. The rhythm would somehow unlock her.*

A: She would talk about playing the piano and say, "The tips of the fingers are the only other place besides the brain where there's gray matter." I don't know if that's true or not! But that's what she said: that your fingers think, so that disciplining yourself on the piano feeds your discipline as a writer.

*Q: Did you swim with her?*

A: No, because for her swimming was a solitary discipline, like writing. She did the breaststroke and sidestroke. She never did the crawl. She never put her face in the water! She would swim laps, I don't know how many. In that rhythm, she would find a sense of relaxation.

*Q: Did you have a last encounter or series of last encounters with your grandmother near the end of her life?*

A: The last year or so of her life she lived in a nursing home in Litchfield, Connecticut. We visited often, my mother the most often because she lived fifteen minutes away. Maybe 90 percent of the time we'd visit and she wouldn't really care or acknowledge the visit or it was depressing and frustrating and saddening because she just seemed not to be living a life. But 10 percent of the time she'd really be there, and it was wonderful when she was. One of the hardest things about her decline was that she had a great many friends who felt very close to her and a great many friends who felt they knew her better than the family did, and some people felt no compunction about telling us what they felt we were doing wrong. It was really quite amazing. It points to how difficult aging has become, and how hard it is to do right by someone who is in decline.

My grandmother had always cultivated and struggled for and wanted deep connections with people. In 1998 or 1999, for example, at the time when she broke her hip, she was close to a religious group called the Bruderhof Communities. They were founded in Germany in the 1930s as an antifascist group and had left Germany early and reestablished their communities here. They're kind of like the Amish. Marriages are arranged. They have a business of making wooden toys for disabled children. They're highly trained folks. When my grandmother broke her hip, they offered one of their members who was a licensed practical nurse to come and live with her. At one point the nurse took me aside and said, "Well, I want you to know that I had this conversation with your grandmother. She told me that I'm like the daughter she never had." It was a speech designed to make this person feel incredibly connected and special to my grandmother. But she said she was telling me this because she thought it was very strange, you know, that my grandmother would be soliciting that kind of intense and intimate relationship.

*Q: When I interviewed your grandmother, I asked her if there had been a moment when she realized that she was no longer a child, and she recalled a time when she walked in on her mother crying and was surprised to realize that her mother had the same vulnerabilities as other people. Did you have a comparable experience with your grandmother?*

A: I think I'm continuing to come to that realization. I have a relationship with her that is still evolving and growing. I get more insight and understanding of her needs, and as a parent myself I continue to learn what it's like to balance family and work.

*Q: What would be an example of something you've learned?*

A: Just how little absolute control she had. I used to think she made the world. So much of her worldview and beliefs seemed self-evident. Yesterday I read Katherine Paterson's introduction to the fiftieth anniversary edition of *A Wrinkle in Time*, in which she recalls the time when they met at a conference at Simmons College on the theme of disturbing the universe. My grandmother's response to the theme had been "Absolutely! We have an obligation to disturb the universe." Katherine's response had been exactly the opposite. Reading the essay yesterday made me realize, Oh wow. There's another way of approaching big questions like that. I always felt insufficiently bold if I wasn't *out there*, like my grandmother. On a more mundane level, I felt somehow wrong for preferring Jane Austen to Dostoyevsky, which she didn't, or for enjoying musicals, which she disdained because they weren't "real theater." I am just coming to understand what a big shadow she cast.

# MENTOR

# WILLIAM ALEXANDER JOHNSON

William Alexander Johnson is a professor emeritus of philosophy, the history of ideas, and Near Eastern and Judaic studies at Brandeis University and a canon at the Cathedral Church of St. John the Divine, New York.

*Q: How did you meet Madeleine L'Engle?*
A: I was appointed a canon of the Cathedral of St. John the Divine in about 1970. A canon is an ecclesiastical title, and it was left to me to define my particular role. It was a full-time appointment, and I took it on while I was employed as a professor at Brandeis University, which was also a full-time job.

While I was searching for what I should be doing at the cathedral, Paul Moore, who was then the bishop, said, "Why don't you become canon theologian?"* This meant that I would be involved somehow in the cathedral's intellectual life. It was about this time that I met Madeleine. She either was already the cathedral's librarian or was soon to take on that role. Because I was going to do something theological—in the end, I started a school, an institute of theology at the cathedral—and she was the librarian, our lives immediately made contact.

I found that Madeleine was very much interested in seeking after a deeper understanding of the Christian faith. I directed the

---

*Paul Moore was bishop of the Episcopal Diocese of New York, 1972–89.

cathedral school for thirty-plus years, and Madeleine was there for almost all of that time, until she got sick and weary. She and I would see each other often. She would call me up from the library and say, "I have tea brewing. Let's have a talk."

The school provided theological education in Christian ethics, church history, the liturgy, preaching, and theology and was intended both for people who might be interested in going on to be ordained and for those who simply wanted to learn more about the Christian faith. We tried to make it rigorous and enlisted professors from Union Theological Seminary, NYU, General Theological, and Columbia University. I asked Madeleine to teach at the school too. She said yes immediately.

Because of her busy writing and travel schedule, she was unable to teach full-time, but she would teach a course whenever she was available. Often it would be something like Great Books and Theology. She would take on Augustine and Luther and Thomas Aquinas. I think that Madeleine was an autodidact as a theologian, but she was very smart, and she had read a lot and had gotten a good general education. So she fit in very nicely.

Madeleine's primary association at the cathedral was with a man named Edward West—Edward Nason West. He was the canon sacrist, and I used to joke that he had been at the cathedral since the time of the Anglican Reformation, which is to say for the last 350 years. Madeleine was very much drawn to the cathedral because of Canon West. He was her spiritual adviser.

Being the cathedral librarian wasn't a terribly demanding job, the real work with the cathedral's collection of books having been done in the nineteenth century. There were tens of thousands of books, most of them in subterranean vaults. Nobody had seen them for years and years! Madeleine tried for a while to make them available to readers. But it was not a cathedral made up primarily of intellectual clergy or intellectual laypeople, so there were few requests. Nonetheless, Madeleine would be at her desk in the library almost every day except when she was traveling. She would resurrect certain books and put them out for people to discover. There was one shelf in the library of books handpicked by Madeleine. They were important books, some of which she donated, some of which she got from others, including myself. These were the lively texts, though sadly there was not a great demand for books among the cathedral clergy. The library for her was also a place where she could meet with people with whom she wanted to meet.

Q: *What were your first impressions of Madeleine?*

A: I liked her immediately. She was extremely personable in genuine ways. She had no agenda. She was famous, but there was no aura about her. We got along very well at a very basic human level. We talked a lot about the cathedral, a lot about religion, a lot about the Christian faith, a lot about the future of the church. She worried about Canon West because he lived alone and was getting on in years and beginning to have some physical problems. Occasionally, she talked about her own family, but she didn't want to reveal too much about her personal life.

She was very pleased when her daughter married Alan Jones, who had been a monastic in England and come over to General Theological Seminary to be in charge of a program called the Center for Christian Spirituality. Zen Buddhism and Hinduism were becoming very important in the West then. The center was meant to provide a kind of Christian counterpart. It became very popular. Eventually, Alan Jones was invited to San Francisco, where one of the important deanships in the Episcopal Church U.S.A. was open, and he became the dean at Grace Cathedral and remained there for a long time. The marriage broke up—this was late in Madeleine's life—and I have heard that she was totally devastated by that. Then she moved to Goshen, and I didn't see her for several years. Near the end of her life, when she had had strokes and was so disabled, I went up there to see her and really just to say goodbye. She died maybe six months later. She was in terrible shape by then. I liked her very much and felt she was an authentic human being, searching just like the rest of us for some kind of true meaning in this world of ours. And I think she got most of her Christian belief from Canon West. But then I remember once preaching at a church on the West Side—All Angels'—and she was in the congregation. So I think she kept up her Christian faith and Christian participation even after Canon West was no longer there.

*Q: Would you describe Canon West?*

A: He was a unique human being. He was the son of a Boston butcher. There's still a sign for "Edward Nason West, Butcher" in Quincy Market. He went to Boston University, not Harvard. He had been the rector of Trinity Church, in Ossining, New York, during the 1930s. Nobody there now would remember him, but if you go up to Ossining, you will find photographs of all the rectors, and there among them is Canon West. Then, in 1941, Bishop Donegan summoned him to the cathedral to serve as canon sacrist—the man in charge of the conduct of sacred worship. On a good day, three or four thousand people came to worship at the cathedral, so you needed to have someone in charge of it all. He did his job very well.

Canon West was always his own man. He wrote an authoritative book on Christian symbolism. He was an expert on church architecture and would be invited by different churches around the country as a consultant. We went through a great liturgical change in the 1970s, when the altar, which traditionally had been set against the wall, was instead brought out to face the people. He traveled the country to help with these liturgical changes.

*Q: Did Canon West favor changes of that kind?*

A: Yes. He gave the impression of being a die-hard conservative, but he wasn't one, really. Bishop Donegan, who was very austere and Victorian in manner, was also a social liberal. Canon West avoided controversy, but he recognized where the church was going. He also taught at the school I started—every semester, I think, for fifteen years. He taught the liturgy course, and *everybody* took his course. He also taught the preaching course. He gave good solid sermons himself that showed awareness of both the Christian faith and the secular world.

At one point he became very much interested in the Russian Orthodox Church tradition, grew a long beard, and wore a cassock like Rasputin! I didn't understand that at all, but somehow it made perfect sense to him—spiritually, liturgically, theologically. He was a very good man and, as I said, a unique individual: someone who figured things out for himself. And he had such a magnetic personality that I think that everybody who met him was changed by the experience.

*Q: What would have attracted Madeleine to him?*

A: It's only supposition, but I think she was very much interested in becoming a Christian. Madeleine had a Christian background and may have gone to church on Easter and Christmas. She wanted to put it all together and to make her Christian faith a dominant theme in her writing as well as in her life. She saw Canon West as the person who could do that for her, who could transform her lukewarm Christianity into something profound, as he had for so many other people.

*Q: What did this transformation entail?*

A: First of all she needed to be confirmed. It's the bishop who confirms—following elaborate preparations. Canon West prepared me for confirmation. It took nearly a year, meeting once a week. I think that he prepared Madeleine too. These sessions would take the form of conversations. "Today," Canon West might say, "I'm going to talk about the liturgical meaning of Maundy Thursday." Madeleine admired the quality of his mind, the wisdom that shone through, and the strength of his commitment. You could tell he wasn't fooling around! This was no closet socialist. He had no other agenda. I think she accepted their relationship as that of teacher and student. She was a famous writer, and yet he was her teacher. I had two Ph.D.'s and he had none, yet he prepared me for confirmation. He was that kind of person.

*Q: Did Madeleine show you her books as works in progress?*

A: Occasionally, she did: the books of personal reminiscence, not the children's books. She would give me a chapter to read and ask: Was she going in the right direction? We would have these conversations over tea. At most I made a modest contribution.

*Q: Were you ever invited to her apartment?*

A: Lots of times, usually as one of a group of guests. I could tell that playing the host was great fun for her. Hugh would not be there an awful lot of the time, which I thought was rather strange. Hugh did not become involved in the life of the cathedral. He may have come on Christmas Eve. Years before I met Madeleine, I had seen him on Broadway as the cardinal in John Osborne's play *Luther*. It was a while after I met Madeleine that I realized that Hugh and she were man and wife. Madeleine was what one would call in the profession a true believer, in the best sense, and I don't think Hugh shared in her spiritual quest. Her faith was completely straightforward, almost in a naive kind of way. Where I trained philosophically, we learned to ask questions about everything. Madeleine didn't have that questioning mind.

*Q: Really?*

A: Not that I could see. It was not that Madeleine accepted everything right away. She had to work her beliefs out for herself. But she didn't come to the Christian faith through doubt. She came to it—it sounds terribly clichéd—through a search for meaning in her own destiny.

*Q: During the 1960s, the cathedral took a public stand against the Vietnam War and involved itself in the civil rights movement. Did Madeleine play a role in any of that?*

A: The clergy were demonstrably opposed to the war. We marched on Washington. Sermons condemned the war. We held symposia on "just war" theology. I chaired that committee. In conversation Madeleine made it quite clear that she herself was opposed to the Vietnam War, but she didn't take part in public protests of any kind. She did not want to be politically visible.

*Q: Would she be at the cathedral on Sundays?*

A: Yes, but she also went to other churches. Sometimes she went to All Angels', on West Eightieth Street, near Zabar's. The original pulpit is now in the American Wing of the Metropolitan Museum. It had the reputation for being a charismatic church, which seemed so unlike her. But more than that I don't know.

Technically, a charismatic church is one where the focus of the preaching and of the congregants' religious experience is very much rooted in the emotions. Hands will go up, and people will call out "Hallelujah" and "Amen." The emphasis is an anti-intellectual one. You don't want to get involved in ideas, because they'll take away from an authentic relationship with God, which comes from the emotions or rather the spirit. The human spirit meets the divine spirit, prompting suprarational behavior such as speaking in tongues.

When Madeleine did worship at the cathedral on Sundays, she would usually come to one of the early services. There was an eight o'clock, a nine o'clock, and then the big eleven o'clock service, which was attended by hundreds of people. Madeleine preferred the earlier services, where there would be Holy Communion and a short sermon or perhaps none at all. Canon West conducted one of these early Sunday services. I did the other one. Dean Morton did the eleven o'clock—the spectacular service where there might be Sufi dancers or the blessing of the animals.

*Q: In her speeches and lectures Madeleine searched for connections between religion and science.*

A: Yes, but I don't think she did that very well. Her idea was: If people are becoming commodities on the world scene, let's acknowledge and affirm again the individuality of the Christian faith. And if science is now dominant in our view of the world, let's somehow insert the Christian faith into the discussion and talk about "world spirit." She uses that term, and I don't know what it means. Her intentions were honorable, and they fit very well into the way she looked at the world. She wanted to make the Christian faith intelligible for modern, scientifically oriented, secular human beings. It was a worthy goal, but she didn't know enough about science to pull it off. I think the butterfly effect does not make an awful lot of sense, that that is really just a romantic idea.* I had done some work on the concept of transcendence. If you're a deterministic, mechanistic, materialistic scientist, is there any sense of transcendence? How can you find a sense of transcendence? A Christian would say that the scientific, mechanistic, materialistic view is a limited view of life, because there's another dimension. I look at science more as one intellectual discipline that does some things very well. I look at religion as another kind of intellectual discipline that does other things very well. And I think you only get confused if you try to integrate the two of them. Madeleine thought that if science is the dominant intellectual ideology, somehow we've got to bring the Christian faith back into it. That was an agenda of hers, and as a popular writer she thought she would command attention. But I don't see her as a great apologist for the Christian faith in those later books.

*Q: Tell me about your and your family's first reading of* A Wrinkle in Time. *It must have been before you met Madeleine.*

---

*The butterfly effect is a concept originated by the MIT meteorologist Edward Lorenz. Working in the 1960s with an early computer model for predicting weather patterns, Lorenz noted the unexpected finding that even minute shifts in atmospheric conditions had the potential to trigger dramatic changes in a long-term forecast. Popularized, this counterintuitive notion proved to have widespread appeal, whether as a metaphor for or a supposed demonstration of the interconnectedness of every constituent element of the natural and/or spiritual realms.

A: Yes, I think it was. My three children were born two years apart. We tried in our home to read to them every night. My wife must have found *A Wrinkle in Time*, and rather than read it to one child—they were two, four, and six at the time—we read it to all three of them. When we finished the book, we started it all over again. I thought it was a great book, and it became the Holy Bible to our children. When they were able to read on their own, they got their own copies. I gave them each a copy, signed by Madeleine, for Christmas one year.

*Q: Having seen the impact of her book on your children, you must have been thrilled to meet her.*

A: I was kind of awed. I didn't know important people before her, and she was as nice and as friendly and pleasant and common as anybody. It made me feel very good to be with her. And then of course we got to know each other and we shared ideas.

I remember once I was asked to become a college president and wasn't sure what I wanted to do. I had been a university professor for ten years at that point, and the job I was being offered was at a very good school. Canon West thought that I should probably take the job, but Madeleine disagreed. She said, "What will happen is that you'll become a fund-raiser and administer a faculty that really don't like you. You'll have students with whom you can't have a real relationship." Not long afterward, the members of the search committee flew into Logan Airport to formally offer me the job, and I turned them down. I later ran into the man who did take the job, and he told me that it had all turned out for him just as Madeleine said it would. That was around 1980.

*Q: Do you think she considered her involvement with the cathedral to be the center of her life?*

A: It certainly was for some years—during the 1970s and 1980s.

*Q: She wrote a novel for teens called* The Young Unicorns *that is set in New York and with a canon in the story who is modeled on*

*Canon West. In it she describes a crime- and drug-ridden city in decay. It's a disturbing vision of contemporary city life. Would you say that that is how Madeleine herself felt about New York?*

A: The cathedral is all gussied up now. It is like a great museum piece. But in the 1970s and 1980s the neighborhood of Morningside Heights was in terrible decline. A canon who came into work early one morning was assaulted by a mugger. Where had the mugger learned how to attack someone? As an American soldier in Vietnam. People would come into the cathedral and steal things—including one of the rare seventeenth-century Mortlake tapestries. One morning as I arrived for the eight o'clock service, I was met by thieves running out the door carrying this huge rolled-up tapestry under their arms! People would throw rocks at the stained-glass windows. People would get mugged by the Peace Fountain, on the cathedral grounds. Madeleine knew that the neighborhood was becoming increasingly poor and drug-ridden and dangerous. It appalled her.

Canon West probably attributed this decline to the work of the devil, but I think Madeleine was a lot more sophisticated than that. She believed that we lived in a world in which there were natural laws and natural processes and that God did not intervene directly on that level. You know: You start with a world of human beings who have free will. If drugs are available, and there's no work and no green cards, buildings will crumble, people will behave badly, and there will be muggings in the streets. I think that that is what Madeleine thought. Canon West had more of a mystical streak, but Reinhold Niebuhr and Paul Tillich, who both taught at nearby Union Seminary, and the Scottish theologian John Macquarrie, who visited the cathedral, were all opposed to mystical theology. They believed it was too subjectivistic. Canon West, in any case, had no choice but to stay at the cathedral. He had been at the cathedral since the 1940s. He never married, and he had an apartment there for life. That also is why his friendship with Madeleine was so important for him.

*Q: Do you see a connection between Madeleine's life in the theater and her attraction to church liturgy?*

A: I think so, and Canon West would emphasize, in his conversations with Madeleine about the Christian faith, the role of the liturgy.

*Q: There are hundreds of photos of her at Wheaton College. Do you think she enjoyed being photographed?*

A: I don't think she was a vain person, if that's what you're asking. Wheaton College is a very good evangelical college. It had been a fundamentalist, rather anti-intellectual place, with a reputation, earlier on, as an intellectual disaster zone. There was a real intellectual shift there, however, one that, I think, was influenced theologically by C. S. Lewis. That is why Madeleine was invited to lecture at Wheaton College. They had begun to realize that you could be an evangelical and a reader of literature and philosophy too.

## JAMES PARKS MORTON

James Parks Morton is president and chairman of the board of the Interfaith Center of New York and dean emeritus of the Cathedral Church of St. John the Divine, New York.

*Q: How did you meet Madeleine L'Engle?*

A: I met her in 1972 when I was called to be dean of the Cathedral of St. John the Divine. My wife and I were living in Chicago at the time, and Pamela and I were visiting New York to look at the deanery. Eddie West gave a lunch for us and Madeleine at a Greek restaurant near the cathedral, called Symposium. That was when I first met her.

I had known Eddie long before that, and so it was more of a conversation with him than with Madeleine. But she was in a very serious way his sidekick, and when he had special events and wanted to impress people in a certain way, Madeleine would be brought along. I of course knew who Madeleine was. I had read some of her books. Eddie probably brought her along to get her take on me.

I had first gotten to know West when I was a teenager. I grew up in Iowa City, where my father ran the University of Iowa's theater. The rector of Trinity Church there was a man by the name of Richard McEvoy, and he and my parents were good friends.

Then McEvoy was hired to be rector of St. Mark's in the Bowery, in New York, and when I went east to visit various prep schools I was thinking of attending, I stayed with the McEvoys at the rectory of St. Mark's on my way up to Exeter. During that visit, McEvoy said to me, "You must meet Canon West. He's very odd and he's a fixture of the cathedral and he knows everything about liturgy." So I headed uptown, and I did meet him—long before I had any notion of being at the Cathedral of St. John the Divine myself.

In 1954, after graduating from Harvard and studying in Cambridge, I was ordained, married, and went to Jersey City to work with Paul Moore in the inner city. I saw West in all of the years that I was in Jersey City because people would take groups of acolytes to the cathedral to see it, and West was always there. Not long after that, every denomination decided to establish at the national level an office of inner-city work, and I was asked to run it. For two and a half years I was Mr. Inner City at the headquarters of the Episcopal Church in New York. Then all of the urban executives of all of the denominations decided that just having an office at their national headquarters was not sufficient and that we also needed a training program for inner-city clergy in order for them to really know what the problems are and how to deal with them. So the Urban Training Center was established in Chicago, and I was asked to head that. Eight years later, when Bishop Paul Moore called me to the cathedral, he said, "I have an empty cathedral. It's as dead as a dog, and you're crazy enough to do something with it." So back we come to New York and move into the deanery and are there for twenty-five years. That's when we really got to know Madeleine.

I was sort of a frustrated architect, having studied architecture at Harvard before turning to theology for my graduate studies at Cambridge. While living in England and visiting the cathedrals of Europe, and with my knowledge of their architecture and medieval society, one of the things that dawned on me was that the reason the cathedrals were so monstrously big was that they were intended to be big enough to hold the entire city. That was the reason they were so big. And that realization led me to think about the role of a cathedral: that it was not so much a denominational institution as it was an urban one. Its role was to be the holy place for the whole city. So I decided to make St. John the Divine a place in which the issues of the city were discussed and where everyone felt welcome to come and take part.

When I opened up the liturgy to more contemporary matters, West was very supportive of what I wanted to do. In the late 1970s, for example, when I came to the realization that the environmental crisis was *the* crisis of this period of history, we initiated a big environmental program at the cathedral. Throughout the 1980s, the cathedral became the green think tank for New York City. West and Madeleine were both supportive of that.

Canon West was the subdean and the man in charge of the cathedral before I appeared, there not having been a dean there since John Butler retired in 1966. West had great passions, which he energetically pursued. One of these was his love for all things English and especially all things aristocratic. He traveled to England every year and was intent on having the liturgy of the cathedral be as English as it possibly could be. His vision was for St. John's to be our Westminster Abbey or St. Paul's. I found all this rather delightful.

Bishop Donegan, who was very close to the queen, was himself rather Low Church, whereas West was High Church. Eddie took it upon himself to school the bishop in what the bishop should do. Also under West's influence, the venerable Order of St. John of Jerusalem was brought in, and the cathedral became its American headquarters.

One of the things I discovered when I lived in England was

that the Church of England is full of odd ducks, and Eddie was very much that kind of creature. He always wore his cassock, when no one else did, and he wore a sort of square velvet cap that stood up, sort of like a biretta but without the pompom. It was a very English choice. His parties were legendary. After the Christmas midnight Mass, he would have a big party in his apartment to which everyone was invited. It went on till two in the morning, with tons of alcohol consumed. His lifestyle was his lifestyle. In fact I was hugely fond of him. He was a very special guy. He was a brilliant man, a very wise man, very learned, and very humorous. And he really was Madeleine's father figure and personal spiritual adviser. They just dovetailed very nicely.

Madeleine too did whatever she wished at the cathedral and was used to that freedom. She preached regularly—perhaps twice a year for twenty-five years in the main service. She was a very inclusive person in her theology, and she was very eucharistically centered. We started a series of Lenten meditations that she and West led together, on Wednesday nights, starting with Ash Wednesday. I would always introduce their conversations. Fifty people would come, sometimes more. Madeleine had a big following.

I think that Madeleine saw everything she did as part of her religious life. It wasn't, Here I do my writing, and here I do my religion. She was called the cathedral librarian, which was kind of funny because what she really did in the library was write her books. The library was totally unused, as it is to this day. It is a collection of the libraries that various clergy who died left to the cathedral. So it really was her library, with Canon West's office adjacent to it. She had her own professional Madeleine L'Engle life, and she did it from the base of the cathedral, though not in the name of the cathedral. It was in the name of Madeleine L'Engle, which was fine with me.

Madeleine revered West as a highly spiritual human being.

Eddie was deeply respectful of her talents and gifts and imagination. They were also very close friends. I think he loved being made into a character in her books. He loved the freedom that Madeleine showed in doing that. Their relationship was a wonderful one, and everybody at the cathedral was happy to be in their presence. It was like having a pair of giraffes in your backyard. Not everybody has that.

## PETER GLASSMAN

Peter Glassman is the owner and president of Books of Wonder, the independent children's bookstore he co-founded in 1980 in New York City with the late James Carey.

*Q: How did you meet Madeleine L'Engle?*

A: In the fall of 1978, I was an eighteen-year-old freshman at Brown University. One day in either late October or early November, I was going down to New York City to visit my then boyfriend, James Carey, who later became my partner in life and co-owner of Books of Wonder. I was waiting on the platform at the Amtrak station in Providence when I saw a woman carrying a stack of books, all the same title. I noticed that the books said "Madeleine L'Engle" on the spine. It wasn't a book I recognized, which focused my attention even more because I thought I knew Madeleine L'Engle's work well, and so I wandered over to see what book it was. It turned out to be a new book of her poetry published by Harold Shaw, *The Weather of the Heart.* The back cover was visible at the top of the stack, and what I saw next was the author photograph of Madeleine L'Engle that was printed there. It was then that I looked up and realized that the woman holding the stack of books was the woman in the photograph! I was so dumbfounded that all I could think to say was "Oh my! You're Madeleine L'Engle!" To which she replied, "Yes I am. Who are you?"

MENTOR

I introduced myself, explained that I worked part-time in a bookstore and that I loved her books. After that, we just started talking. We were having a lovely conversation for a few minutes when for the first time in recorded history the Amtrak train arrived on time. Madeleine had a first-class seat and I did not, so we parted company as we prepared to board the train. She was one of my childhood heroes, and I desperately wanted to continue my conversation with her. So I made my way up to the first-class compartment, and with the chutzpah of youth I did my best to explain the situation to the conductor, assuring him that I didn't want any first-class service, or first-class food, or anything. All I wanted was to finish my conversation. Thank goodness I looked so innocent in those days. He let me in.

Madeleine and I talked for the next hour and a half. I told her—she reminded me of this later—that I wanted to open a bookstore. I told her about James. She talked to me about Hugh. We talked about *A Wrinkle in Time*, and I told her that the very first hardcover book that I bought with my own money was *A Wind in the Door*, when it first came out. I had seen the ad for it in *The New York Times Book Review* and saved up my allowance.

This was the first time I met someone I had known only as a reader, someone I considered a hero. She was everything I would have wanted her to be: intelligent, vivacious, and very strong in her opinions and her beliefs. You could see bits of her characters in her. It was just wonderful.

Madeleine had been in town to give a talk at Providence College, one of her many, many workshops. As I came to learn, she was one of the most generous souls in the world. She loved sharing with other people, particularly young, aspiring writers.

I left Brown at the end of the semester and moved to New York to be with James. About a year later, I heard that Madeleine was having an event at Eeyore's, the city's only children's bookstore at the time, and so I filled two shopping bags with my copies of all her books and headed off to have them signed. I expected a gigantic line, but by the time I arrived, not many people were waiting to meet her. The next thing I knew, Madeleine had caught sight of me and said hello. I was so amazed that she remembered me. When she saw how many books I had brought along, she asked if I wouldn't mind waiting until the end. Then she said, "In the meantime, why don't you keep me company?" Just as I made my way behind the rickety little table where she was signing, a teacher showed up with fifty or sixty kids, all clutching their Scholastic paperback book club editions. She was unfazed, and she proceeded to sign all their books. It seemed that no one was supervising the class, and I noticed that some of the kids were blocking Madeleine's light, making it hard for her, especially with her weak eyesight, to see what she was doing. Finally, my camp counselor training kicked in, and I clapped my hands loudly and announced, "Okay, come on, kids. You know how this is done. Get in line single file!" I just sort of took charge. That cemented our friendship there and then.

A year later I opened Books of Wonder. Originally, it was going to be an antiquarian bookstore. But I didn't have enough books to fill my shelves, so I went over to Bookazine, the book distributor, and picked up several shelves' worth of my favorite children's books, to fill out my bookcases, including of course *A Wrinkle in Time*. People responded very strongly to this handpicked selection. The next thing I knew, our tiny store was half new books and half old ones. After two years we moved to a bigger store. It was still tiny, but the extra space allowed us to carry all of Madeleine's books. So at that point I contacted Farrar, Straus and requested that Madeleine come to Books of Wonder for an appearance. Arrangements were made, and when she came to the store, she once again greeted me warmly. She met James that day, and after her signing we all went out for dinner, which became a tradition for us, as did having an event for every book she published from then onward.

Fast-forward to 1989, the year that Farrar, Straus published *An Acceptable Time*. As always, I was very excited to have a new book by Madeleine. This time, however, when I put in my request for an event, the answer came back that no, Madeleine was not available. I thought at first that she must not be going out on tour for the book or that she had plans to be out of town. But when it turned out that she did have a signing scheduled at a nearby Barnes & Noble, I was furious. I called the publicist at Farrar, Straus and said so. In the end, Madeleine did come to Books of Wonder to sign *An Acceptable Time*, and over dinner that evening, when I told her the story of what had happened behind the scenes, Madeleine said, "I guess they didn't tell you the real story." I said, "What do you mean?" It seems that Madeleine had gone into Farrar, Straus a few days earlier to review the publicity plans for the book. She had been shown the list of stores where she would be signing during her very extensive tour. When they reached the end of the list, Madeleine had asked, "Where's Books of Wonder?" and was told that it couldn't be fitted into her tour. To which Madeleine had replied, "If we can't fit Books of Wonder into the tour, let's cancel the tour." When I thanked her for the grand gesture and told her she should never have said something like that to her publisher, Madeleine said, "Of course I should have. You are my number one bookstore, and right is right."

As a fellow Farrar, Straus author, Madeleine had met Maurice Sendak on a number of occasions, and at some point they began to talk about collaborating on a book. Then Madeleine wrote a manuscript for Maurice to illustrate—*Dance in the Desert.** She sent

*Dance in the Desert*, illustrated by Symeon Shimin, was published by Farrar, Straus and Giroux in 1969.

it to him, he read it, and then he gave her a call. Maurice told her that he loved what she'd written but that there was just one problem: she had described *everything*, leaving nothing for him to illustrate. He explained that as an illustrator he looked for what he could add. In this case, she seemed to have left no opening for illustrations. Madeleine said she had not considered that possibility, that it hadn't occurred to her before. But, she said, she couldn't help it; this was simply how she wrote. At which point they both concluded that they were not a good match for collaboration after all, much as they liked and respected each other.

Madeleine was such a loving and loyal friend. She introduced me to T. A. Barron and did a joint appearance with him at the store when his first book, *Heartlight*, was published in 1990. When Hugh passed away, she was devastated. It was amazing to see how she soldiered on. I remember saying to Madeleine that James was my Calvin because James was the brilliant child in a family of people who were not nearly so brilliant. To which she replied that I was his Meg. I loved that! She kept her sense of humor even as her health began to fail. Once, after she had started to lose her memory, we went out for dinner, and a couple came by our table who recognized her. "Oh, Madeleine, how lovely to see you!" After they had moved on, Madeleine turned to me and said, "Do you know who those people were? I have absolutely no idea. Oh well!" She just carried on. She was not going to let it bother her.

She had a different special phrase for each book when she autographed it. For *An Acceptable Time*, the phrase was "Even now." She would write it on the title page, just above the title: "Even now—*An Acceptable Time*."

# T. A. BARRON

T. A. Barron is the author of the twelve-volume Merlin
saga and other books for young readers and the founder of
the Gloria Barron Prize for Young Heroes.

*Q: Tell me how and when you first met Madeleine L'Engle.*
A: It involved a cruel hoax and a teddy bear. Let me explain.

While at Oxford, I took a year to travel and blew every penny
I had to my name on an epic trip to Russia, Nepal, India, Japan,
and East Africa. In Japan, I worked as a roof thatcher in a remote
village. The villagers called me "O Choku-choi," which roughly
translated means "Honorable Butterfingers," because I'm so clumsy
that I single-handedly caused more damage to that village than
several monsoons. Well, in the course of those travels I wrote my
first novel, a fantasy heroic quest set partly in the Rocky Mountain West, where I grew up, and partly in an imaginary world.

Once back at Oxford, I thought, This is my big chance to become a writer! That had long been my dream. I expected to find a
publisher, return home, and enter into the glorious life of a writer.
This book had a terrific reception—thirty-two rejections—which
I now agree that it deserved. At the time, though, this was more
than a little discouraging. All I could think to do was to paper the
wall of my bathroom at Oxford with those letters.

So after coming back from Oxford, I moved to New York, put
on a business suit, and started work. As a Colorado kid, I would

much rather have been stomping around in the Rocky Mountain wilderness. Meanwhile, I was also recovering from a first marriage that had fallen apart. Put all that together, and I was not happy!

One day I happened to speak with a friend who was the curator at a children's museum. She said, "I have something that will cheer you up, Tom. I have finished an exhibition called *Collections* about all the things that famous people collected as kids. The best thing in the show is something from Madeleine L'Engle." Well, I lit up at the mention of her name because she had always been one of my favorite authors. "What is it?" I asked. And my friend explained that Madeleine had sent a beat-up old teddy bear she had played with when she was seven years old. It was missing an eye but was clearly well loved. Best of all, Madeleine had sent not only the bear, whose name was Alphonse, but also a biography she'd written about the bear's life and times. My friend offered to send me a copy of Madeleine's story. I didn't think any more about it until a week later, in my stack of mail at home, I found a thick envelope from my friend containing the story of Alphonse. Written on the stationery of Madeleine's publisher, Farrar, Straus and Giroux, it was endearing, funny, fascinating, sad, and wise all at once—typical Madeleine L'Engle. What a joy to read!

Then, as I looked through the rest of the mail, I came to an envelope addressed to me from someone at Farrar, Straus and Giroux. After all those rejection letters, my feeling about publishers was so dark that my first reaction was, Oh, hey, that was one of the publishers I have not sent my book to yet. So I bet they're writing to reject my manuscript in advance!

With trepidation I opened this envelope, and lo and behold, it was a letter to me from Madeleine L'Engle herself! It said, "Dear T. A. Barron"—I was following the Oxford style of using just my initials—"My friend at the children's museum has told me that you have a dream of becoming a published children's book author, but have met with no success. I just want you to know that *A*

*Wrinkle in Time* took forty-two tries before I found a publisher who finally accepted it." My heart soared as I read this, and I thought, Well, that gives me at least ten more tries! Seriously, it was the most encouraging letter you could imagine. It was as if someone had reached out and given me a big hug. It ended with something stirring like "Just persevere. Keep writing. Someday I promise that you, too, will find your voice."

Thanks to Madeleine's letter, I was so happy that I called everyone I knew to tell them about it. I even took the letter downstairs and read it to the doorman of my building. I was just thrilled. My friend at the museum had not been home when I'd tried to call her, but a few days later we finally connected. I told her the great news. To my surprise, she seemed strangely silent. When I asked her what was wrong, she sighed and said, "I just didn't think you were that gullible."

Suddenly I understood. She had made up the letter as a kind of joke. Unfortunately, the joke didn't seem all that funny. I was just crushed. Even worse, all my friends kept asking about my new pal Madeleine L'Engle. And every time I went outside, the doorman would slap me on the back and congratulate me. It was the worst.

Two or three weeks went by before I finally found a way to make myself feel better. I sat down and I wrote a handwritten letter to Madeleine L'Engle. After all, I now knew her publisher's address. The letter said, "Dear Madeleine L'Engle, This is a thank-you letter. I'd like to thank you for two things: First, for those wonderful books you've written, which have inspired me, enlightened me, delighted me both as a reader and as someone who has dreams of someday being a writer. Second, for sending me the most lovely letter I've ever received, which is attached." I enclosed a copy of my friend's forged letter. Then I said, "This letter really lifted my spirits. There was only one problem with it. You didn't write it." Then I said, "The truth is your letter really did mean a lot to me because my deepest dream is to be a writer. Although I haven't had any success, I still hope there might be some way, someday."

At the end of the letter, I wrote, "If you are ever in New York City and have time to be taken out to lunch by someone who wears a business suit and has a day job but would much rather be a writer of children's books, I would love to do that." At the very bottom of the letter I put, "P.S. If you by some miracle do write back to me, please have your signature *notarized*. I just absolutely can't deal with another forgery ever again!"

I went out and mailed the letter to her. Immediately, I felt better. Still, I felt certain that never in a million years would she reply. But it felt like good therapy just to have done that. Well, almost a month later, I received a reply. It was a postcard with a picture of Crosswicks on the front and a typed message on the back: "Dear Mr. Barron, I live in New York and would love to have lunch with you. Please call this number. Sincerely yours, Madeleine L'Engle." And the postcard was stamped, "Signature notarized."

Later, I found out that she had walked it down to the local bank to get a notary to stamp it. The very next day I called Madeleine at her office in the cathedral library, and we made a lunch date. We met at 12:30 p.m. at an Indian restaurant, and we were still there at 7:00 p.m., when the waiter finally kicked us out. There was so much to talk about! We hit it off immediately. That began a wonderful friendship.

At that point, I still wasn't ready to write again, but Madeleine did her best to encourage that. She and Hugh would invite me to Crosswicks for weekends. Sometimes I would work in the garden there. One weekend, we planted a lot of trees at the far edge of the meadow to create a screen from the road. Late in the day we'd come indoors and play Ping-Pong, or I'd chop vegetables while Madeleine made a wonderful big stew. She liked to put more garlic in a stew than anybody I've ever met. We would talk about life and literature. If I was confused about something, she would relentlessly probe my heart and say, "Tom, what do you really want?" After a conversation with her, the right decision usually seemed clear.

One evening in 1985, Hugh, Madeleine, and I were having dinner at their apartment on West End Avenue. I had just brought out a bowl of spaghetti from the kitchen and placed it at the center of the table. We were starting to serve ourselves when Madeleine and Hugh began talking about how important their godparents had been to each of them. After a while, as we were eating our spaghetti, Madeleine turned to me and said, "Tom, tell us about your godparents." I replied, "I don't have any." Then she turned to Hugh, and they exchanged a nod. Turning to me, she announced, "You do now!" We put down our knives and forks, joined hands by candlelight, and Madeleine improvised a little ceremony that made me an adopted godson. That was Madeleine. It was always her instinct to go right to the place of compassion, to fill a gap, to make things better.

Another time I was at Crosswicks, we were talking about the power of nature to inspire, teach, and heal. Madeleine said, "Tom, there is a place I need to take you." We got in her car and drove to Cathedral Pines, a nature preserve in Cornwall, Connecticut, with towering old trees. Madeleine and I wandered in the woods for the rest of the afternoon. People were out hunting for mushrooms, and she told me that a year or two before, the head of the local mushroom hunters' society had died from eating a bad one. She couldn't resist the dark humor of that, and neither could I.

As we walked, we kept noticing things: a butterfly, a mound where some small animal lived, a twisted branch. Finally, we came to one of the oldest and tallest trees, and Madeleine said, "This is where I go when I really need solace." Then she walked up to the tree, and she put her arms around its trunk and said, "Come here. Put your ear to the trunk and listen." I remember thinking skeptically, Okay . . . But then for a timeless moment we just stood there *being* with the tree. The beauty of that moment, what I witnessed right there, was Madeleine moving seamlessly from reality into fantasy, from a normal walk in the woods to a realm beyond the senses. That was when I realized she was showing me something even more remarkable than a great tree. She was showing that it was possible, as well as desirable, for someone of any age to be full of wonder and imagination and spirituality.

While her husband, Hugh, was dying in the hospital, she started writing *Two-Part Invention*, the story of their life together. In that book she recalls going for a walk in Connecticut on the road to Dog Pond with a young couple who were thinking about getting married. That couple was Currie and me. Later, she wrote a blessing for our wedding, which spoke about the importance of each partner respecting the individuality of the other.

Six months after Hugh died, when I asked her how she was doing, Madeleine took a deep breath and said, "I'm doing all right. I feel a little less terrible today than I felt yesterday." Then she said something deeply wise. "You know," she said, "the only thing I've really learned from this process is that grief is like a tunnel. You have to go through it to get to the other side. If you try to ignore it or if you try to find a way around it, you will *never* get to the other side. You have to go straight through it." Her eyes were at their widest as she said this.

A few years later, when a serious hip problem had landed her in a wheelchair, I took her down from her apartment to dinner at Henry's. Pushing the wheelchair, I said, "You know, Madeleine, despite everything, you seem to be in good spirits." She replied, "What choice do I have? Either I can mope and groan and suffer, or I can just do fine. I prefer to just do fine." That was Madeleine at her wise-woman best.

*Q: Did you ever take one of her writing workshops?*

A: No, but I did take part in two of her silent retreats at the Holy Cross Monastery in the Hudson River valley. At these retreats, there were twenty or thirty people. Madeleine was the only person allowed to speak. After a morning of complete silence, we went to the chapel, where Madeleine spoke for an hour. Sometimes she would read from one of her books, such as *A Swiftly Tilting Planet*. Other times she might read from an ancient Chinese philosopher. Or she might speak about the size and shape of the universe. She built one talk on the observation that, starting from opposite ends of the cosmic spectrum, particle physicists and astrophysicists were asking many of the same questions. Both groups, she pointed out, were exploring the wonders of the universe with physics as their common language. She concluded by talking about how much still remained mysterious—and how great that was.

We were then sent off to have lunch in silence. The only sound was the clattering of forks and knives. Then came an afternoon of silence during which one could sit in an alcove and read or go walking on the trails along the Palisades. Later, we would receive a fresh infusion of Madeleine L'Engle, rich in ideas and literary allusions and scientific riddles, and be sent off into silence to think about it all. This went on for three days. It was a marvelous experience.

The first time I went to one of her silent retreats, in 1985, I still had my day job. I left work early that Friday, drove up along the Hudson to the monastery, and traded my business suit for my Colorado clothes. Because we were a small business, my partners and I would always leave a phone number where we could be reached on weekends. Just in case of an emergency. So I had left the monastery's number. But in all those years, no one had ever needed to call me on a weekend. Until that particular weekend.

One of my partners, a financially savvy but very impatient guy, decided he needed to speak to me. He called the monastery on Sunday. The monk on duty, Brother Boniface, was well acquainted with the rules of the silent retreat. My partner, thinking he was calling some country inn, asked, "Is Tom Barron there?" Brother Boniface scanned the list of people attending the silent retreat, then replied, "Ah, yes, Tom Barron. He is with us now." My partner was a little taken aback by this response. "Us? Who is us?" he demanded. Whereupon Brother Boniface, who had only recently come to the monastery, proudly said, "Why, we are the Brothers of the Holy Cross!" By now my partner, I'm sure, was beginning to doubt my sanity. He said, "Well, I don't care who you are. This is urgent. I need to speak with Tom Barron now!" Brother Boniface, however, did not budge. He knew the rules. "I'm sorry," he replied, "but this weekend Mr. Barron is speaking with no one but God." At which point Brother Boniface heard a dial tone.

I knew nothing about all this until the following morning. Heading for work, I walked into the office-building lobby, and the security guard greeted me from behind his desk with a twinkle in his eye and called out, "Ah, Brother Barron. It is so good to see you!" That was the start of a rough week at the office. It was also the first inkling my partners had that there was another side to me, though it wasn't one they understood. Madeleine loved to hear me tell that story to friends.

*Q: Did you turn to Madeleine for advice about whether or not to leave your job in order to write full-time?*

A: Yes. All that time in New York, Madeleine was quietly encouraging me to try writing again. Sometimes not so quietly, because she knew it was what I really wanted to do. But after all those rejection letters, I was a bit afraid of putting myself out there again as a writer. So I led a bit of a double life. I would get up at four in the morning to write in my journal, to play with story ideas, or to write a poem. Then I'd go off to work. Yet sometimes at the office, the urge to write was so strong I couldn't resist sneaking in some more creative writing. People thought I was taking copious notes at those long, dreary meetings with lawyers and investment bankers, because I'd sit in the back of the room and scribble away. (The lawyers in the room always thought I was taking notes to prepare for litigation!) But the truth was I was writing character sketches of the more flamboyant types—what they were really like when no one else was around. Maybe they inspired some of the ogres, goblins, and trolls in my books! No wizards, though.

Madeleine gave me the kick in the pants I needed. She was well aware of my situation and urged me to figure it out. Finally, after a long talk with my new wife, Currie, I walked into a meeting at the office, gave my report to the partners, and then told them I was going to resign as president of the company. "Why?" they asked, shocked. "To move back to Colorado and try to write a book that somebody would like to read," I answered. They were even more shocked. It was great fun. And I knew that whatever happened, I was following my passion.

A few days later, Currie and I went over to Madeleine's for dinner. When we walked in, I declared, "It's done." Madeleine, who was in the kitchen, whooped and clapped her hands. Then she said, "I am so happy for you! Wherever this leads, it's going to be good." Her phrase "Wherever this leads" was perfect because it acknowledged the risks but also honored the importance of doing what you love in life.

When I had completed the manuscript for what became my first published book, *Heartlight*, Madeleine put me in touch with Patti Gauch, the editor in chief of Philomel Books. She knew that Patti enjoyed fantasy and might take a chance on a new, undiscovered writer. In 1990, when Philomel published that book, Madeleine hosted a dinner for me at her apartment to which she invited librarians, booksellers, reviewers, and others. They all came, of course, to have an evening with her. But she really wanted them to know about this new writer and his book. She was so generous and loving. Throughout the course of the dinner, she turned to me and asked, "Now, Tom, what do *you* think about that?" That was just the kind of person she was. Madeleine really loved to help people. And she did so with her customary flair and grace.

I had moved back to Colorado in 1989. Several years later, Madeleine came out to visit. Walking had become hard for her, so we only went to the wildflower meadow near our mountain cabin. I had strung a hammock between two aspen trees. She lay on it and gazed at the mountain. We were there in time for the first bloom of the wildflower season, and it was all just spectacular. She seemed truly at peace. It was great to give that little moment to Madeleine, who had given me so much.

Trish Marx is the author of *Elephants and Golden Thrones*, *One Boy from Kosovo*, and other nonfiction books for young readers.

*Q: How did you meet Madeleine L'Engle?*

A: I need to start with the backstory. I grew up during the 1950s, in a family of readers, in a small southern Minnesota town with an old Carnegie library. We did a tremendous amount of reading in our house, and when *A Wrinkle in Time* came out, it hit us like a bomb. My mother, my older sister, and I all thought it was fabulous. Madeleine L'Engle was a new author to us, and we thought her book was different from any book that we had ever read: it was science fiction, not realistic fiction in the usual sense, and yet it was infused with the most realistic emotion. Ordinarily, I didn't enjoy science fiction, and I would not have chosen the book on my own. But there was something about the way she had put it all together: the combination of realistic emotion beautifully described and the theme of time travel, and the other world of possibilities she had created. It had been my mother, most likely, who was an artist, who first heard about *A Wrinkle in Time*. She was always telling us about books to read.

My mother was taking art classes and painted at home. Later, she sold some of her paintings. Reading about Meg's mother reminded me of her. In turn I think my mother was inspired by Mrs. Murry. The book really did have a big impact on us.

After I married and was living in Minneapolis, I met a woman at a party one day who said she was about to visit New York. "While I'm there," she said, "I'm going to have dinner with Madeleine L'Engle." I was probably twenty-eight or twenty-nine at the time, and I was absolutely floored by the news. At home that evening I said, "I can't believe that somebody gets to have dinner with Madeleine L'Engle!" I wanted to be there. I wanted to be a mouse in the corner so I would know what she would say and do.

Then, fifteen years later, after living in London for a time, my family and I moved to New York. Somehow I found out that Madeleine L'Engle was giving a writers' retreat in Brewster, New York, and that anyone could sign up for it.* I signed up immediately. Then I called my mother, and she signed up for it too.

There were about seven of us, all women, and we gathered on a Wednesday in a lovely old house that was kept up by Episcopal nuns, who cooked all our meals. We helped set and clear the table, and we ate all our meals together and were basically together all day long for the next three days, from breakfast until evening Vespers, which was celebrated in a monastery across the road, with the monks singing. It was all very medieval—and lovely. Every evening, we would follow Madeleine across the way to Vespers, after which she retired for the night and the rest of us would stay up and talk. I regret not staying on for the silent retreat that followed over the weekend, but I had three small children at home, and getting away wasn't easy. At that point I had published one book, and my goal was to do what I could to move my writing career along.

---

*L'Engle led the workshop referred to here, and others like it, at the Melrose house, a retreat center maintained since 1961 by the Sisters of the Community of the Holy Spirit.

The house had a front porch with a woodpile. We would sometimes haul in wood for the fireplace. Madeleine always had a big fire going. Her chair was positioned directly in front of the fire, and she would take her place there very regally at the start of each session. She would sit with her back perfectly straight and her head held high and with her hands folded neatly in her lap. All her movements were slow and deliberate. Her hair was short and white, very severe around her face. She was utterly composed. At first glance you might in fact have thought her unfriendly.

She would start each session by simply looking around the room. As she did so, you would feel that she was taking in every aspect of your being. You wanted to say, "What is it you see?" It was a little unnerving—that total composure, that regal manner—and it didn't come with a smile. Warm and friendly and smiley she was not. Nonetheless, she *cared* about you. During those three days, you came to feel that she cared about you both as a person and as a writer.

When I think about the pieces I wrote during the retreat, I can see that they were a very different kind of writing from what was usual for me. I still don't know exactly how she got that out of me. Some of the other participants were writers as well, while others were just people who wanted to be around Madeleine. Somehow she drew very good writing out of everybody. She made it a very safe place to be and a very special place to be, so that you would share things that you might not share otherwise.

We worked the whole day, with breaks between sessions. Madeleine would give us exercises. Once she had us write a sonnet. Other times she would tell a story from the Bible and give us twenty minutes to write an essay, a poem, or a character description based on it. She would prompt us just enough that we'd all be scribbling in our notebooks. Twenty minutes later, we would pass our papers to the person to our right, and everybody would read the other person's work. I remember writing a story about Jesus in which I melded the biblical character with details from the life of my own son, who was then a young child. Writing this exercise had suddenly made me think of Jesus not as a mythic figure but rather as an individual with real emotions. When my story was read to the group, Madeleine said, "That's really nice." This was the *highest* praise you could hope for from her, a few modest words of praise with perhaps a look of surprise thrown in, instead of just a nod. I lived for those moments!

People were always bringing Madeleine her shawl and draping it around her and fixing it for her. She cut a very dramatic figure and seemed to encourage this kind of response from the others. It seemed a bit much. People would help Madeleine sit down. People would help her get up. I couldn't tell if they were being solicitous or if she really needed help. Some people would literally sit at her feet and gaze in adoration of her.

Not my mother, however, who was about Madeleine's age and something of a grande dame herself. She was not in the least bit in awe of her and would even talk back to Madeleine in a friendly, teasing way. Madeleine would say, "Now we're all going to do writing," and my mother would pipe up, "But, Madeleine, I *can't* write. You know that I'm an artist. I don't see things the way you do." To which Madeleine would respond in her firmest voice, "Jean, you *can* write! And you will write *something*." That was all it took to get my mother scribbling away. Madeleine was different with my mother than she was with the rest of us. It was funny to see these two grandes dames go at each other. My mother thought it was wonderful.

The retreat was intense, and it was intimate. The Melrose house felt like a home, but Madeleine created a working atmosphere. We were expected to participate in every one of the sessions, which were more like conversations in that she spent much of the time talking on some topic, as a prologue to the next assignment. There were no formal lectures, and nothing all that extraordinary was said. But I think that when someone like Madeleine L'Engle is sitting close to you in a room and is expecting you to write, and she wants to listen to it being read aloud and is prepared to say a few words about it afterward, well, you try to do your absolute best. You forget about everything else. All distractions fall away.

*Q: How well did she get to know you?*

A: She didn't waste a whole lot of her strength or energy on that. She just assumed you were there to work. That was my feeling. She totally respected that part of you. I don't think I ever talked with her about my own book. Attending the retreat didn't entitle you, I didn't think, to stay in touch with her later. But then I was kind of shy, and I remember being surprised at how familiar some of the others were around her. There were those who had come back again and again.

*Q: Her groupies!*

A: Yes, the true aficionados, people who loved every word that came out of her mouth, and for whom it always was "Madeleine this, Madeleine that."

*Q: Even so, it sounds as if you found the retreat genuinely useful.*

A: Absolutely. I went for two years in a row, and I was ready to go back for a third time when she became ill and had to stop giving retreats.

*Q: Were the retreats for Christian writers only?*

A: Absolutely not. It was more that she found the stories and the characters in the Bible so richly compelling. In fact I wasn't all that aware of her religious side, and she certainly wasn't playing the evangelist. I would say that she was taking the Bible as a common frame of reference and as a source of material from which to launch some of our writing exercises.

*Q: Why do you think she gave these retreats?*

A: I have no idea why she gave them. They were very unusual, now that I look back on it: to have that kind of sustained contact with such a well-known writer. How often does that happen? She seemed to thoroughly enjoy herself. Maybe she felt the retreats were a way to impart her wisdom to others. What I learned from her is that if you write from your heart instead of writing about a topic that you think is going to sell or work with the school curriculum, it somehow frees you.

Madeleine may have seemed intimidating at times, but I don't remember being afraid or ever once feeling stupid as a member of the group. I am sure that that was because of the tone she set for us. She insisted that we respect each other's writing. There were some very good writers and some who were not so good. But as Madeleine would remind us, everyone has a point of view. So to her there was always something in everything.

## DON LUNDQUIST

Don Lundquist served for more than twenty-five years on the administrative staff of the Cathedral Church of St. John the Divine, where his posts included executive assistant to the subdean (later master of ceremonies) Edward Nason West, managing director of the Cathedral Events and Time Space Use Calendar, and managing director of the Cathedral Columbarium Facility and Arrangements.

*Q: How did you meet Madeleine L'Engle?*
A: I started working at the Cathedral of St. John the Divine in 1982 as an assistant for the Reverend Canon Edward West. His office was next door to the cathedral library, where Madeleine worked, so I would have met her very early on. I knew her until she died. After Canon West died in 1990, Madeleine carried on in the library, and I continued to work in the office next door. So we had almost daily contact.

Madeleine was a stately woman who seemed comfortable in any situation. I don't recall that she and I were ever formally introduced. That would not have been necessary with her. She was always rather creatively dressed. She wore big jewelry, for example: long, dangly earrings, which she was able to pull off because of her long neck and short hair. Her gait was solid, but as she got older, it was as if she had to think about where to place her feet. I don't know the exact medical reason for that, if there was one. In any case, it didn't get in the way of her travels: from taking off to give writing workshops or to lecture or preach, not until her last few years, when she was confined to a wheelchair. Before then, she was always on the go.

A great many people came to see her, too. A large percentage of those who came to the library were school groups—groups of children who were studying writing or literature. They would come in to talk with her or to interview her. She would sometimes give them direction in writing or have them do a short paragraph and then go through it with them and tell them what she thought. Friends would also come and go, sometimes friends of long-standing from any number of different walks of life. Madeleine was also a confessor, or spiritual adviser, for a lot of people, including some priests, who would come to her to discuss theological issues. Young, old: anybody could come by for a talk with Madeleine.

At the library, she somehow also found plenty of time to write. She always kept a big box full of blank white eight-and-a-half-by-eleven paper on one side of the desk, and across from it, on the other side, a second box that she gradually filled with her latest manuscript pages. Quite frequently, she would pick up the latter box and stuff it into her shoulder bag and take it home. So it was easy to see that she was doing work. Taped around her desk were hand-drawn pictures, cutout figures in felt, and banners that had been presented to her by individual children or classes.

I started at the cathedral in the days when everybody still wrote on typewriters. Not long after that, somebody convinced Madeleine that she needed to write on a computer. Personal computers were brand-new then. One day Madeleine turned to her assistant at the library and announced, "This is what we need to do. Go buy me a computer." I accompanied this young woman to the store, and we picked out something. When the store clerk asked, "What kind of program do you have?" we had no idea how to respond. It was suggested that Madeleine might want to start with a program called Symantec's Q&A. It took her a while, but once she got the hang of it, Madeleine thought the computer was wonderful. Editing became so much easier.

Madeleine could be so generous. She said, "Don. You should get one yourself." So she sent us out to buy another computer just like hers. She had given us a blank check. Madeleine was also responsible for my staying on at the cathedral following Canon West's death, as well as for one of the other priests.

In addition to my regular duties at the cathedral, I worked closely with Madeleine on her correspondence. She responded personally to every letter, whether it was from an adult or a child. We would sit together and go through twenty or thirty letters at a time, with Madeleine dictating to me. Her responses would be short, but still there would have been this direct contact. She had the uncanny ability to pick out some detail or reference in a letter that she could respond to in personal terms. Oftentimes, she would make a connection to one of her books. So there was an element of creativity in her writing even in these letters to fans. I would take the dictated letters home to type them up or print them out. I had to learn to forge her signature! One of her famous sign-offs was "Tesser well, Madeleine." It was fun to be in on that part of her life. Periodically, we would bundle up copies of all of her responses, together with the original letters, and send them off to the Madeleine L'Engle archive at Wheaton College, which one of the professors there, Clyde Kilby, had been instrumental in establishing.

Madeleine loved to celebrate her birthday. If it fell conveniently on a day when she was at the library, we would go up to Canon West's apartment, which was in the same building as the offices, for a noon champagne-and-caviar birthday lunch. It would be wonderful. I would have spent part of the morning hard-boiling the eggs and chopping the onions—preparing a whole variety of things to go with the caviar. Madeleine, pretending not to appreciate the effort, would say, "I don't know why you bother. I just want a spoon and the caviar and the champagne!" Madeleine didn't especially care about presents. What satisfied her more was the presence of people wishing her well. If all else failed, the tried-and-true gift was some sort of unicorn or giraffe. Her desk was loaded down with these miniatures.

Her husband, Hugh, was always concerned about money. I remember him saying once, "If you ever find any clothes catalogs in Madeleine's mail, immediately pull them out so that she doesn't start ordering a lot of stuff!" They both had a theater background and knew what it was not to have the next gig. It colored their attitude to the point that they lived pretty closely. In Connecticut they rented a meat locker from a local butcher and would keep a frozen turkey or a roast beef stored away. One time when I was up visiting, Madeleine was going on and on with Hugh, giving him instructions about what to bring home from the locker for dinner. Hugh had a tendency to roll his big eyes when he was getting perturbed, so I could see what was coming. He and I got in the car and drove to the butcher shop. When we got inside, Hugh turned to me and said, "You know, I just can't remember a thing she said. What am I supposed to pick up?" Even so, I would say they had a beautiful life because while they clashed openly like that at times, they still loved each other and cared for each other.

They enjoyed having people at Crosswicks. Weekends there were a time to relax, to take a walk down through the meadow to the stargazing rock after dark or to just sit around talking or playing the piano.

Madeleine was at her best in the kitchen shaking spice after spice into the pot for whatever she was making. Hugh would be out in the living room pouring the drinks for the cocktail hour, after which we'd all have dinner. When it was bedtime, Madeleine would say, "Everybody's invited into our bedroom," and we'd all file in there, plunk down on the bed, and talk for another hour or so. Madeleine would tell stories about the friendly ghosts of Crosswicks, which supposedly you could hear if you listened carefully or which you might see if you went outside and put a candle in the grass and did sort of a *Midsummer Night's Dream* dance around the candle.

Canon West officially retired in 1982, and I arrived some time later that same year—in the late summer or early fall. Prior to my coming to work there, I had known the cathedral primarily for its magnificent music and for the preaching of the canon. I had also taken evening courses at the cathedral's Institute of Theology, where Canon West was on the faculty, and had had the chance to meet him. So when I came in one day and said simply, "I have time on my hands. Could you use some assistance?" the timing was right. Following his retirement, the cathedral no longer provided him with a secretary. What he did still have there was his rather grand apartment—and Madeleine was responsible for that, together with the cathedral board of trustees. The dean made good use of him, giving him a sort of honorary position as master of ceremonies, which meant that he was still involved in planning the big services. If a special visitor was expected—the Dalai Lama or the Armenian patriarch, for example—it was Canon West's job to know the proper protocol. Protocol was one of his areas of expertise. In the time I worked with him, he was kept busy thanks to his expertise in so many areas: theology, church history, church architecture, church heraldry. He always had some project. If a church out in Ohio was thinking of remodeling its altar area, he might be called in for a consultation. If a new design was needed for the bishop's signet or sealing ring, or the pectoral crosses worn by bishops—that too was a job for Canon West. He designed a coat of arms for Trinity Parish. What would be the correct combination of elements for a shield intended to proclaim in the formal language of heraldry: "This is Trinity." He would sit for hours with his colored pencils and finally come up with the perfect design! He would say, "If I don't know something immediately, I know where to look it up." That is why he and Madeleine got along so well. They were always bouncing ideas off each other and always learning from one another, each one making the other one think.

For six weeks every year, during the liturgical season of Lent, there would be a soup supper in the Cathedral House following the little Mass that was celebrated in the cathedral at 5:30 or 6:00 p.m. After supper, Madeleine and Canon West would sit at a table together in front of the sixty or seventy people who would have come to hear them. Canon West would pick the topic for the evening in advance but keep it to himself, not saying a word to Madeleine about it. One night, for example, they sat down, and Canon West began by saying, "Okay, Maidel"—he called her that, never Madeleine. "Tonight we're going to talk about Saints Damian and Cosmas." She responded, "Oh, Edward, where did you ever get *that* idea?" "Well, just tell me what you know about them," he said. And off they'd go—for forty-five minutes. Sometimes they veered off on a tangent or two, but they always circled back to the evening's theme. Whenever Madeleine went off into her imagination, Canon West knew how to refocus the discussion. Those informal sessions were a remarkable course in theology.

They both had a lot of fun doing it. Sometimes, in response to one of Madeleine's more offbeat comments, Canon West would say: "Well, do I hear you correctly, or did you really mean . . ." To which she would snap back, "Of course you heard me correctly! And that is *exactly* what I meant." "Well, well . . . ," he would say. "No, Edward. Now, don't correct me!"

It was always a very sensitive time when Madeleine turned to Canon West for help in editing her manuscripts. She would come into his office and sit at the side of his desk. He would have spent time going through the thick pile of manuscript pages, and once again he would start with "I think that perhaps you meant to say . . ." I cannot recall a single time when Madeleine took his criticism with grace. There was always an argument, and quite frequently she would just storm out of the room, leaving the manuscript behind. Canon West would turn and look at me across the room and say, "Just like a mother giving birth to a baby!" It never bothered him in the least. He had said what he had to say. She had responded in the way she had to respond.

Canon West's office and the library each had access from the main hallway. But it was a quirk of the building's design that both offices were connected from within, by a "secret" passageway in the rear. This worked out very well for Canon West and for Madeleine too whenever either of them needed to disappear in a hurry, perhaps to avoid an unwanted visitor whom the receptionist had announced.

I don't know how often Madeleine showed Canon West her manuscripts, but one that I remember specifically was *Certain Women*, which was one of her later novels. That book was so much involved with the emerging women's lib philosophy. Canon West didn't have a lot of sympathy for women's lib. He thought the women priests had a sort of perpetual chip on their shoulder whereas someone like Madeleine didn't need women's lib to earn respect. It was what she had to offer, and it had nothing to do with whether it was coming from a man or a woman. Madeleine herself would often say that she hated labels of all kinds. "I can be anything," she said. "In my mind there's no such thing as Christian or non-Christian. I can be Buddhist, I can be Catholic, I can be Jewish, I can be Muslim." She hated being called a children's book writer, too. She would say, "I don't write books for children. I just write what I have to write."

Among the major influences on Madeleine's religious thinking was Agatha Christie, who in addition to her well-known mystery novels wrote a number of really probing theological works—*Star over Bethlehem* and others. But I don't think that Madeleine was in direct contact either with Agatha Christie or with another English mystic who appealed to her, Evelyn Underhill.*

She would talk about her visits to Wheaton College, which, when I graduated from there in 1966, was still a very conservative, right-wing Christian evangelical institution . . . call it what you will. It is not so much like that anymore, but it was back then. The first time Madeleine visited Wheaton, she was asked to sign the pledge, which every student was required to sign at registration. The pledge committed one to a life while at school of no smoking, no drinking, no card playing, no dancing, and no theater attendance. Madeleine of course thought the whole thing ludicrous. She would joke, "That's why they need the front campus," which was a big sloping green in front of the old main building, landscaped with low-lying bushes and hedges. She said, "There was nothing else for the students to do but to go out with a date and lie under one of the hedges."

It might seem surprising that Madeleine would have given her papers to a college that had the pledge, to which she objected so strongly. But she was impressed that two members of the literature faculty, Beatrice Batson and Clyde Kilby, had sided with her. The pledge was not the only issue there, either. A couple of the churches and the library in town had attempted to take her books off the shelves. If anything drove her up a wall, it was any sort of censorship. In the end, I think she saw her involvement with Wheaton as an opportunity to broaden some minds. She liked to talk about human beings as "co-creators." Her belief was that we have the ability to be co-creators with the Creator of the universe, provided that we don't get bogged down in religious dogma or closed-minded, political thinking. At Wheaton she saw strict limitations, and she thought she could help encourage change there.

*Evelyn Underhill was an English Anglo-Catholic writer on Christian mysticism.

Madeleine arrived at the library at 9:30 or 10:00 in the morning, five days a week, usually with her Irish setters in tow. I would sit with her for the first couple of hours and take dictation. Then it would be lunchtime. Madeleine always had lunch plans, usually at one of the neighborhood spots like the V&T Italian restaurant just across the street or the Columbia Cottage, which is a Chinese restaurant. For special occasions there was Butler Hall, a penthouse restaurant with a magnificent view south to the city. She would go there with Bob Giroux or with out-of-town visitors. Then she would return for the afternoon. If Madeleine wasn't expecting a student group or other visitors, she would get to work writing. She always kept a supply of herbal tea on hand to offer visitors.

Both Madeleine and Canon West had Irish setters. At one point, Madeleine had to put one of her setters to sleep. I escorted her to the vet, who, when it became clear that Madeleine wanted to witness the whole procedure, said, "We don't let the owners stay here during the euthanasia." Madeleine as usual just stood her ground. "What do you mean?" she said in her best indignant manner. "I saw this dog born. I'm going to see this dog die." And so she did. When it was over, she shed a little tear, then she turned to me and said, "Okay. Now let's go back to the library." This would have been in 1986 or 1987.

One of Canon West's Irish setters got into rat poison on the cathedral grounds and died. Another died of old age. Then, one day, Madeleine decided she wanted a golden retriever, so she made arrangements with a breeder in Maryland. From the same litter from which Madeleine got Doc, whom she named after Dr. Tyler, the character that Hugh played on *All My Children*, Canon West took a pup he named Tino, which was short for Marcus Antonius. These were wonderful large-structured golden retrievers. Madeleine's son, Bion, who was living at Crosswicks, kept a third pup.

When Canon West retired, he had just turned seventy. He was

very much involved in the New York social scene. It was not just that he knew all of the Social Register people. He himself was a member of the St. Nicholas Society, St. George's Society, Mayflower Society—at least a dozen different lineage societies. Madeleine loved to say about him, "Oh, he was just a greengrocer's son from Charles Street in Boston." But in fact his father had been an officer in the military. It was after that, I think, that he had a grocery store. I have two swords, one that dates back to the middle of the nineteenth century, which belonged to Canon West's grandfather. He kept them around the office.

He claimed to be an only son of an only son of an only son, back some five generations. Once his mother died, which would have been in the early 1970s, he had no family. So his family became a group of people he called his godchildren, who were basically of student age, a good many of whom were those who came into the cathedral while studying at Columbia or Union Seminary or elsewhere. He would take them under his wing and sometimes literally feed and clothe them if they were not of ample means. So he usually had company, and on evenings when he was home, he made a point of never dining alone. The reason he gave for this was a theological reason. I had asked him once, "In all of your years as a clergyperson, is there any one subject or experience that you can think of that has been a disappointment to you?" His answer surprised me, to say the least. "Yes," he said, "the thing that distresses me the most is never to have had the chance to see my Lord face-to-face, as a human being." I thought to myself, Well, *that's* interesting. Then he said, "You see, Duckie"—Duckie is what he called me—"that is why I always have to break bread with someone: it is as in the story of the two disciples on the road to Emmaus, who met a stranger. Then, when they sat down to break bread, they recognized who it was." He said, "I keep hoping that sometime as I break bread with one of these people who join me for supper, I am going to see my Lord sitting across from me." Remarks like that would just stop you in your tracks, just as things that Madeleine said sometimes made a deep impression.

Everybody assumed that Canon West was a very crusty and curmudgeonly man, which he could be at times. But all that was really just a defense. In reality, he was an unusually sensitive human being. He would sit for hours with students who had been turned down as not qualified for ordination. They would be weeping, baring their souls, and he would offer them encouragement and comfort. Occasionally, he was able to have the decision reversed.

He had a marvelous way of probing the meaning of words and ideas. "Do you know what a lie is?" he would say. "A lie is the withholding of truth from someone who has the right to know it." In his course at the Institute of Theology he would go through the Lord's Prayer or the Apostles' Creed phrase by phrase, devoting an entire evening to each one. He would remark that "Thou shalt not kill" applied equally to the teacher who screamed at a child in school, thereby killing his or her desire to learn, as it did to an actual murderer. He used to say to me, "Duckie, I'm not good at time. All I understand is the difference between God's time, *kairos*, and our time, *chronos*." He and Madeleine were alike in the depth of their thought and in their powers of empathy, and I think they always saw each other as equals.

Canon West *loved* vestments. In his last few years he designed vestments as well as altar hangings. He loved cloth of gold and once had a huge golden cope designed for Paul Moore, when he was still bishop. The design called for intersecting crosses in the metallic weave that made the entire cope look almost iridescent, especially when it was seen under the cathedral's special lights. Canon West had one chasuble that he wore only one Sunday a year, for the Feast of the Transfiguration. It was all a brocade of fake diamonds and emeralds, and it just shimmered when he got in the lights. In his later years, he had a long beard, so that when he would get into one of his antique vestments, he looked the part! His thinking about all this was that if he was going to be acting as a priest of God, he wanted to be dressed his best! It wasn't a Liberace kind of thing. He took it very seriously. He always made a big point of sitting up straight, too. He said, "The queen never touches the back of the chair!"

He had had a tailor make him a full set of Scottish regalia in the clergy tartan, complete with the socks and the dagger and the little pouch. He visited Crosswicks once dressed in this way. It made quite a picture, especially when he pulled up in his black Thunderbird!

Most of Madeleine's writing is about herself and the people she knew, so it's not surprising that she modeled Canon Tallis on Canon West. This must have amused him, and perhaps especially that she linked Canon Tallis to Interpol. He would have understood that as a private joke. Canon West always seemed to know everything, not just about theological and liturgical matters, but also about the people around him. Sometimes he would even poke fun at himself about this. "My mind is like a kitchen sink," he would say. "Everything gets stuck in the drain." On a more mundane level, people would sometimes wonder out loud just where he had gotten this or that tidbit of information. Canon West never divulged his sources! He would only say, "My spies report to me . . ." So, no, he was not literally an agent for Interpol. But like the fictional Canon Tallis, he was a chevalier of the French Legion of Honor as well as an officer of the Order of the British Empire. His decorations filled two large cushions that were carried in procession behind the casket at his funeral. After his death, Madeleine would often say to me, "I miss Papa." Or she would say, "Where's Edward?"

I had dinner at Madeleine's West End Avenue apartment on

many occasions. She would usually start the dinner with grace in the form of a song that the children knew.

This is the day
This is the day
Which the Lord hath made
Which the Lord hath made
Let us rejoice and be glad in it.

It would end with a big "Hip hip hooray!" Then she'd bring out one of her favorite dishes, lemon-flavored chicken, and the first time we had it, we said, "Oh, how do you make it?" and she said, "Oh, it's easy. You just take a lemon and stick it up its butt." The apartment always had the appearance of being well taken care of and lived in. Because of the presence of at least one cat, some of the furniture had gotten a little scratched. My most vivid memory of the apartment is probably the long, long hallway of floor-to-ceiling books—the hallway that went all the way back to the bedrooms. And one entire wall of the living room was lined with books, although after Hugh died and she had the apartment redecorated, that wall became blank except for a huge portrait of her as a little girl.

The real crisis times in Madeleine's life came after Canon West had died. I'm thinking of Bion's illness and death and of her own decline. Madeleine remained pretty much in a state of denial about Bion, which was a big problem for the family. Finally, at Bion's funeral, his widow, Laurie, stood up and point-blank told the congregation what Bion had died of, saying that as unfortunate as it was, it should be a lesson to everyone to do their best to make sure that any friend or loved one who was suffering from alcoholism got the help they needed. Bion was the apple of Madeleine's eye.

In those later years, I went with her on Friday nights for a subscription at the Metropolitan Opera. I would drive the car from the cathedral over to West End Avenue, pick her up, put the wheelchair in the trunk, and then get us down there. Most of the time we went just for the opera, but now and then we also met friends at the Grand Tier for supper beforehand. There was no handicapped access in those days for people in wheelchairs, so we would have to go up through the office area to get to the Grand Tier. On one of these occasions, the restaurant happened to be offering caviar on toast points as an appetizer, and we all knew that that was what Madeleine was going to order. We usually split the check among ourselves, and by the time Madeleine had ordered, she had also observed the look of panic that spread around the table. "Don't worry!" she said. "I'll pay for it!" It hadn't been hard to read our minds. After that, we all relaxed and had a very nice time. Her own mind had started to fade a bit. She wasn't very talkative that evening. And when it came time to pay the check, she had forgotten all about her promise.

Another time I was having dinner with her at Henry's, a favorite restaurant on Broadway and 105th Street. This was before the city's no smoking ordinance had gone into effect. Madeleine saw somebody light up a cigarette on the other side of the restaurant, and she took an ice cube out of her water glass, hurled it across the room, and said in a loud voice, "You're killing all of us!" She would just say whatever popped into her mind. There must have been other times that I didn't see when it was clear that she was losing it.

I visited Madeleine when she was up in White Plains at the rehab center. I would see her granddaughter Charlotte quite regularly when she took over at the cathedral library, after Madeleine had moved permanently to Connecticut. I would always ask, "How's Madeleine?" Then one day she came in and said, "Don, the family decided last night that we had to put Madeleine in hospice care." So I knew the end was near.

I attended her funeral in Goshen, at which Luci Shaw and

another old, old friend got up and read a piece together in Madeleine's honor. Then Dana Catharine, whom Madeleine had first met when she and Hugh were helping out at St. Hilda's & St. Hugh's with the Christmas pageant, got up and spoke. Then came Bion's widow, Laurie. After the ceremony, there was a big reception downstairs. Apparently, the church ladies had anticipated a mammoth crowd. Food was everywhere. Alan Jones was there. I had gotten to know Alan because early on, when he and Josephine were dating, Madeleine had introduced Alan to Canon West, who of course immediately took to him because he was English. I paid my respects to Josephine and didn't stay long.

I think it was hard at times for the grandchildren and the children as well to deal with Madeleine because like everyone there's always another facet. There was an article about Madeleine in *The New Yorker* a few years ago, in which her children were quoted as saying in effect that a lot of her autobiographical writings were fabrications—pure fantasy. But this is how Madeleine lived. If she couldn't figure out something, she would create a fantasy to describe it somehow—which I don't think is bad. It may have made some of the inner circle of family uncomfortable at times, but I think that has to be weighed against the immense creativity that benefited so many people. She certainly paved the road well for the family for the rest of their lives. Personally, I can count on one hand the important people in my life, and Madeleine L'Engle and Canon West were two of them.

# ELSA OKON RAEL

Elsa Okon Rael is a playwright and the author of *What Zeesie Saw on Delancey Street* and other children's books.

*Q: How did you meet Madeleine L'Engle?*

A: A friend of mine, Shellen Lubin, had attended her silent retreat, in Brewster, New York, which to this day I'm sad I didn't know about in time.* Apparently, it had an incredible effect on her. When Shellen heard that Madeleine was doing a workshop at St. Hilda's House, she invited me.† This was about 1990. I was incredibly impressed with Madeleine from our first meeting. She was warm and accepting and encouraging. We saw her once a week for five weeks, and each week she'd give us an assignment. We would sit around and read aloud what she had assigned the week before.

One such assignment Madeleine gave us was "Pick a character from the Bible and write for one hour—no more than that—about that character and bring it in next week." I wrote about a character from Judges named Jephthah, who makes a terrible bargain with God that ends with him having to kill his own daughter. It was a really gorgeous piece, and Madeleine asked for a copy, which

---

*Shellen Lubin is a director, performer, writer, and teacher of music and theater.
†The original St. Hilda's House, the convent house of the Community of the Holy Spirit, was opened in 1950 on Manhattan's Upper West Side.

she rarely did. Another time she had us write a sonnet. She wanted us to learn the sonnet form, and we did. You knew from her face, from her expression, that she approved. She would say, "That's a lovely piece," or "I liked that one," but not much more than that. If Madeleine felt that someone's piece was too long, she would cut it off. She would say, "I told you only to write for an hour!" She was strict when it came to that! Of course I adhered to the one-hour rule. She truly meant it.

The cost of the workshop was quite reasonable, and we would have dinner as a group with the Sisters at St. Hilda's and even attend evening services, which to me was all a delight. I'm Jewish, and everyone at St. Hilda's was very welcoming to me. There was never an attempt to get me to convert to Episcopalianism! But in order for my group to remember that I was not Episcopalian, I found myself telling them stories about my Jewish upbringing on the Lower East Side. They kept insisting, "Write it! Write it! Write it!" Ultimately, I did—which resulted in a series of picture books published by Simon & Schuster.

After the five weeks were up, the students in our group decided we wanted to continue on our own, and so we did, meeting at my apartment. We continued to meet for eleven years. Madeleine would handpick about a dozen of her former workshop students, the ones who were really good writers, to come once a year to have dinner at her apartment. Happily, I was one of them! We would write her notes, and we would get notes from her. It was a loving relationship. At the beginning none of us were published, but eventually all of us were.

# FRIEND

## DANA CATHARINE

Dana Catharine teaches foreign languages at Poly Prep Country Day School, Brooklyn, New York.

*Q: How did you meet Madeleine L'Engle?*

A: After Madeleine and Hugh got married, they moved to Connecticut. Hugh gave up the theater and took on the role of general-store keeper, which he always said was his "longest role." He missed the theater, and after about ten years they decided to come back to New York. Madeleine recounted this in many of the talks she gave.

The only place they could afford to live was the Upper West Side, which at the time was not the trendy place it is now, and so they took an apartment at 924 West End Avenue, which is diagonally across the street from where I grew up.

The best school on the Upper West Side at the time was St. Hilda's & St. Hugh's, which is where I went to school and where they enrolled their three children. Josephine, their oldest daughter, is a year or so younger than I, so she was my schoolmate, though not my classmate. By the time I was a sophomore, Madeleine and Hugh had become teachers at the school, teaching speech and drama once a week. We were a small group of kids who had been together forever in the very small and incredibly demanding British-style traditional school, where we had classes from eight to four. Anything extra at school started *after* four. We were all fairly nerdy kids, and we loved the school. We loved the nuns. We lived for our books and our studies. And then in walked Madeleine and Hugh, who were amazing bright lights. They posed topics for us in speech class intended to make us think about life. It was all very exciting.

I spoke about this at Madeleine's funeral and have expanded on it in an essay for the book *A Circle of Friends*.* At the beginning, they were alien presences to my classmates and me in the sense that when they presented us with a thought-provoking topic, we didn't know how to respond. One time they challenged us with "Suppose creatures from outer space come and take over the earth, demanding that you have to say why you deserve to live. They're going to kill all those who can't say why they deserve to live." Having been saturated in the stories of the saints and early Christian martyrs, we were all ready to be fed to the lions, but not one of us could say why we should live. I think Madeleine and Hugh were devastated that we didn't understand what they wanted us to consider. We thought they were suggesting that if we gave a convincing reason why we should live, then someone else would die. But that wasn't what they meant at all. It wasn't that you had to prove yourself better than the next person. It was simply that they wanted us to investigate why we were worth living. Finally, we all understood that! The responses were thoughtful and heartfelt. I remember referring to Thornton Wilder's *Our Town*, including Emily's "Oh, earth, you're too wonderful" speech, as part of my defense. For me, it was a memorable experience. It was forty-six years ago, and I still remember it strongly.

*Q: Did they team-teach the class?*

A: Yes, they did so as long as Hugh wasn't in a play. Hugh was lovely, and they both cared about us. Once they asked us to talk

*A collection of reminiscences about Madeleine L'Engle edited by Katherine Kirkpatrick.

about a dramatic moment in our lives. On another occasion they asked us to speak about something we cared about. I wanted to be an archaeologist, and so I talked about why I didn't want the Aswan Dam to be built. They were also funny. On April Fools' Day of 1961, Madeleine came in and began writing out the questions for a test on the board. We were horrified. She wrote several questions, and the last question she wrote in Greek. Then she wrote: "April Fools!"

In 1963, the year she won the Newbery Medal, I was the editor of our school newspaper. One evening I walked across the street to their house and interviewed her at their dinner table. I think I may have been the first person to interview her on that occasion!

*Q: Prior to that time had you been aware of her as a writer?*

A: No. A lot of kids think that their teachers are hung up by the backs of their necks in closets at the end of the school day. We knew Hugh was an actor, which was quite something to us, and I guess we knew Madeleine was a writer. But we didn't really give that a lot of attention. Hugh and Madeleine—"Mr. and Mrs. Franklin" to us—were people first.

*Q: Were they full-time faculty?*

A: No. In addition to our weekly class, they must have taught a couple of others.

Madeleine told us that she hadn't thought she could help out at the school in the usual ways that parents did—by volunteering to be a chaperone or by baking cakes. (She later wrote that she was a terrible baker. I know that her oven could be a source of disaster. Once, she put frozen butter in the oven to soften it for garlic bread. She went back to the Tower to write and forgot all about it. You can imagine what happened!) So initially, she and Hugh offered to direct the Christmas pageant.

The Christmas pageant was not something with cute little children in bathrobes. It was spectacularly beautiful. It was given at the main altar of St. John the Divine. As a child, you grew up knowing that after Thanksgiving you would be assigned your part and that a chunk of your life was going to be devoted to a really amazing production of the story of the birth of Jesus, done as tableaux, a student reading from the Gospel of St. Luke, and different choirs of students and nuns singing Christmas hymns appropriate to the tableau. The hymns were often medieval and little known. The nuns sang the Magnificat at the scene of the visitation of the Virgin Mary to her cousin Elizabeth, for example.

The pageant was a very serious thing. In my experience, no child ever messed with it. You didn't disgrace the Christmas pageant. It existed before Madeleine and Hugh came along, and it was already something beautiful, but they made it even more so. A lot of the kids got to know Madeleine that way.

Then, in the summer of 1963, Madeleine's daughter Josephine and I got to know each other well because we both took a job with the nuns at their summer place, where they ran a summer camp for kids. We worked hard all day long, organizing games and looking after kindergartners. We spent our free time discussing the immortal questions in a nearby cemetery!

Here I should explain that when I was fourteen, I was diagnosed with systemic lupus. Everyone was told that I would be dead by the time I was seventeen. I never believed it myself, but I became, from the outside, an "object of interest," you might say, and I think Madeleine and Hugh as faculty in a small, caring, and loving Episcopal school cared particularly about me. The nuns prayed for me every day.

It is also true that Madeleine and Hugh "collected" children. They always said that they had wanted to have a lot of children, but Madeleine had almost died after Bion's birth, so there would be no more natural children. They absorbed the actual and the adopted godchildren, and they absorbed me, and I think their eye was on me for some time. After that exhausting summer camp experience, they invited me to come and spend some time with Josephine at Crosswicks. That was the beginning of my really getting to know them.

I first read *A Wrinkle in Time* that summer in the attic of Crosswicks, in the bed that Meg was supposed to have slept in. I did nothing all weekend but read that book. When Hugh and Madeleine drove me to the train, I was still reading it. But I don't think I had a sense yet of who Madeleine was, because she was so real as this other person, my teacher and dog-walking companion—the one who listened to me and encouraged me and sang songs and played charades. It's just a strange thing. It really was as though we were part of the same family. I remember once coming home from church with her and noticing that she had a run in her stocking and saying to my friend Julian, "This is why I love Madeleine. She's come to church with a run in her stocking. She's not perfect!" I guess we all knew that.

*Q: Would you tell me a little more about the young people Hugh and Madeleine gathered around them?*

A: There were the Connecticut neighbor children, Polly Kinsella and Margie Krukar, who sat out on the stargazing rock at night and shouted every time we saw a shooting star. There were the children of dear friends, the Hannas and the Chases. There were students from our school. Julian, who is three years younger than I and was still a student at the school when I had graduated, became very close to Madeleine. Just imagine, a teacher who had time to listen to you and with whom you could discuss the great questions! Plus, she was exotic and everything we wanted to be when we grew up! Julian and I were good friends. One day she took me to the cathedral library—and she *gave* me to Madeleine. That is exactly how she put it. She said, "Madeleine, here. Here's Dana!"

*Q: But you already knew Madeleine . . .*

A: Yes, but I had never sought her out in the way that Julian did. It wouldn't have occurred to me to do that, and besides I would have been too shy. After that, beginning in 1963 or 1964, Madeleine started inviting both of us to accompany her to the talks she gave in the city. She'd simply say, "Come along," which we were thrilled to do. And that way she had company too.

Then, because of my health, I was not able to go away to college. I was very unhappy about that. So I called Mother Ruth, headmistress of St. Hilda's, and said, "May I please take Mrs. Franklin's writing class?" And Mother Ruth said, "Of course." I was probably eighteen by then, and I went to the classes, and from then onward I became more and more part of Madeleine's life. She occasionally asked me to teach a class (thrilling!) when she began what became a serious speaking career.

Q: *What was her writing class like?*

A: She was very generous and giving. And these classes, I think, were the first classes she ever gave. She was not all that famous yet. The Newbery Medal certainly propelled her career, but she still wasn't the big thing that she became later. And so it seemed to us in her class that Madeleine was ours. Her writing class was very democratic—which felt unusual then. The atmosphere was very positive. Conversation and helpful criticism were encouraged. She would always come up with a springboard idea that we were to develop. She said she loved talking to young people because they were not afraid to ask the big questions. She was beloved by the kids not just because of who she was but because of *how* she was with us. She was completely there, present.

Q: *Would you say that Madeleine had a dramatic manner?*

A: Absolutely! She did not seem to be afraid of anything. You couldn't beat her at charades. It was rumored that she once threw herself on her knees on Park Avenue to get a taxi!

On Sundays we went to church together to the Church of the Resurrection, on East Seventy-fourth and Park Avenue. Leo

Damrosch was the rector, and he was a wonderful man. John Farrar, the publisher who acquired *A Wrinkle in Time*, went to church there too. Nobody oohed or aahed over Madeleine then. She was just another member of the congregation. But she was noticeable!

Madeleine had a wonderful old collie named Oliver that she would walk in Riverside Park every evening after dinner. She would sometimes call and say, "Come walk with me." Sometimes we would talk, and sometimes we would just walk, enjoying the beauty of the city at night. If there was anything on my mind, I shared it with her. Sometimes, when she and Hugh went away, I would take care of Oliver for them.

Another thing that brought us closer was her son Bion's illness in the springtime of 1964. It may have been because he missed his dad, who was away on tour playing the cardinal in John Osborne's *Luther*. Hugh and Madeleine were both very worried because no one could diagnose the illness. So to cheer Bion up, I illustrated a set of the elephant jokes that were very popular then and sent them to him.

Something else Madeleine and I shared was keeping a commonplace or, as she called it, a "goody" book—a book of quotations you came across as you read and then wrote down. Over the years we would exchange our current goody books and copy from each other. Anywhere I traveled, I would bring her back a hardcover notebook for quotes or journaling. It just seemed that she and I loved to do the same things.

In 1967, for my birthday, Madeleine and Hugh gave me tickets to see Hugh on Broadway in *What Did We Do Wrong?* After the play, we went backstage to see Hugh, and then we rode home on the bus together. My world was very small compared with theirs, but being around them allowed my world to expand. It brought out a rascally part of me, and so knowing how they "collected" children, and because I had been born three months before they were married, I used to tease them that I was their "oldest illegitimate child." They thought that was very funny. So as we were boarding the bus that evening, there was an older couple on line who were excited to recognize Hugh from the play. They turned to me and said, "Are you one of his children?" To which I replied, "Yes!" "How many children does he have?" "Ten," I said. It turned out the man was an obstetrician! Before long he and Hugh were deep in conversation on the bus. Ordinarily, I would not have done anything like that, but there was something about being around them that brought out a mischievous streak in me. I think they got a kick out of it too. Years later, Madeleine was meeting at the cathedral with Norman Lear about the sale of *A Wrinkle in Time* to the movies, and when I happened to walk in on their meeting after school, Madeleine said, "*Dana*, tell Norman who you are!" So I said, "I'm Madeleine's oldest illegitimate child." Everyone else I had ever said that to got the joke. But not Norman Lear. He didn't think it was funny, and he looked sort of stunned.

Then, in the summer of 1967, Madeleine invited me to live with her family in Connecticut and to take care of her mother, Madeleine Barnett Camp. My job was to read to Grandmama and be her companion. I loved to read and was a very quiet person, so I was a perfect companion for an elderly lady. She told me stories about her family in the South, and I loved to hear them.

*Q: Tell me more about Madeleine's mother.*

A: Grandmama was a very lovely southern lady. Madeleine always said that she was sorry I met her after she had had a stroke. But that's the only Grandmama that I knew, and I loved her. She told me stories of her life in Jacksonville. Madeleine describes the place where her mother had lived, the old family home, in *The Other Side of the Sun*. Her mother's father, Bion Barnett, was president of the Barnett Bank, and Grandmama said that in Jacksonville a Barnett was buried in each corner of the church.* They were old southern aristocracy. Grandmama told me about being a young woman when Jacksonville burned to the ground, and how they had had to run out of their beautiful house and try to save what they could.†

*Q: What did you and she do together?*

A: We had a great time. I would read to her from these dreadful books that she loved by a romance writer named Howard Spring. She and I watched soap operas together, and in 1969 we watched the moon landing on television. I remember thinking, How cool is this to be sitting on the end of the bed of a woman who was born before electricity, telephones, and cars! But Grandmama said, "I really don't like this. It's messing up my soap operas." The moon landing was just a bother to her. But of course by then she was not her wonderful complete self, because she had had a stroke two or three years before.

*Q: Did you see something of Madeleine in her mother?*

A: I would say the only similarity that I could see was the love of storytelling. Madeleine loved to tell ghost stories and silly jokes, and she liked pranks in those days. Madeleine used to say that she was not comfortable in the South of her growing up because she was too tall and she was too clumsy. And she was a bookish person. She wasn't going to be a lovely southern belle or fit into a society of coming-out parties and things like that. When she went to school at Ashley Hall, she was very happy, and from there she went to Smith, and I think that that was so much more her world. She began writing plays there. She always told us that she loved Smith.

---

*In fact, the Barnetts are buried in Jacksonville's Evergreen Cemetery.
†On May 3, 1901, the city of Jacksonville was largely destroyed by a fire that began with a spark at a mattress factory. Nearly ten thousand city residents were left homeless. Seven people died. Madeleine Hall Barnett had just turned twenty.

*Q: Tell me about Madeleine's nanny, Mrs. O.*

A: She was a wonderful person, no-nonsense but very loving and affectionate. Mrs. O. knew people who had traveled on the *Titanic*. She said that if Grandmama was fixing a bouquet of flowers, she would walk through the house trailing petals and leaves, and Mrs. O. would be picking up after her.

*Q: How did Madeleine spend her time at Crosswicks?*

A: She would get up early and go out to the Tower—she had a room built over the garage that was called the Ivory Tower—and she would come down at noon and make lunch, which was usually a huge quantity of soup and big fat sandwiches, and we would all talk. It was never just two people. There was always a horde of visiting priests, visiting artists, and friends of Bion's. By this time Josephine had gotten married, so she wasn't there, and Maria was away too. But Bion was there. He was seven years younger than I, but age didn't seem to matter to us. It didn't matter to Madeleine either, and we often said that we had gone to school together because we seemed to understand each other and have similar likes. I think she must have been as nerdy a kid in school as I was. I wasn't looking for another mother, but I did need someone with whom I could share the great ideas or whatever was going through my head at the time. And Madeleine enjoyed it too.

After lunch, Madeleine would go back up to work until about five o'clock and then come down again and start making dinner. There were usually ten people at dinner at Crosswicks every night. Dinner was preceded by Baroque music and cocktails and appetizers and a game of charades or mah-jongg or Murder in the Dark. Grandmama would join us. And then we'd all have dinner together, usually with a sung grace or a said grace—we collected graces—or people taking turns, always holding hands. And then Madeleine would go off and get ready for bed and leave the cleaning up to us because she said if she cooked dinner, she didn't need to wash the dishes. And the dogs got to lick all the pots and pans. Sometimes we would put on the ratty old fur coats in the hall closet and go out to the stargazing rock. She wrote about this in *A Circle of Quiet*. We decided to sing out any hymn or song with a hallelujah in it for each shooting star. And then we'd go back to the house and make hot chocolate and sometimes climb into bed with her and talk for a while. And that was Crosswicks in the summertime. It was all so idyllic and, I have to say, so very lovely.

Q: *Tell me about Madeleine's religious life.*

A: At a certain point—I think in the mid- or late 1960s—she became very close to the Sisters of the Community of the Holy Spirit, an Episcopal teaching order, in New York, as did my friend Julian and I. We all became associates of the community, which meant that we had certain spiritual responsibilities such as praying for the Sisters. Madeleine was the most advanced kind of associate. I think she began this deep involvement with the church primarily because of Edward West. He was an incredible person. Madeleine got to know him when she was directing the Christmas pageant.

He was a stickler for not celebrating Christmas until midnight, December 24. He kept all his Christmas cards, and there were many—he had friends all over the world—in a basket until the twenty-fifth. Of course our world doesn't work that way. He was visibly annoyed that the children of St. Hilda's & St. Hugh's were celebrating the birth of Christ a week or so before the actual day. And so Madeleine met with him when she was directing the pageant to talk this over, because he had been fussing over some arrangement or other. She told us that she went to him and said, "This is the only real Christmas that some of these children are going to have. It's very important!" After that, they became friends. I think she had been searching for a long time for a spiritual life and that she began to find one with the Sisters at the community and with Edward West, who became her really deep, profound friend and confessor. He was a great, great preacher and a fierce kind of person.

*Q: Fierce in what sense?*

A: He had a deep voice, and he cultivated his scariness! He could pretend to be a bit of a basilisk at times, absolutely freezing you with his eye. But he also loved dogs, as did Madeleine, and in later years he was surrounded by a flurry of Irish setters.

He was a celibate priest surrounded by students and friends. He was the confessor to the Sisters of the Community of the Holy Spirit. But one of the main things about him was that he was such a presence. I remember Bishop Donegan of New York complaining in a jolly sort of way that when he and Edward West had traveled to India together, "When Edward West got off the plane, everybody in India knew *who* the bishop of New York was!" He was quite a character.

*Q: Madeleine must have gotten a kick out of that.*

A: Of course, he was very theatrical, but also real and alive. By 1967, Madeleine was deeply involved at the cathedral. So much so that the bishop would come to her apartment on West End Avenue for Christmas dinner.

She would say that she had written *A Wrinkle in Time* as a way of finding her spiritual life because she hadn't been able to find spiritual meaning in anything else that she had experienced or read until that time. And then she discovered the Episcopal Church and then, through St. Hilda's & St. Hugh's, the Sisters of the Community of the Holy Spirit. Then she began to go much more deeply into Episcopalian life, by saying morning prayer and evening prayer, by going on retreats. Then she began to give retreats herself.

In the summer of 1970, she wrote her first nonfiction book, *A Circle of Quiet*, a book that at first she resisted writing but which, she said, "kept asking to be written." And I think it was at that point that she became really well-known, because a great many people who had read *A Wrinkle in Time* when they were young were older then and were perhaps wanting something more. She became the big ticket then because she was writing about herself, and her family, and about what she thought about life. I remember that summer particularly well for many reasons, but one reason was that book, because after that she began to be asked to speak a lot more and things really changed for her.

Madeleine had discovered a brook on their property, two fields from the house. We would walk down to the brook and say evening prayer sitting by the brook, and we would stretch out on the rocks at night and sing the hymns. How many people can you do that with? We loved doing simple things like that. And I never thought this was odd: *of course* this was how to spend an evening! I always thought how lucky I was to have her to sing hymns with, but maybe I was good for her in that way, too, because, again, I don't know how many people you could do that with. Over the course of her life, as she got older, she met many more people who became dear friends with whom she shared these experiences. But back in those days, there maybe were not so many.

Then I fell in love with Mario and was about to get married and go off to Mexico, and everybody was very happy for me. Hugh and Madeleine asked me what I wanted for a wedding present. I said I wanted to have my honeymoon at Crosswicks. So they gave me their own house. They held my wedding rehearsal dinner at their apartment in New York. Knowing that my parents were divorced, Hugh said, "*I* will give you away!"

They were who I wanted to be. They were the models for me of a perfect family. They were the models for me of a marriage. The image I always pictured—and we talked about this all the time— was the image of a dining table that was full of love and always ready to include one person more. And I took that absolutely whole. I based my life on that, and I think I still do.

I got married and went to live in Mexico, and the next summer they sent us plane tickets so that I could come up and read to Grandmama. Hugh and Madeleine also sent us money for plane tickets to be with them for Christmas. That was lovely. Later, when things got really bad in my marriage, I would call Madeleine collect, practically every other day, for weeks and weeks. And both Madeleine and Hugh were incredible supports to me at that time. I wrote to her and she wrote to me.

*Q: When your marriage ended and you came back to New York from Mexico in 1979, did you see Madeleine often?*

A: Yes, I would see her about once a week. We had corresponded at least once a week while I was living in Mexico, so she knew all about my life there. I would go up to see her at the cathedral and talk. Occasionally, I would have lunch with her and Canon West. She was a mainstay for me, not only in advice and good company, but also in joy and light.

After Hugh died, I spent much more time with her. I think she was very lonely. There were many times when my sons and I would go with her to the airport and keep her company until she boarded her plane for one of her many speaking engagements. We would just sit with her, chatting, because she didn't like to be alone. She increased the pace of her speaking trips, and I think she did that because she missed Hugh so much. I would say, "We never get to see you. You're traveling all the time!" It was exhausting, but I think she missed Hugh so much that it was better to keep busy by traveling.

It was after Hugh died that Charlotte and Léna came to live with Madeleine, just as they were both starting college, and that made her very happy. She welcomed all these young people into her house—Charlotte and Léna and their friends, and also my two sons and their friends, who were all in high school at the time. My sons and I had Thanksgiving with Madeleine after Hugh died, and we also saw her at Christmas.

Madeleine loved Christmas, and she was very good at it. We loved to sing Christmas carols together, rejoicing in the fact that we knew the second verses of many of our favorites. We would both get very excited when we came upon a new carol. Every present I received from her came with a poem she had written specifically for that present! They were silly poems, for the most part, but some were serious. Once when I asked her to write me a birthday poem, she pulled out a list, a schedule that had been put together by the Episcopal Church of other churches to pray for. She took the first letter of the name of each church on the list and began the first word of each line of the poem with that letter. I do have to add that the presents were sometimes very odd! She was a master of re-gifting! Once she gave my ten-year-old son a yellow apron from Africa. Hugh commented that Eduardo was extremely polite, not only for accepting the gift, but for thanking her for it.

Dinner was important because I think she felt it was a sacrament. The sharing of food and friendship around the dinner table was the foretaste of heaven and a symbol of the love that holds together the universe. She would often have ten guests over for dinner: priests, musicians, and writers. She was a great hostess, and we had happy times around the dining room table. We would play word games, Botticelli, for example. Hugh had invented word games, and Madeleine had a game where you would choose a famous writer and redo his or her name; for instance: "Who is Everybed?" "Louisa May *Alcott*." We sang a lot. We told jokes.

Here is a joke that Madeleine once told me: "Jesus needed a new robe, so he went to the local man and said, 'I need a new robe. Can you make me one using this pattern?' The man said, 'Sure, come back tomorrow and I'll have it ready for you.' Jesus returned the next day, and when he saw his new robe, he was so pleased that he said to the man, 'This is magnificent! This is wonderful!' 'You know, Jesus,' the man replied, 'we could go into business together. We could call ourselves Jesus and Solomon.' To which Jesus replied, 'Hmm. Better yet, let's call ourselves Lord and Tailor.'"

She was often, although not always, a very good cook. Once I made for her a Mexican green chili dish with green tomatillos and jalapeños and softened by sour cream. Madeleine loved it, and so I gave her the recipe. Years later when she made the dish herself, she would put in anything green, just so that it became green sauce. But it did not taste the same!

*Q: Tell me about her seventieth birthday party, which took place in the fall of 1988.*

A: The story that Madeleine often told about her seventieth birthday party was that Charlotte had announced that she thought Madeleine should have a big seventieth birthday party and that she was going to make all the arrangements and invite all of Madeleine's friends. Madeleine said, "That's lovely, Charlotte. Who's going to pay for this?" And Charlotte said, "Well, *you* are, Gran!" Charlotte worked devotedly on the party with great attention to every detail. I believe she felt that Madeleine should have a big celebration while she was still vital and healthy enough to enjoy it. The party was held in Synod Hall at the cathedral, which is a great medieval-style hall, on Tuesday evening, November 29. It was beautifully catered with food everywhere. Madeleine, sitting next to Canon West, was enthroned near the stage as a hundred or more of her friends, who had come from as far away as Hawaii, stood in line to hug her, give her presents, and wish her happy birthday. My two friends and I, who played in a music group together, gave her the present of a performance of medieval music, which I introduced by saying, "The pieces we are about to play were performed in the court of Alfonso the Tenth of Spain. For this evening, Madeleine is the queen of the court." It was a beautiful party. She had a wonderful time.

*Q: Canon West died a little over a year later.*

A: His death was a disaster. Madeleine was really angry at him for dying—angry for abandoning her, which is a normal human response. She was devastated, partly because he didn't take care of himself. I worked for him for a very short while before Don Lundquist came along, and he would ask me to run up to the kitchen and start the chili. I would say, "But, Canon West, you're not supposed to be eating red meat." And he'd say, "It's not red when you cook it, Duckie." He called everybody Duckie. He had said to me, so I'm sure he said it to Madeleine too, "You know, Duckie, I am going to live for a very long time. I know these things." Usually, he *did* know.

Madeleine always had lots of friends and family around her, but only a few people who were on her level of intellect and spiritual development: people with whom she could share who she really was. After Canon West died, I think she closed up a lot and she stopped talking about a great many things.

Then, when Bion died in 1999, she really started to go downhill. I made an effort to see her more often. Over the next few years, many of the people she had known drifted away. She could no longer be the gracious hostess she once had been. When I went to see her, I would bring food and do the cooking, or we would order Chinese. At dinner she would be very quiet—not the sparkling hostess, full of fun, I had known before, who loved to talk and tell jokes and play silly games.

I think she often worried about the diminishment of old age. More than once I had heard her say, in earlier years, "When I am old, put me on an ice floe and send me out into the Arctic, as the Eskimos do!" That seemed utterly heartless to me then, but I think, in the end, she might have preferred it!

Luci Shaw is a poet, lecturer, writing workshop leader, and, with Madeleine L'Engle, the co-author of *Friends for the Journey* (1997). She co-founded Harold Shaw Publishers, where she published several of L'Engle's books, and later served as that firm's president.

*Q: How did you meet Madeleine L'Engle?*

A: We met in Illinois at Wheaton College, which is a Christian liberal arts college with a renowned English department. Wheaton hosts an annual language and literature conference. One year in the early 1970s Madeleine and I were both invited as speakers. That was my first exposure to Madeleine. We clicked immediately and exchanged books. I gave her a book of my poetry called *Listen to the Green*, and Madeleine gave me a copy of a book she had just published, *A Circle of Quiet*, and signed a copy for me. After that, we started to correspond. Of course, Madeleine had many, many correspondents, and she knew a great many people. But that was the beginning of a close and wonderful friendship for us both.

*Q: What were your first impressions of Madeleine?*

A: She was a presence, such a dramatic person. She was a tall woman, and she commanded attention. She had the most remarkable, exotic clothes. There was a kind of magnetism about her.

And she was warm and generous in her approach to people. Other conference speakers could be rather forbidding, but Madeleine welcomed response and conversation.

As we got to know each other, we found that we had a lot in common. We both loved the color green. We both loved Bach, and we both played Bach on the piano. We both loved comfort food like pea soup, which of course is green! These sound like trivialities, but they served as points of contact at the beginning.

Madeleine had published a book of poems called *Lines Scribbled on an Envelope* that had gone out of print because it had not been particularly well publicized or advertised. I am a poet, and my husband and I had just started a publishing company and had decided to publish good poetry by poets of faith. So I asked Madeleine if she would like us to bring her book back into print. I told her that we would make all the necessary arrangements with her agent and that there would be room in the new edition for some of her more recent poems. Madeleine's response was immediate. "Oh, that would be wonderful!" she said. That was the beginning of our relationship as editor and writer.

We called the book *The Weather of the Heart*, and Madeleine was very pleased with what we had done with her poetry and the format and the cover. It was a beautiful little book. I then asked her to write a book reflecting on the relationship of Christianity and the arts. About six months later, when she was staying with us, she presented me with a rather large, untidy manuscript and said, "It has no shape. Can you do something with it?" For the next few weeks, I sort of went into seclusion, which was a little difficult because I also had our five children to look after. Soon my living room floor was covered with piles of her manuscript pages, and I cut and pasted and reordered the whole thing into a coherent sequence. That was *Walking on Water*, which became a bestseller and is still in print.

Madeleine's husband, Hugh Franklin, was delighted with what we had done, and he advocated that we become the publisher for her books about her faith and Christianity. Not the novels, of course, which Farrar, Straus and Giroux continued to publish.

*Q: Did you get together with her fairly often during the first years that you knew her?*

A: One time she was at Wheaton when she heard the news that her older granddaughter, Léna, had been injured in an accident and nearly lost her life.* I remember taking Madeleine to a nearby park and just sitting and talking with her and praying with her for the recovery of her granddaughter. She was very grateful for that. I think after that incident she realized that we were friends in a more than casual way. My husband was in Sweden just then, and he brought back a beautiful, large, but simple silver cross, which I gave Madeleine as a token of our friendship and of my concern for her family.

*Q: I think I saw her wearing that cross at a book party, about fifteen years ago.*

A: Yes, she wore it often. It was one of her favorites. Madeleine loved jewelry. We often exchanged earrings, and when I would visit her in New York, she would always wear earrings I had given her. She remembered who had given her what.

My office here at home is full of things that Madeleine gave me. I have wall hangings and all kinds of tokens that she would send me for my birthday and for Christmas. We were almost exactly ten years apart in age. Her birthday was November 29 and mine is December 29, and so we always kept those dates in mind and often celebrated together.

*Q: Would you describe one or two of the other things she gave you that you keep in your office?*

*Memories vary as to L'Engle's whereabouts when the news reached her of her granddaughter's accident. See pages 171 and 185.

A: Well, she gave me a beautiful glass figurine of the Virgin Mary and Jesus that stands on the windowsill. She gave me a gargoyle—"to keep things from getting too holy!" She also gave me one of those faceted crystals that can hang in a window. I call it my light catcher. That was very much what Madeleine symbolized for me. She reflected light from different angles of understanding and perception—more so than any of the other fine writers I have known. The way she looked at life, her understanding seemed to be unique, fresh, original.

*Q: Your religious background was somewhat different from hers, wasn't it?*

A: Yes, I came from a fundamentalist background. Both my parents had been in the Plymouth Brethren, which is a very conservative Christian group, where women have no voice and have to be in submission. Madeleine of course had an Episcopalian background. Her parents, I believe, were both Episcopalians. I became an Episcopalian, not because of Madeleine, but simply because that became to me a place where my gender didn't matter and where I would be able to use my gifts, whatever they were, for the benefit of the church congregation. We found a meeting place between her left-ish, liberal Christianity and my right-ish, conservative Christianity. We sort of met in the middle. I think we both contributed a new dimension to each other's faith.

*Q: When did you become an Episcopalian?*

A: Nineteen eighty-five.

*Q: Were any of the people associated with St. John the Divine involved in your training?*

A: No. At that point we lived in Illinois, and Madeleine lived in New York City. I once did an Advent retreat at St. John the Divine, but my association with the cathedral was as a visitor and a communicant. When I visited Madeleine, we would always go at noon for Communion to St. Martin's Chapel in the cathedral.

*Q: Did you meet Canon West?*

A: No, but he was a figure shimmering in the background of our conversation. I knew of course that he was Madeleine's spiritual adviser and great friend, and I learned a lot about him from her references, but I never met him.

*Q: Do many Episcopalians have spiritual advisers, or was her relationship with him an unusual one?*

A: It was a little bit unusual for the time. More recently, people have been turning in a spiritual direction and to spiritual counseling in a way that had been quite common in the Catholic Church but not so much among the Protestant denominations. I have benefited greatly from a spiritual director and rely a great deal on the counsel and prayer with that person. When I was living in Chicago, the Episcopal presiding bishop, Frank Griswold, was my spiritual director for several years. For Madeleine, I think it was a mutual thing. Edward West cared for Madeleine, and he learned from her as well as her learning from him.

*Q: He was an authority on liturgical matters, and I wonder if you think that might have appealed to Madeleine's sense of drama?*

A: Well, the sacraments are very dramatic in their enactment. That was a part of what drew me to the Episcopal Church—that show-and-tell aspect—the kneeling in veneration, crossing oneself, and standing: it's a very bodily, incarnational way of worship. Liturgy has become very important to me, as it was to Madeleine. In fact both of us were friends with Alice Parker, who is a composer who became quite well-known for getting congregations to learn to sing as choirs. She was the arranger for the Robert Shaw Chorale, and Madeleine and I attended a conference in New York where she was getting poets and writers together with composers to try to write new hymns and other new material for the church. That was a very interesting three-way friendship. We were all somewhat of the same age and same kind of musical background. I would say this happened about twenty-five years ago, at Grace Church, in Greenwich Village.

Madeleine and I often took part in a conference at Laity Lodge, a secluded retreat center in the Hill Country of Texas, and we watched the stars from there, too. To reach the retreat, you have to drive off the road and along the river. That was one of Madeleine's favorite places. Writers, creative people, people who wanted a spiritual dimension to their work, would gather there for retreats. It would be quite a diverse group.

Madeleine had fans who would show up wherever she was scheduled to speak, and I think this was a bit of a struggle for her. Everybody wanted a piece of Madeleine. Everybody wanted to be counted as a close friend. Because she was so generous and warm-hearted, she had many, many friends. She said that some people viewed her more as some kind of hero rather than as a real person. And it is true that when you are famous, you are on a pedestal that removes you from the real life that you live. It becomes hard for the other person to understand that you can be tired or cranky or quixotic, all of which Madeleine often was.

*Q: Later in her life Madeleine started going to a church in New York called All Angels'. Why do you think she wanted or needed a church other than the cathedral?*

A: All Angels' is an Episcopal church. On the scale of things, it is more conservative than the cathedral. It is a smaller but wonderfully friendly church, and Madeleine was very much involved there. She was on the vestry, and the rector, Colin Goode, was a friend of both of us. She had a monthly dinner with several of the parishioners. She became their close friends, and they in turn were a big help to her in the later years of her life, when she was unable to live a full life.

St. John the Divine is huge. She had friends there too, of course, but I think she wanted something more like fellowship and a less formal way of worship. All Angels' is in an upstairs hall that used to be a union hall. It welcomed artists and actors and street people. Madeleine was drawn to these people because they were so real and so warm. They were flawed human beings, and she found that she could be a flawed human being there too, whereas at the cathedral she was viewed as an icon.

*Q: In* Friends for the Journey, *you say you asked Madeleine what she wanted for her seventy-fifth birthday, and it turned out to be a trip.*

A: We had a belated celebration, in the summer of 1994. I had a little house in Bellingham, Washington. Madeleine flew into Seattle, and she stayed with us there for about a week. Then we drove up into the Canadian Rockies. It was all rather funny. We had booked our hotels in advance without bothering to find out how good they were. As a result, we stayed in some pretty funky places! Madeleine hated cigarette smoke, and some of our motels just reeked of smoke. We made up for all that, however, by staying in a fantastic resort in Jasper National Park. We had ten lovely days together that summer.

At one point as we drove along, we stopped by a lake to enjoy the view, and I managed to lock us out of our car. I had to hitch a ride in a truck to the nearest town for help. Hours passed, and Madeleine, seated on the bench in the viewing area, gamely awaited my return. She was such a good sport. By then, she was walking with a cane. Even so, the two of us walked all around Lake Louise. I was tired out, and she must have been exhausted, but she never complained.

*Q: Did she write while she was traveling with you?*

A: She did not bring her computer along on that trip, but she was certainly thinking about writing. She would suddenly fall silent, and I would know that she was forming an idea for a story or novel. This might last for some time, and I knew better than to interrupt her.

*Q: In 1995, you took another trip.*

A: We went to Ireland, where Madeleine was speaking at a

children's literature conference.* A close mutual friend, Barbara Braver, accompanied us on that trip. We drove around Ireland, then took the ferry to England. In the Lake District we visited Beatrix Potter's house and Wordsworth's house, Dove Cottage. We visited the island of Iona. Then we made our way down to London.

*Q: What did Madeleine like best about traveling?*

A: She loved the scenery and was intensely interested in the history of the places we visited. She loved being driven! Madeleine had a driver's license, but she hardly ever drove. People did not encourage her to do so, because she might get engaged in conversation and drift a little to one side of the road. We had a habit, whenever I visited her at Crosswicks, of going out for a drive in the afternoon. She'd say, "Let's just take the first right turn, then the first left turn, and the next right, and see where we end up!" I would be a little afraid of losing Madeleine L'Engle in the wilds of Connecticut, of not being able to bring her home again, but she loved adventures like that.

*Q: Was it on that second trip that the idea for you and her to collaborate on* Friends for the Journey *was first discussed?*

A: It came about gradually. It was certainly part of our conversation, and Barbara was a big help in working out the schema of the book. It grew organically out of our friendship and the experiences we shared.

*Q: Is it possible to say whose idea it was?*

A: As a publisher, it was probably mine. I wanted to do a book from which people could learn about friendship. We found that our own friendship could be a good model for people who want to maintain a friendship while living far apart.

*L'Engle was a featured speaker that year at Children's Literature New England's annual summer conference, which was held at Trinity College, Dublin.

*Q: Did you and Madeleine go on tour together?*

A: We did a number of public conversations, including one at the Sheldonian Theatre, at Oxford. Two wing chairs had been set out, and a table with two cups of tea. Madeleine would say something, and I'd respond. Then I would say something, and Madeleine would respond. It flowed very naturally. We would surprise each other and ourselves by the turns the conversation took.

I had wanted to call our book "The Table of Friendship" because we spent so much time together at tables: playing Scrabble, playing Ping-Pong, sharing meals. For both of us the Communion table was a primary metaphor for friendship. We both hated the multiplication table! And Madeleine nixed the title because, she said, she disliked the multiplication table so much!

*Q: Where did you play Ping-Pong?*

A: At Laity Lodge. Madeleine was a formidable player. She had such reach! She would advance upon the Ping-Pong table like a ship in full sail and demolish her opponent. She liked to win at Scrabble too, and of course she had a huge vocabulary and an etymological dictionary so we could research word origins.

*Q: Your husband and Madeleine's husband died in the same year. Going through that experience as friends must have brought you closer.*

A: Very much so. Both men died of cancer, and so our emotions and responses at that time were very similar. We did a lot of cross-continental phoning, asking for prayer and sharing our sorrow—or our jubilation when some test turned out better than expected. That was a bonding experience.

*Q: Do you recall the article that appeared about Madeleine in* The New Yorker?

A: Yes, that was very troubling for many of us. The thing I liked best was the full-page cartoon of Madeleine, which was perfect.* But the fact that some of the family members aired the

*The caricature of Madeleine L'Engle was by Tullio Pericoli.

family dirty linen in front of the public was horrifying to us. Not that it was all false, but we just didn't see how it was helpful. There was a lot of correspondence back and forth. At that point I don't think Madeleine cared one way or the other. She was so used to being in the public eye and having interviews and articles published about her. I don't know that she even read it very carefully. But there was a lot of buzz among her friends about that article. It felt cheapening, demeaning, a betrayal. One thing that that article said that was true was that in Madeleine's memory the plots for her novels and the events of her real life sometimes got confused. She would conflate her own life experiences and the experiences of her characters. I think that that was the first sign of a mental deterioration that took place in the final years.

*Q: You see it more in that way rather than as simply what fiction writers do?*

A: Well, I'm sure that that was part of it, too.

*Q: Do you see Madeleine as belonging to a particular tradition of religious writers?*

A: She was a contemplative writer. She loved George Mac-Donald's writings and his philosophy of life. Like him, she was a Universalist. She believed that in the end every human soul would be redeemed and "join the party" in heaven. Madeleine's Universalism alarmed some conservative theologians. My feeling is that if it was a heresy, it was a wonderful heresy!

*Q: Was her work well-known in England at the time that you and she spoke together at Oxford?*

A: It became more widely known partly because of her appearances at Oxford and Cambridge. But no, she was not known there at first, whereas in the United States almost anyone you talk to has read *A Wrinkle in Time.*

*Q: Did you first read* A Wrinkle in Time *as an adult?*

A: Yes, I did. My youngest daughter was in elementary school, about eight or nine, and her class was reading *A Wrinkle in Time.*

The school was just across the fence from our house in West Chicago, and by coincidence Madeleine was visiting with us. This would have been about 1979. One day, Madeleine was walking down our front walk, and Kristin caught sight of her through the window at school. She stood up in class and said, "Oh, look, there's Madeleine L'Engle now!" This caused quite a sensation.

*Q: Were you at the memorial gathering for Madeleine in Goshen?*

A: Yes, I spoke at that. I had been planning to go to Florence on vacation when the news came of Madeleine's death. So I canceled my trip and was able to fly into Connecticut and be part of that gathering at the little church in Goshen. So many friends came together, with so many memories of Madeleine. It was a beautiful day.

The pastor told a funny story. He said that when Madeleine came to church there, she would always sit in one of the very last pews, directly under the light switches by the door. On days when she thought the congregation needed more spiritual enlightenment, Madeleine would reach up and switch on the lights.

Barbara Braver retired in 2006 after serving for eighteen years as assistant for communication to the presiding bishop of the Episcopal Church.

*Q: How did you meet Madeleine L'Engle?*

A: I met Madeleine in 1984 or 1985 when she gave a retreat for clergy in the Episcopal Diocese of Massachusetts. At that time I was the communications director for the diocese and also did some freelance writing. When I discovered Madeleine L'Engle was going to be with us for several days, I arranged to interview and photograph her for *The Christian Century.*

The best time to take Madeleine's picture turned out to be during her rest period between sessions, and I remember being a little chary about interrupting her rest, especially as I was some-what in awe of her! But Madeleine said, "Oh no. That's fine. Come on over." We had a marvelous conversation, and I still have the photo I took of her that afternoon—propped up on one elbow on her bed, wearing a granny-style smock. She was grinning and in a playful mood. It was all so comfortable. Madeleine was ap-proachable and down-to-earth—so apparently candid, and so very present. I had a sense we might become friends.

After the retreat we corresponded and talked on the phone from time to time. We found we had many things in common, including that my son and Madeleine's granddaughter Charlotte were both about to graduate from Northfield Mount Hermon School, in Mount Hermon, Massachusetts. We discussed the possibility of attending the graduation together. Then Hugh became ill, and she couldn't go. Another time, when Madeleine was leading a writers' retreat at Holy Cross Monastery in West Park, New York, I signed up for it and picked Madeleine up at Crosswicks and drove her there.

In 1988, I took a new job as assistant for communication for the presiding bishop of the Episcopal Church. The national office of the Episcopal Church is in midtown Manhattan, but my husband and I were not about to move from Massachusetts, so I commuted to work, spending a few days each week in the city. When I was in New York, if Madeleine wasn't off traveling somewhere, we would often have dinner together and perhaps go to the ballet.

For a time I shared an apartment for my overnight stays in married student housing at General Theological Seminary. One evening I had Madeleine in stitches describing how my pleasant but rather hapless roommate had a way of trailing me around when I was trying to accomplish something, chatting on about fascinating things, such as how long it took her iron to heat. At this, Madeleine interrupted my tale and invited me to come and live with her. She said she was not meant to live alone in her enormous space, and now that Charlotte and Léna had left, she prayed the right person would come along. We talked about it, and I thought about it, and in the end that's what I did. For the next twelve years I lived with Madeleine in her West End Avenue apartment. It was a grace-filled situation and so much fun. We talked and prayed and laughed and cooked and ate together often when we were both in New York. We were completely at ease with each other, and I think it was in part because, as Madeleine would say it, "You love me, but thank God, you do not *adore* me." That is, I was a friend and not a fan.

Madeleine was impatient with technology, and the results

were often amusing. I remember her being quite frustrated trying to learn the ins and outs of a new computer. When the message on the computer screen required her to click "OK," Madeleine would call out in an exasperated voice, "It is NOT okay, and I'm NOT going to say it is!" Once when we were at Crosswicks and she was having a particularly difficult computer moment, she declared, "I am going to *find* a goose, and *kill* it, and *take* one of its feathers, and *make* myself a quill pen! I will not use this computer!" I laughed, of course, and so did she, and she persisted with the computer.

She could find amusement in ordinary domestic situations and was very good at laughing at herself. One of her most quoted remarks is "I take the Bible too seriously to take it all literally." In the same way, she took her life too seriously to take it too moment-by-moment literally. Perhaps that is one reason why she made such a distinction between fact and truth. Something might be factually correct but still lead you to the wrong conclusion.

In the summer of 1995, I was on sabbatical, so Madeleine and Luci Shaw and I decided to treat ourselves to a trip, with the holy islands of Iona and Lindisfarne as special destinations. I volunteered my husband to research good places to stay, and he found some absolutely marvelous old inns for us. I told Luci and Madeleine all about them, including the cost. Well, I got the dollar-to-pound conversion rate backward, so everything actually cost two and one-half times more than I had thought! I realized my error after bookings were made. Madeleine and Luci thought this very funny, and we all believed it was a gift that we had quite accidentally splashed out for ourselves. We never regretted our luxurious journey. Madeleine wrote about this fortunate error in *Bright Evening Star*. In retrospect, now that we are no longer making memories of what Madeleine called our "trinity of friendship," I am so grateful it all sorted out as it did. So many memories—mostly of visits to holy places, those "thin" places where one seems particularly in touch with the transcendent reality that is all around.

Madeleine was a very disciplined person—particularly with regard to her work. She carefully structured her day: getting up in the morning, making her bed, dressing, having breakfast, going to her office at the cathedral, and so on. That was the framework. In *A Wrinkle in Time*, one of Madeleine's wise characters, Mrs Whatsit, compares our lives to a sonnet: a strict form, but with freedom within it. As Mrs Whatsit says: "You're given the form, but you have to write the sonnet yourself. What you say is completely up to you." She had the structure, and within that there would be distractions and surprises: welcome and often stretching, and full of grace.

When she was writing (which she often was in some form—even when she was to all appearances chopping onions), she allowed her imagination to take her where it would. She called this "riding the wind." She even allowed her characters to surprise her.

Madeleine believed that what is at the center of the universe—its animating force for good, one might say—is love. This certainly comes across in *A Wrinkle in Time*, and her other writings are shot through with it as well. Madeleine understood that love to be the essence of God. She knew that something big is always trying to happen: love is trying to shine forth, to be manifested, and we are meant to cooperate with that effort. As a collect in the Episcopal Church's Book of Common Prayer would have it: "Direct us to the fulfilling of your purpose." Madeleine must have prayed that prayer thousands of times.

She would also say that everybody had their part in serving God's larger purposes. She was faithful and intentional about trying to discern what her part in it all was. She often said, "I'm not called to be Shakespeare. I'm called to be Madeleine L'Engle. I'm called to write what I can write." And she believed that about the rest of us too: we are called to be who we are and write what we can write. She understood that if you're wide-awake and alert to the life around you, then stories will occur to you—stories that nobody but you can tell. I think her sense about all this explains in part why she encouraged so many people to write and led all those workshops, why she relished being a mentor—something she was good at and had an instinct for.

Madeleine was a sacramental person, by which I mean that objects had meaning because of their connections—to memories, to particular people. Sacraments are outer and visible signs that point beyond themselves. So her possessions weren't just *things* in themselves. They signified something. She had them around her not simply because they were useful, or beautiful, but because of the memories they held: what they pointed to. That mattered more than their monetary value. The apartment was full of the treasures of memory, and so many photographs. Photographs were important to her because the people in the photographs were important to her.

It was a delight to share Madeleine's space with her and in so doing to share something of her life in its richness, and by that I mean what was sad, painful, and difficult as well as what was joyful and life-giving. I recall those years with great joy, as well as sadness at relinquishing what had been. However, Madeleine understood impermanence and that you can't clutch on to joy—and so do I. One season turns into another.

Mira Rothenberg is a psychologist specializing in the treatment of autistic and other severely disturbed children and is the author of *Children with Emerald Eyes*.

*Q: How did you meet Madeleine L'Engle?*

A: Madeleine knew about me before I knew about her. I had written a book called *Children with Emerald Eyes*, in which I described my work with autistic and schizophrenic children, and Madeleine had read it. She knew that I was working with the child of a friend of hers, and at some point she decided she would pay that child's bills. So at first the only thing I knew about Madeleine was that she was the person from whom I was receiving a check. Finally, we decided we should meet. I came to her house and we talked for a little while, and—just like that—we became close, close friends.

Thinking that I would one day do another book, I was writing a series of articles at the time about Lithuania and the persecutions of the Jews there. I was also fighting to get back my land and houses in Lithuania. And I was lecturing at the University of Vilna (where I am from) about autism and how to work with these kinds of children, and I was helping the Lithuanian government to set up centers for severely disturbed children in the SOS villages.*

*Founded in 1949, SOS Children's Villages is an independent, nongovernmen-

For all these reasons, I visited Lithuania periodically—seven times in all—and each time on my return home I would write down my impressions of what I had seen and also fill in the historical background. This had started out as a series of articles for a Jewish magazine. Madeleine was fascinated, and whenever I saw her after that, she would ask me to bring her the latest article for her to read. She was always urging me to turn my articles into a book.

Madeleine would tell me about her family's life in the South, their role in the Revolutionary War and later the Civil War. She knew all about her family history and was very into it all. In her apartment she had old family portraits and several beautiful pieces of family silver. One time she told me the story of how the silver had been buried during the Civil War to hide it from the enemy. It was all so fascinating to me because I had no relatives at all, as all had been killed in World War II, whereas Madeleine had a past—a past that went back, back, back. Madeleine had a history!

I visited her quite often at her apartment. By the time that I met Madeleine, she only "sort of" liked to cook, and I found her kitchen to be an odd combination of "missing things" and "having things." Whenever I would come to visit, she would give me one of her books.

I was running a treatment center in Brooklyn for autistic and schizophrenic children, and we talked a lot about that. We talked especially about the common perception of autism and schizophrenia: how silly it was, and how out of tune it was with the reality that these children were in fact treatable.

Toward the beginning of our friendship, I needed to have an operation. As a get-well present, Madeleine gave me some stones, on each of which she had written a word. One stone, for example,

---

tal development organization that works throughout the world to provide for the basic needs and to protect the rights of children.

said "Wisdom." While I was recuperating, another friend brought me a copy of *A Wrinkle in Time*. I read it twice from cover to cover. At first, I could not connect the book to her. But after that, we became even better friends.

I went to hear her give a sermon at St. John the Divine. Then we started going out to dinner, to the theater, to the ballet. Usually, it would be just the two of us. When she could no longer walk, her assistant or her daughter would come and push the wheelchair, and we would go down to Henry's for dinner.

Madeleine would tell me about her marriage to Hugh and about all her adopted children—the children, that is, that she adopted in spirit. There seemed to be quite a few of them. She had their photographs up on her apartment walls. It was not, I think, that she needed so many children. My hunch is that she would meet somebody and immediately see his or her need. That would be it for her. She was very alert to anybody who needed help. We recognized that quality in each other, and it was one of the reasons we connected.

We would talk about philosophy, religion. I told Madeleine stories about the first few years of my life, when I was looked after by a Polish peasant woman who couldn't read or write and did not even own a pair of shoes but would simply wrap her feet in paper. She took care of me and was very warm and kind to me. I learned from my peasant woman that religion was not in ritual but in actual living. I grew up wanting to be like that woman, even though I also wanted to be like my mother, who was a beautiful and educated Jewish woman, a dentist with a good singing voice. I think that Madeleine must have had someone in her life like that woman too.

*Q: Yes, she did—her childhood nanny, Mrs. O.*

A: Madeleine was fascinated with the fact that I picked mushrooms, that I knew which were the poisonous mushrooms and which were the ones that were good to eat. I had learned to do this from my Polish peasant woman.

We talked about how wasteful and idiotic religious dogma was. I am a Holocaust survivor, and Madeleine identified with all of us, the injured ones, philosophically and religiously. I'm Jewish. She was Christian. We understood each other so well despite how different we were. I think we were both just looking for a human connection.

I was busy with my clinic at the time that my son was little. One day at a gathering at the nursery school he attended, they asked each of the parents how many children we had. When it was my turn to answer, I said without thinking, "I have twenty children." Everyone looked at me as if I had just fallen out of a tree! So then I said, "I mean I have one child." "So, which is it?" someone demanded. "Well," I replied, "it is really *both*."

I had all these autistic and schizy kids who lived in my house. Who had the time to bother about *whose* kids they were? They were *kids*. It was also through our not needing to differentiate between "my kids" and "other people's kids" that Madeleine and I really connected.

*Q: Did Madeleine consider writing about child characters like the children you have worked with?*

A: In a way, her child characters are *all* like them. If you read her books, the kids she writes about all have two sides to them.

*Q: Both Meg and Charles Wallace are misjudged as slow learners. And Madeleine would often say, "I am Meg."*

A: I would tell Madeleine that the people who think the kids I work with are dumb are nowhere near as smart as those kids are.

I am now working on that book about Lithuania. Madeleine wrote the introduction to it. The piece she wrote—unlike the book itself—is all about the Holocaust. In it, she describes a girl who was faced with a terrible choice. She could either go to the right or go to the left. Because she chose left, she survived. This was a story from out of the blue. It was not a story that I had ever told Madeleine, and it had nothing directly to do with my book. Yet it also had everything to do with it. It was a very surprising thing to both of us, this friendship of ours.

# THOMAS CAHILL

Thomas Cahill, a former director of religious publishing at Doubleday, is the author of the Hinges of History series, a wide-ranging chronicle of the founding and development of Western civilization, and other books.

*Q: When did you meet Madeleine L'Engle?*

A: I met her in about 1980. My family and I went to a Catholic church in Greenwich Village called St. Joseph's, which had a Vespers series during the weeks before Christmas for which I was asked to invite a number of guest preachers. Madeleine L'Engle was one of the people I invited, and she said yes.

In a sense, my first meeting with Madeleine had been my reading of *A Wrinkle in Time* to my daughter. In that period, unlike today, there were not all that many interesting books for adventurous girls like my daughter. *A Wrinkle in Time* was a real "wow" for her, and we followed it up by reading the rest of the Time trilogy. It was obvious to me from those books that Madeleine's view of religion was extremely broad. I could also see how much she had absorbed from the great Western tradition and how deeply she cared about it, as did I. It was on that basis that I had invited Madeleine to speak at St. Joseph's. After the sermon or homily that she gave, my wife, Susan, and I took her and her husband, Hugh, out to dinner. And that was the beginning of my friendship with Madeleine.

*Q: What were your impressions of her?*

A: Meeting the author of a book you find extraordinary can be a great disappointment. But Madeleine in person seemed just like her books: she had the same openness of manner, the same breadth in her frame of reference. As I got to know her better, I learned that she had grown up not only as an only child but also as a very lonely child. I'm sure her parents thought they had done right by her. But all that loneliness had its effect on Madeleine. It left her feeling secretly awkward—maybe "hesitant" is a better word—with people. In some ways, it put her at a disadvantage in really close relationships. Family life was always difficult for her. Madeleine would make an effort to put everyone else at ease, but she herself was never at ease. Yet she covered her discomfort up with a genuine warmth that was also a learned warmth. She had been an actress. She knew how to play a part. She had so many followers, so many people who were absolutely crazy about her and thought her magical. She had to learn how to deal with their adoration, too.

Madeleine had a very good sense of what is called in theology "Christian incarnationalism," which is the notion that the significance in ordinary lives of God becoming man is that everything is divinized in some sense. *All* bread is divine. *All* wine is divine. It's not just what takes place in the little ritual at the altar. *All* human beings are incarnations of God. I think she really believed that and that it propelled her notionally toward other people, almost before she would have been drawn to them at the gut level. Maybe that was a part of what I saw, the disjunction between her beliefs and her own abilities. Certainly her many female followers were completely unaware of that side of her. They didn't see the hesitancy at all. What I find so admirable about Madeleine is that she was largely successful at disguising it.

Madeleine herself idealized some people—Canon West, for

example—and she idealized her son, Bion, who was the model for Rob Austin. I knew Bion as an adult and seldom saw him with Madeleine. But when I did see them together, they seemed like a team. He seemed to second her opinions on everything and would be almost *too* polite: "That's right, Mother . . ." At least that was my impression. When Bion and I were alone, he would be more negative about his mother.

*Q: When you and Madeleine got together, what would you talk about?*

A: Madeleine and I often talked about literature. She would not want to talk about the book she had just read. She would want to talk about the great books. She'd be interested in having a long conversation about Sir Thomas Browne. Once Madeleine told me about her student days at Smith College and recalled her work on the literary magazine with Betty Friedan. Smith had probably come up in the context of talking about Friedan's books. Madeleine said that Betty Friedan didn't understand literature. She said that what she understood was bookkeeping!

At the time that Madeleine and I met, my wife and I had a mail-order business called Cahill & Company. Through our Reader's Catalog, we sold books as well as literary greeting cards, calendars, things like that. Very often Madeleine would have a whole page in the catalog, and she liked it so much that at one point she told me that she wanted to invest in the company, which I let her do. When Cahill & Company went bankrupt in the mid-1980s, she lost all the money she had invested. I was very upset about that, but all Madeleine ever said about it was "It's only money." Her response to the bankruptcy was one of the most extraordinarily generous things that anyone had ever done for me.

Madeleine liked having a beautiful house in the country, but she did not have a moneyed appreciation of beautiful things. She didn't like things because they were expensive. She was a real celebrator of the beautiful and the good, a humanist in the Renaissance sense. Most people would have a hard time saying, "It's only money." But Madeleine lived her stated beliefs in a way that most people are not capable of.

She is one of the people to whom I dedicated my book *Sailing the Wine-Dark Sea: Why the Greeks Matter*. I had dedicated the first three books in my series the Hinges of History to my wife and two children. *Sailing the Wine-Dark Sea* was the fourth book, and I wanted to dedicate it to the people who had been the greatest influences on me. It's a strange list: Desmond and Leah Tutu, Pauline Kael, and Madeleine L'Engle. In my dedication, I call them "mentors and models of life and art." Each is there for a different reason: the *New Yorker* film critic Pauline Kael for having taught me to say what I mean and not beat around the bush about it; the Tutus for the incredible courage they had shown throughout all the years of their opposition to apartheid, when at any moment they or their family might have been killed.

I included Madeleine because of her kindness. Yes, the writing was great, but she was such an incredibly *kind* person. Our children both went to St. Hilda's & St. Hugh's, a private school on the Upper West Side of Manhattan. After the bankruptcy, we were in very bad straits financially, and Madeleine arranged for scholarships for both of them. In fact I think she paid for the scholarships, though she never said as much. She did a great many things of that sort and was always quiet about it.

I didn't see Madeleine much toward the end. Even before she went to the nursing home, it was harder and harder to be with her. When *Sailing the Wine-Dark Sea* was published in 2003, I brought her a boxful of copies for her to give to friends. She was already fading, and I was aware of the fact that there was something dim about her response.

The profile of Madeleine that appeared in *The New Yorker* the following year really shocked me. What shocked me was not whether this or that detail in the piece was true. What was said about Bion, for example, sounded more or less accurate. It would have been fine to say those things once she was gone. What shocked me was that Madeleine's family had talked about her in that way while Madeleine was still reading.

Susan Buckley is the author of *Journeys for Freedom*, *Kids Make History*, and other nonfiction books for young readers and is the editor of *AppleSeeds*, a social science magazine for children.

*Q: How did you meet Madeleine L'Engle?*

A: My three stepchildren, who came into my life in 1973, had all read *A Wrinkle in Time* and loved it. My first awareness of Madeleine and her books came to me through them. Then, sometime in the mid-1980s, Dana Catharine came to work for me on a project at the big book-packaging company CCI, where I was a vice president and project manager. Dana is quite a wonderful person, and we soon became friends as well as colleagues, and that is when I discovered that Dana was Madeleine's "god friend," as they both liked to say. Dana was not her official goddaughter, but Madeleine and Hugh had become close friends of hers after first meeting her at St. Hilda's & St. Hugh's, where Dana was their student. Dana is a close friend and contemporary of Josephine's and is the actual godmother of Léna. Then, in 1987, Madeleine was going to be giving one of the very first public lectures at the New York Public Library's newly restored Celeste Bartos Forum. Dana and I attended the lecture together, and afterward I was invited to accompany her to dinner at Madeleine's apartment. So that was how I first met her.

Madeleine's talk that night was fascinating. She described the trajectory of her career: how she had come to write her books and in particular *A Wrinkle in Time*, how she had coped with that book's many rejections, and what she had wanted to accomplish by writing it. I had not yet begun to write children's books and wanted very much to do so, so everything she had to say was of great interest to me. During the question-and-answer period at the library, some unsuspecting soul had walked up to the microphone and asked, "Ms. L'Engle, what made you decide to write children's books?" Whereupon Madeleine drew herself up to her full height and in her most imperious voice replied, "I do *not* write children's books!" A big crowd had turned out to hear Madeleine that evening. Now everybody gasped. Then, breaking the tension, Madeleine explained, "I just tell the story I want to tell. If it happens to be about children, people think of it as a children's book. But that isn't my intention."

Then we all traipsed over to Madeleine's apartment for dinner. There were about ten of us, including various friends of Dana's. The gathering had the atmosphere of a salon with Madelcine at the center holding forth. She was large-boned and rather heavy by then, but I could see that she had once been beautiful. It's always interesting to see how an aging beauty carries herself. I thought that Madeleine exuded a kind of pride in her past glory. She also struck me as a little scary because if you said something that she considered silly, she just cut you off. There was no trying to make the other person feel better. She told you exactly what she thought. She was a brilliant conversationalist, and if you were there, you too were expected to be witty and smart.

Madeleine and I never became friends, but I was so intrigued by her that I took any chance I could get to be around her. My husband, Peter Buckley, and I were invited to three or four parties at her home.* Peter, like Madeleine, was a well-traveled writer with a vast circle of friends, and the two of them immediately recognized each other as kindred spirits. Peter too could be quite imperious, and he always spoke his mind. They got along famously and would always sit next to each other at parties and be naughty together by commenting on everyone around them.

Madeleine was always good company, but I did not sense that she was an especially kind person. She could be very demanding, and she had lots of expectations for the people around her. And she would be so absolute about her likes and dislikes. None of these qualities make for a very nurturing mother, so it is not surprising that there were problems between Madeleine and her children.

My response to the *New Yorker* article was that it was absolutely horrifying, that the people who spoke to the reporter should not have done so while Madeleine was alive. I was also distressed by the atmosphere at Madeleine's funeral at St. John the Divine. The service was so cold—literally and figuratively. It's true that there had been another, more intimate funeral in Goshen for family and friends, where some of the people who were closest to Madeleine told stories about her. But still! You could have had all the solemnity and pomp and circumstance of the formal Mass and still have had two or three people speak about Madeleine from the heart. Just to make it a little more personal.

*Peter Hays Buckley was the author and photographer of *Bullfight* (1958), *Greek Island Boy* (1965), and other books.

# JAMES VANOOSTING

James VanOosting is a novelist, the author of *And the Flesh Became Word: Reflections Theological and Aesthetic*, and a professor of communication and media studies at Fordham University.

*Q: How did you meet Madeleine L'Engle?*

A: I met Madeleine in 1985 when I did a telephone interview with her for a tiny academic journal for college and high school teachers of speech and drama called the *Journal of the Illinois Speech and Theatre Association.* The interview focused primarily on the relationship between acting and writing, which was an interest that she and I shared.

Madeleine went into the procedure of writing a book, how she needed to hear the words, although she also said that she did not work aloud, as many writers do. She simply went into her experience as an actor as she wrote. When she'd finished a manuscript, she would have her husband, Hugh, read it to her. That for her was the final stage of revision. I thought about how often a writer will read a newly completed manuscript to some poor audience but that Madeleine had this good actor who could read it to *her*.

I'm a great admirer of Madeleine's fiction, but even more so of her nonfiction, and I think the real strength of all her work is her thinking: it's not the voice of her characters. She felt strongly that the voice was a great strength of hers, but I find that so many of her characters sound alike.

I asked her about writing as an "incarnational act"—a term she had used elsewhere. That is when she talked about being in the audience when Hugh was performing, and losing a sense of him as her husband, of momentarily not recognizing him because he had so fully become his character, and of him in turn being so thoroughly vested in the role that he felt he embodied his character. She compared this experience of performing a role with the writer's experience of creating characters. In both cases, she said, you have to let go of your own self. She made another connection between the theater and fiction writing. She said, "The kind of novel that I like to write and the structure of a play are very similar."

We talked about the "young reader": her admiration for young readers' greater willingness to plunge in and participate than that of adults. She said she got very upset about the view that novels written for children weren't quite real novels, that so often there was the sense that people looked down at them. I pressed her about who it was who felt that way. When I added that children's literature was rarely taught in the literature curriculum of an English department, Madeleine went off on Smith College, her alma mater. She said that Smith had asked her for her papers and in the course of doing so had proudly said that they had introduced a children's literature course in the English department. They told her this, she said, as if they felt they were doing something radical. Madeleine said she was very happy to say, "You're too late." She had already given her papers to Wheaton College, where Clyde Kilby had taken both her children's work and her adult work.

I sent Madeleine the transcript of the interview, and she didn't make any revisions. After it was published, I got a little note from

Hugh saying he thought it was the best interview that had been done with Madeleine, which I think merely meant that it focused on acting, which of course was *his* thing.

At the end of the interview, maybe because I was teaching Umberto Eco's *Name of the Rose* at the time, where the monks in that novel are disputing whether or not Christ laughed, I asked Madeleine what she thought about that. "Oh yes!" she said. She said she thought the parables were very funny stories. Soon thereafter, when I was visiting New York, she and I met at St. John the Divine and afterward went to her apartment, where we continued to play out the question: Was Jesus funny?

We began with the hypothesis that he must have been hilarious. Otherwise, would people have remembered his stories at a time when they had not yet been written down? We began with the idea that his sense of humor was responsible not only for making his stories memorable but also for giving them the compact structure of a joke.

The test we gave ourselves was this: Madeleine had two Bibles, two different translations, neither of which was the King James. Seated across from each other in her living room, we read certain parables back and forth, alternating translations while asking ourselves, Well, if this is funny, where are the laugh lines? How would you deliver it? Do you give a wink at the beginning of the story so the audience knows what's coming is actually something of a tease? Or halfway through the story do you give that sort of verbal wink—or a literal wink, saying, Now, go back to the beginning and revise what you've been thinking about this, and then move forward? Or do you do it at the end? Or is it the sort of stable irony where the tongue is firmly in the cheek from beginning to end, and you never give the wink, and you leave it to the audience to decide, well, was he teasing or was he not teasing?

The story I remember doing quite well with was the one where

Jesus says, "It would be easier for a camel to fit through the eye of a needle than for a rich person to get into the kingdom of God." A camel trying to squeeze through the eye of a needle? That's a terribly funny image, if you think about it. We agreed that to think of it as a funny story didn't diminish what Jesus was saying about the dangers of wealth. If anything, it made it better.

ICON

Wendy Lamb is vice president and publishing director of Wendy Lamb Books, an imprint of Random House Children's Books.

*Q: When did you meet Madeleine L'Engle?*

A: Long before I met her, Madeleine L'Engle was a big influence on me. I first read *A Wrinkle in Time* at the proper age, and I thought it was an astounding book. This was perhaps two years after it won the Newbery. I can still picture the blue cover with the green- and white-lined circles on it. I found the pronouncements of Mrs Who, Mrs Whatsit, and Mrs Which to be just thrilling. After I read the book, I shared it with my father, who was always interested in spiritual things. I was a big reader, and this was the only time during my childhood that I shared a book with him. I knew he would love it, and he did.

Later I went off to Brown, where I majored in creative writing. I wanted to write fiction. I had never been much of a science student, and Brown's academic requirements were such during the early 1970s that I could have graduated without ever taking a science course. But in senior year I decided that I *needed* to take at least one science class anyway. The reason for this was my love of *A Wrinkle in Time*. I had convinced myself that I needed to understand the basic laws of physics in order to be able to make creative use of them in my writing. I wanted to reflect on the nature of the physical universe because, well, look what Madeleine L'Engle had done! In senior year I found a course called Physics for Poets. It sounded perfect! First, though, I had to meet with the dean of women. "No, no," she said. "You don't want to take physics. You want to take this new engineering course in which you'll learn to build your own stereo!" She talked me into it. But by the time I had left her office and reached the stairway, a voice was telling me, "You are never going to be able to build your own stereo!" So I returned to the dean's office and enrolled in Physics for Poets.

It proved to be a very hard course: all formulas and labs, with no mention of fun concepts like tessering. We had a cool professor, though, who was interested in holography, and when I botched a lab, I asked if I could write a short story to replace it. He said, "All right, as long as it's physics related." I had an idea for a story about a plane crash, about a man whose father had died in a crash and who wanted to understand what had happened to him— including the physics of what had happened. The story was really about grief. About two years later, it became my first published short story, "Snow Geese." In a funny way, all this came out of my love of *A Wrinkle in Time*.

After college I moved to New York and took an entry-level job reading the slush pile in the Harper children's book department. The work was pretty boring, but I got to sit at a desk just outside the office of the great Charlotte Zolotow.* That fall I wrote Madeleine L'Engle a letter. I began by saying, "I'm in this job because of you." I told her everything: the story of my physics class and the story of my dad having loved *A Wrinkle in Time*. Then one day the phone rang—and it was her!

---

*Charlotte Zolotow, a much-honored writer for young people, served as vice president and associate publisher of Harper & Row's Junior Books division from 1977 to 1981, when she became editorial director of her own Harper imprint, Charlotte Zolotow Books.

Madeleine said that she had loved my letter and that she wanted to meet me. She said she would call me again when things were less hectic for her, in the spring. When she did call the second time, she told me that her agent had recommended a very good restaurant just across the street from Harper. It seemed so generous of her, to be reaching out to me in this way. On the day of the lunch I came to work all dressed up and excited.

I had loved the Austin books, and at lunch I told Madeleine about the time when as a child I had taken out *Meet the Austins* from the New Canaan Public Library and then somehow lost the book at home. When the library found out about this, they took back my card and would not let me borrow any more books until I had paid the fine, which grew to be enormous. I was a voracious reader, sometimes reading four books in a single day, so for a while I was in a terrible kind of limbo—-again, because of Madeleine L'Engle! Finally, I scraped together the thirteen dollars and paid the fine. Then I found the book. I still have it, that horribly expensive book, now with my old library card tucked into the front pocket as a kind of souvenir. It was an amusing story about a child's devotion, and Madeleine must have enjoyed it.

Colleagues at Harper had told me stories about her: that she'd been an actress, that she always traveled first-class, that she was considered "glamorous." At lunch, she talked about her family, and I must have asked her to tell me about her husband because I remember feeling embarrassed not to know that he was a famous actor. Suddenly I felt unprepared—for what, though? I'm not sure what I was looking for. Maybe a fairy godmother!

The real problem was that I hadn't read all that many of Madeleine's adult books. As we talked, she seemed to grow impatient with me for not being more familiar with that other side of her work. I had never sat down before with someone I worshipped, and here I was running out of things to say! I learned that when you meet someone as a fan, beyond expressing your admiration, you don't necessarily have a lot to say to that person. After that, I would hear about her from time to time from mutual friends, but I never saw her again.

In college, I had wanted to write a book as good as *A Wrinkle in Time*. Then, when my career took a different path and I became an editor, I wanted to publish a book that good. Ha! Impossible, perhaps, but *A Wrinkle in Time* has always been my model. When I reread it after having worked as an editor for many years, I was startled to realize how short a book it is compared with so many books that are published now and how comparatively simple the plot is. There aren't that many stages to the plot, and the things I remembered clearly about it were the main events. I was amazed all over again—this time from my professional perspective—to realize that she had created a book that was as simple as it was and yet which had had such a huge impact.

When Rebecca Stead came to me with *When You Reach Me*, in which *A Wrinkle in Time* figures in the story, I told her, "It's weird, but I think I was meant to edit this book."* As we worked together, we agreed that if *A Wrinkle in Time* was to be an element of the story, it should have an important role; it couldn't be done lightly, and it should be useful. It became a tool for introducing and explaining the concept of time travel. Scenes were added with this purpose in mind—conversations about the book and the physics of the story between Marcus, Miranda, and Julia. As Rebecca reread *Wrinkle* from each of her characters' perspectives, it also became a device for delineating her characters. Miranda's private, passionate love of the book is certainly one of her defining characteristics. *A Wrinkle in Time* also helps us see Miranda's mother's boyfriend, Richard, in a new way. His Christmas gift to Miranda is a first edition, inscribed to her by Madeleine L'Engle.

*Rebecca Stead won the 2010 Newbery Medal for *When You Reach Me*, her second novel.

Wow! This incredibly thoughtful, and expensive, gift shows the reader how sensitive he is to Miranda, that he loves her. We hope that Mom will marry him—he'd be a terrific dad. This gift makes the ending of the story even more satisfying.

Rebecca and I did worry that some readers might take issue with the book's role in *When You Reach Me*. Happily, the reaction was positive. We were thrilled that Madeleine's granddaughters, Charlotte and Léna, liked how Rebecca had written about *A Wrinkle in Time*. That meant the world to her and to me.

# COLBY RODOWSKY

Colby Rodowsky, a former teacher, is the author of *Hannah in Between*, *Not My Dog*, and other books for young readers.

*Q: How did you meet Madeleine L'Engle?*

A: I met Madeleine in the mid-1970s when a friend of mine at Maryland Public Television was working on a show about children's books. One of the books she wanted to feature was *A Wrinkle in Time*, and as Madeleine was going to be in Baltimore to give a graduation speech, it was arranged that she would talk to five children about her book on television. My son, who was then in the seventh grade, was one of the children picked. I still remember that they all sat together on a little hill, under a tree, with Madeleine slightly higher up the hill, looking down at them. The children sat at her feet as they talked about *A Wrinkle in Time*.

The next day Madeleine was to give the commencement speech at Notre Dame of Maryland University, and the head of the English department, who was a nun named Sister Maura Eichner and a friend of mine, had asked if I would entertain Madeleine for lunch that afternoon. I thought, Oh my God!—but of course I said yes, and following the ceremony I brought Madeleine and Sister Maura back to my house. On the way we stopped at the home of a good friend who had multiple sclerosis and couldn't leave the house. Because she was a big Madeleine L'Engle fan, I had asked if we could stop by for Madeleine to meet her.

Madeleine said yes, and she went inside and visited with my friend. When my friend asked, "What is a fugue?"—there are various references to fugues in *A Circle of Quiet*—Madeleine went to the piano and played one for her. She really couldn't have been nicer. We proceeded from there to my house. My husband and I had hoped to make it a kind of grown-up lunch, with our six children busy elsewhere. But knowing that Madeleine was going to be there was too big a draw, and soon they were all wandering in and out. Madeleine acted as if it was all fine, and somehow, in a matter of minutes, she knew all the children's names. She announced that she was going to eat the "Sarah cookies" that my daughter Sarah had baked rather than whatever dessert we had planned. She was just a very warm and gracious person.

The next time I saw Madeleine was in 1976, when my Maryland Public Television friend and I were going up to New York. I had had my first book accepted by Franklin Watts, and my friend had arranged for us to see Madeleine at the library of the cathedral. Madeleine gave us tea, we chatted, and just as we were leaving, she said to me, "If you have your editor send me the galleys, I'll write a blurb for your book." That just blew me away. I think I floated all the way home.

Not only did she do this once, but after four books with Franklin Watts I was looking for another publisher, and Madeleine suggested Farrar and even told me to contact her editor there, Sandra Jordan. Well, as it turned out, Sandra Jordan wasn't particularly interested in my next book, but she handed the manuscript to Stephen Roxburgh, who was interested. Stephen published the next twelve or so books of mine. The first of these was called *The Gathering Room*, and once again Madeleine wrote a blurb for it. This was the Madeleine I knew.

The last call I remember having with her was the morning Stephen Roxburgh told me he was leaving Farrar. I was feeling totally bereft. What do you do? You call Madeleine!

The books by her that I liked best were the ones for grown-ups. *A Circle of Quiet* was sort of my bible when I was starting to write. Of her children's books, my favorite was *The Young Unicorns*. When I told my son, who was a huge Madeleine L'Engle fan, that I was going up to New York that time to see her, he replied without skipping a beat, "Oh, good! You're going to get to see Canon Tallis." It didn't occur to him that all those people in the books were not going to be there.

CHRISTINE A. JENKINS

Christine A. Jenkins is an associate professor at the Graduate School of Library and Information Science, University of Illinois at Urbana-Champaign.

*Q: You have a story to tell me about Madeleine L'Engle.*
A: I have to set the scene. In 1976, I had just finished my student teaching and was at the American Library Association conference, looking for a job as a school librarian. You get really freaked out when you're looking for a job because you're scared. I was interviewing, and in the end I did get a job, but I did not know it yet. I was trying to be optimistic. So when I found out that Madeleine L'Engle was at the conference and that she would be having a book signing for *A Wrinkle in Time*, I thought, How cool would it be! I could get a copy of *A Wrinkle in Time*, have Madeleine L'Engle sign it, and then give the book to whatever library hired me, wherever that might be. I lined up to meet her, and when it was my turn, I said to her, "Don't dedicate it to anybody in particular, because I don't know yet where I'm going to be the librarian." And she said, "No, I won't do that. It has to be dedicated to someone. I won't just sign a book." I really was irritated! So I said, "Well, how long are you going to be here? I'll come back." I walked around the exhibit hall, clutching my book and thinking, Oh, jeesh! It seemed so heartless of her. I had

explained, "I don't have a job yet. I can't tell you where I'm going to be." I had told her that I would have her dedicate it to the school if I had one. I finally went back to the place where she was having her signing, and this time I said to her, "Okay, how about 'To all the children.' How's *that*?" She looked up at my badge and wrote, "To Christine and all of *her* children," and handed the book back to me. I was just furious!

Another facet of this is that I had just come out as a lesbian, about a year before, and so here I was planning to go to work in an elementary school. I was anxious about that, knowing that I wouldn't be protected legally, that I could be fired at any moment. As a lesbian, I assumed I wasn't going to have children of my own. And so here she was writing, "To Christine and all of *her* children." So that was there too: all the anxiety I felt at the time. I think she just decided that that was what she was going to write, that "to all the children" wasn't good enough, according to her rule. I was really angry. She had acted like a bully. And finally I did get hired by a school, and about a month later I moved to Ann Arbor, Michigan. I kept the book, but I didn't put it in the school library after all. I was too mad because it had been all about her and not about this person who was saying, "I love your book. It made such a difference to me. I want to give it to the children I'll be working with."

So I had this book at home for years and years, and then finally one day I got out a pair of scissors and I cut off the part of the page on which she had written the inscription, so that all that was left was her signature and the date.

Then, a couple of years ago, I took a number of my signed books to a local used bookstore to sell, and this nice lady was going through them one by one and giving me prices. Then she came to *A Wrinkle in Time*. She said, "Oh my God! What happened? Somebody mutilated this book. Oh, this is terrible!" She was really quite distressed about it. Finally, I had to admit, "Well, it was me. I did it." And I told her the whole story. This was twenty years after I had encountered Madeleine L'Engle at ALA.

When Betsy Hearne was preparing to interview Madeleine for *School Library Journal* at the time of her winning the Margaret A. Edwards Award, I had some questions to suggest.* I was particularly upset about *A House Like a Lotus* because I felt that the portrayal of lesbians was so miserable. In *The Small Rain* she also had a lesbian character whom she calls "it." "Now it wore a man's suit, shirt, and tie; its hair was cut short; out of a dead-white face glared a pair of despairing eyes." The good girl in *The Small Rain*, Katherine Forrester, is taken by her mischievous friends to a gay bar, where she sees this woman . . . "or it, or whatever." And the sensitive good girl says she can't stay at the bar because it's too upsetting for her. It was all so creepy.

Over the years her books were published, and I read every one, but it struck me that the world of her books—and all those different characters and locations—it was all like a closed universe. The O'Kcefes and the Austins and everybody was related to everybody else. She billed the O'Keefes as this inclusive, loving, accepting family. But it wasn't. It was just for the elect. So it ended up feeling the way I feel about some strands of Christianity: they talk about love, but it's really just for them. Why does everybody in her books have to be world famous? Why, in *A House Like a Lotus*, can't Ursula be an ordinary brain surgeon? Why does she have to be a world-famous brain surgeon? Why do other characters have to be important diplomats? Not that there's anything wrong with that, but it's *always* that. Her characters always occupy an unattainable level.

*L'Engle was the recipient in 1998 of the Margaret A. Edwards Award for significant and lasting achievement in young adult literature. The annual prize is administered by the Young Adult Library Services Association, a division of the American Library Association, and sponsored by *School Library Journal*.

*Q: Had you known* A Wrinkle in Time *as a child?*

A: Yes, I read it when I was twelve or thirteen. I had a copy then, and I read it over and over again. That would have been in the early 1960s. My mom was a librarian, and she had given it to me. It was a Newbery winner, so that's probably why she bought it for me. That book and the C. S. Lewis books and what I thought of as serious magic books all interested me greatly because they told me that things were not what they seemed. To me "realistic" books like *Little Women* and the Laura Ingalls Wilder books had a very different flavor.

*Q: Did you identify with Meg?*

A: No! This business about "Oh, I'm so ugly . . ." And she was so crabby! She wasn't nice. Regular kids like her poor twin brothers were just so out in the cold in that book because they're not special. They're not communicating with the great beyond. Meg's mother has violet eyes to die for, but not them! The only aspect of Meg's story that I identified with was that I too have a younger brother whom I love. So when he is held captive by IT on Camazotz, she knows that she is the one who must save him, and she finally pulls him away from IT with her love—I resonated with that.

*Q: When you look at the book now, where do you see it in the scheme of children's literature?*

A: I see that it was groundbreaking, although not in and of itself. The groundbreaking aspect was that it became the Newbery winner. If it had just sat there, it would have been a good book. But the significance of it to me is that it broke a barrier in terms of the common wisdom about the kinds of books that kids like— science fiction, for instance. Robert Heinlein only wrote about guys, and this was science fiction about a strong girl, with a mother who's a scientist. I certainly appreciated all that. But I also felt that I could never *be* Meg because she's in communication with the universe and I'm just a regular mortal.

*Q: Did you read her later books?*

A: Yes, I did—not her poetry, but everything else, even though I would be grinding my teeth at times. I always found her books eminently readable. They really draw you in. It is like: there's this person over there whom I'll never know, and she's really complicated and she makes me mad. Sometimes for nice girls like me, it's good to have the chance to get mad at something in a situation that has no real-world consequences. I never went to a talk of hers. I certainly never went to another book signing. And she called herself a librarian! Ha!

In *A House Like a Lotus*, the main character, Polly, meets an older woman named Maximiliana, who is a world-famous painter of course, who has a world-famous neurosurgeon partner named Ursula. They have been together for years, and they live in Max's family home, a beautiful old plantation-type house that has sterling silver doorknobs and an old black couple who cook and clean and who never speak a word. Maximiliana has been a mentor to Polly. And then Polly finds out that Ursula and Max are lovers and Polly's really upset about it, and one of her brothers taunts her, saying, "Oh, you must be a lesbian too." So her father, good old Calvin O'Keefe, says something like, as long as gay people keep their lives private, they shouldn't be discriminated against. The message is: we live in an enlightened society that has agreed that homosexuality is okay, especially if they keep it private. And Polly is saying that Max should have kept it private from her, that she didn't want to know. It's liberal in the worst sense of the word, as in, Not in my own backyard. It's okay that there are gay people out there somewhere, but just don't tell me that some of the people I actually know are gay.

*Q: Do you think that that was Madeleine's own attitude?*

A: Yes, I think that that is where she would have placed herself. She has a couple of other gay characters in her books, and they too are odd, fey characters. Felix, the priest who is Katherine's friend in *A Severed Wasp*, is gay, and that's his big secret. He tells Katherine, but she is not going to abandon him, because he is such an old, old friend. Isn't that nice! What a pal! So, as far as the O'Keefe family is concerned, there really isn't room for people of all kinds. Not everybody is invited.

I am from a generation that was looking so hard for books that showed an understanding of gay characters. During the 1970s and 1980s, we looked so hard and were finding maybe one book a year. The portrayal of lesbians at that time was *so* dismal. So in *A House Like a Lotus*, Max, the world-famous painter, has a painful fatal illness. Alcohol dulls the pain, but one night she drinks too much and makes a pass at Polly. Polly runs, runs, runs away into a rainstorm and cuts her foot and goes to the hospital. Then she goes to the apartment of her handsome cousin, who's an intern there, and they make love. In case any readers are wondering, Polly responds to Max's pass by asserting her heterosexuality.

*Q: What a soap opera!*

A: Exactly.

*Q: Do you think the books after* A Wrinkle in Time *fell off in quality?*

A: Yes, I do. *A Ring of Endless Light* did a pretty good job, but it got to be very formulaic. All right, Polly knows languages. That's her talent. So she goes and reads this language that nobody knows and picks it up in a day.

After I first read *A Wrinkle in Time*, at twelve or thirteen, I read some of her adult novels. In one of them, *A Winter's Love*, there is a character who says so-and-so loves so-and-so and that person loves somebody else, and that only rarely do two people come together who can love each other equally. That made a big impression on me in a positive way, because it was different from the fairy-tale version. And that is where I felt that she was telling the truth.

*Q: What have you observed about your library school students' responses to Madeleine L'Engle's books?*

A: I have taught young adult literature here at the University of Illinois, and one of the assignments I gave my students was a paper and a Web site about a young adult author. After a couple of semesters I noticed that the students who would write about Madeleine L'Engle because they loved her so much could not be critical about her books. I didn't want them to tear anybody down. But they couldn't achieve *any* degree of objectivity, and all they could do was talk about how wonderful she was. So at the start of the semester I would tell my students that they could write about any author they wished *except* Madeleine L'Engle! I would laugh and say, "I don't know what it is about her. If you really want to write about her, let's talk about it. But it doesn't seem to work very well." So nobody ever did.

Reading that article in *The New Yorker* was so interesting because in it her own daughters talked about how her fiction was more realistic than her journals. In my mind they were rolling their eyes as they spoke to the reporter. And I thought, Well, this doesn't surprise me one bit! Then, because she was still alive at the time, I thought, What is she going to think about this!

## GARDNER McFALL

Gardner McFall is the author of two books of poetry, two children's books, and an opera libretto, *Amelia*, commissioned by the Seattle Opera and premiered by that company in 2010.

*Q: When did you meet Madeleine L'Engle, and how did it happen?*
A: I met Madeleine L'Engle in January 1977. I was living in New York and working as a short story editor at *Ladies' Home Journal*. I had read her books as a child, and I would hear about her from time to time from friends in Jacksonville, Florida, where Madeleine and I both had some roots. I had recently been promoted from editorial assistant to short story editor, and it occurred to me that in my new position at the magazine I might reach out to her and buy one of her stories. I may have had an introduction to her from Harriet Gardiner, a contemporary of hers who had been one of my teachers at the small girls' school where we both had studied, the Bartram School for Girls, in Jacksonville. When I called Madeleine at her office at St. John the Divine, she was friendly and encouraging. She said, "Come on up. We'll have lunch." She also seemed a little concerned for my safety. "Where are you coming from?" she asked. I told her that our offices were on Lexington Avenue, in midtown. "It won't be safe for you to come to my apartment," she said, "so I want you to take the bus up to the cathedral."

I met Madeleine in the cathedral library, and from there we went across the street to an Italian restaurant she liked. My very first impression of her had been that she seemed a little scary— she was such an imposing presence—but I was disabused of that impression right away as we easily fell into conversation. We talked about Jacksonville: where she had spent time as a young girl, whom I knew there, and where I had lived.

I told her that I had been born in Jacksonville but that because my dad was in the navy, we moved all around. I was fourteen when my father died. After that, we moved back to Jacksonville, where my mother was from and where she still had family. My grandparents lived at the beach where Madeleine's grandmother had lived. I knew all the places mentioned in *The Summer of the Great-Grandmother*, which became a very important book to our family. My mother was a big fan of all Madeleine's writing, but especially the books of a spiritual nature, which she would read and pass on to me. I finished out my schooling at the Bartram School, from which my mother had graduated before me.

Finally, Madeleine and I got around to the business at hand: my request for a short story. She explained that she was about to go away on a five-week vacation and that when she came back, she would put a story "in my hot little hands." Those are her exact words! Then we talked about writing and the writer's life. It quickly got to be a personal conversation.

I was in my mid-twenties and had left north Florida to be educated in the North, to become involved in publishing, and in time—I hoped—to find my way as a writer. It interested Madeleine that I was writing poems. There was no precedent in my family for what I wanted to do in the world—that is to say, to be a woman writer—and it seemed to me that Madeleine was very willing, from the get-go, to share her insights and her wisdom, in a very personal way. My conscious purpose in asking to see her had been to secure a story from her for the magazine. But I'm sure my unconscious wish was to meet a real writer in New York and to learn—if I could divine it—how she had gone about creating such a life for herself.

One piece of advice Madeleine offered me that day was that if I wanted to understand how to write a novel, the two books most worth "going to school on," because they were so perfectly structured, were Flaubert's *Madame Bovary* and Tolstoy's *Anna Karenina*. If I could somehow master those two books, she said, I would know everything I needed to know about writing fiction. It was excellent advice, even for someone like me who had no intention of ever writing a novel, and it must have seemed important to me because I wrote it down in my journal. She talked about the many rejections she had received of *A Wrinkle in Time*. She related this to the young writer's need to persevere in the face of rejection. We talked about keeping a journal. She said, "Anyone who keeps a journal faithfully, as truly as possible, will never need a psychiatrist." She cut to the chase on all of these things for me.

When Madeleine returned from vacation, I saw her again, and during what was then only our second conversation I had the presumption to ask her to write a letter of recommendation for me for the Bread Loaf Writers' Conference for that summer. She generously agreed to this. I was accepted into the program, and as a result I met William Meredith, Howard Nemerov, and other poets who encouraged me to take myself more seriously as a poet than I had been doing until then. It was a life-changing experience, and Madeleine had helped make it possible. I must have shown her my poems at the time I asked her for the letter, but I don't recall discussing my poems with her. It was just a connection between us.

As for the short story about which I had originally contacted her, I never did get to publish Madeleine at *Ladies' Home Journal*. Either Madeleine's agent never sent a story, or—more likely—my boss, who wanted only formulaic family stories with happy endings, decided not to run the one we had been offered.

Madeleine could place her stories anywhere, and I don't think she cared a whit about the outcome. In any case, we stayed in touch, having established a kind of younger friend/older friend relationship. She must have been in her late fifties when we first met, and I, as I said before, was in my mid-twenties.

Apart from Madeleine's naturally generous nature, perhaps she also identified with me in terms of the Jacksonville experiences we shared, and in terms of my being at the beginning of my life as a writer and she having once been in my situation. She had things to say to me that would be helpful to me, and she seemed to take a certain pleasure in that. I took pleasure in listening to her, and I knew I was benefiting from it.

Jacksonville is practically south Georgia, and the old families all know each other. The L'Engles belonged in the uppermost reaches of Jacksonville society and were a very well-regarded family. It was a small, one might almost say claustrophobic, world, especially for someone with an independent spirit and mind. I know that I didn't feel I could do what I wanted to do if I stayed in Jacksonville. Imagine how Madeleine must have felt so much earlier. The culture was such that if you were at all different, you were going to be labeled "weird" and there was no way that you were going to fit in happily. Even so, once Madeleine became a famous writer, they loved her in Jacksonville. Jacksonville likes anyone who goes away and reflects well on it.

The Bartram School had been founded in the 1930s by the city's first families, for the purpose of educating their daughters. The headmistresses were Miss Pratt and Miss Miller, who had come to Jacksonville from Vassar and Smith, respectively. It was a small and very idiosyncratic school, with maybe twenty-four girls in each graduating class, and Madeleine thought enough of it to go back and give a commencement address sometime in the 1970s or 1980s. Each year a very few girls went on to college in the Northeast. But most girls stayed in the South, perhaps going to Hollins or Sweet Briar or Randolph-Macon. For the women of Madeleine's generation and certainly of mine, the expectation was that you would go to college and that you would then get serious, which meant marrying and having a family and joining the Junior League and perhaps the Colonial Dames. For the rest of your life, you would do good in the community and be a contributing citizen, but you would not aspire to having a real career, and certainly not one in the arts.

I saw Madeleine a handful of times between January and June of that year—1977—and I soon felt comfortable talking to her not just about writerly matters but also about personal things. That spring, I found myself seriously considering breaking off an engagement and leaving New York. I had just announced my engagement, and the Jacksonville wedding machine was in high gear. What made this particularly awkward is that I was engaged to the son of one of Madeleine's good friends in Jacksonville. The plot thickens! I had begun to feel that it wasn't going to work out but hadn't even told my mother yet. I didn't know whom to talk to or what to do. So I went to Madeleine to seek her advice. I gave her a list of all my reservations and concerns. I opened my heart to her, and her answer was clear: "Well, it just doesn't sound as if you should be getting married to this person." When she said that, I could no longer pretend that maybe going ahead with the marriage was the right thing to do. I knew she was right!

I wrote in my journal: "On May 16, I had lunch with Madeleine. Madeleine was in good spirits, not as reserved as before, dressed for summer. We walked under the full spring trees of the courtyard to a restaurant on Amsterdam. We ate pastrami sandwiches." That was when I told her I had canceled my engagement. In the same journal entry, I wrote: "She apparently wrote *The Small Rain* after the breakup of her first romance, which had been moving toward marriage."

That day we talked about how to manage being a woman writer of whom other things were demanded. She said that she had struck a deal with her husband and family, telling them all that she needed to do her work. Therefore, in the morning, she was going to go into her work space and write, and during that part of the day she would be unavailable to them. Any breakfast that needed to be gotten, lunch that needed to be made, they were on their own. She said that she sometimes felt a certain resentment about that from within the family but that it was necessary for her. She clearly knew where to draw the boundaries, even if it caused some conflict. I told her that I did not like conflict, that I craved calm, and that I worked best when things were calm. Madeleine responded by saying that her life had *always* been characterized by conflict and that she was not sure a life without conflict is even worth living. Maybe her idea was that you had to go through conflict to get to something that was worth having.

I not only ended the engagement but also decided that it was time to leave my job as an editor, to leave New York, and to go somewhere else and become a writer. When I told Madeleine all this, her comment was that it appeared that I was "choosing a creative response to the situation." This was a compliment and, more important, a validation—her making it absolutely clear to me that she didn't look at what had happened as a personal failure on my part, which is how I viewed it. Madeleine then said, "You'll be back—because New York needs good people and it always draws good people back!" I moved to Washington, D.C., and, just as she said, two years later I was living in New York again. But it was eight years from the time of that last lunch that Madeleine and I saw each other again.

In Washington, I met and married my husband. When I returned to New York, we lived in Greenwich Village. I was busy with job hunting and then with graduate school. When I became pregnant, we realized that we needed a larger place to live and that the Upper West Side was the neighborhood where we could find something affordable. I moved into our new building, and one day it suddenly dawned on me that the address—924 West End Avenue—rang an old bell. I looked in my address book and saw that it was Madeleine's address! I had become Madeleine's neighbor. I called her or wrote her a note. She seemed less surprised by the news than I was! She had me over for a breakfast of tea and toast. We sat and talked in the kitchen, which seemed small and modest compared with the rest of the apartment. She invited me to join a writing group that met at her apartment. At that point I not only had a baby to take care of but was feeling all work-shopped out: I was done with being a student. So I declined her invitation. After that, we got together a couple of more times, but I didn't see as much of Madeleine as one might have thought. Of course she was traveling a lot and very busy. I gave her my book of poems, and she wrote a nice note about it. Occasionally, she signed books for my daughter. But we didn't have the same kind of intense conversations that we had had when I was younger. Maybe I no longer presented myself as someone who needed that same kind of advice. Ten years later, we were both in different places in our lives. We were cordial but not really close. So it is almost as though I knew two different Madeleines.

In her last years at 924 West End Avenue, when Madeleine was not well, I did not even think about contacting her, but I would see members of the Community of the Holy Spirit come to visit her. My husband was on the board at the same time that Madeleine was on the board, though she was no longer as actively involved there as she had been in earlier years. The community was not grand like the cathedral. It was a small group of spiritual people with whom Madeleine felt a kinship and with whom she enjoyed worshipping. The Sisters all had talents of one kind or another. One played the piano. Another one wrote poetry. They were all thinkers. They respected Madeleine's spiritual writings. They were a small community of Sisters within the Episcopal Church. You don't find that every day, and that, I suppose, is why Madeleine was drawn to them.

JANE YOLEN

Jane Yolen is a poet, science fiction and fantasy writer, storyteller, writing teacher, book reviewer, and lecturer.

*Q: How did you meet Madeleine L'Engle?*

A: Madeleine and I were both Smith College graduates, and during the 1980s I was teaching children's literature at Smith. When Madeleine was coming for a visit to give a big lecture and work with some of the girls and spend a weekend on campus, the college asked me to be her spirit guide: to shepherd her around and make sure she had everything she needed.* I had corresponded with her before, but this was the first time I actually met her, and it was the first time I had a real touch with celebrity.

When I went to pick her up at the hotel, I found that the number of incoming phone calls from people wanting to speak to her—requesting to interview her, wishing to kiss the hem of the garment—was enormous. I finally had to say, "It's time to leave." Otherwise, she would have been stuck in her room for hours fielding all these calls.

When she and I were alone together, she was absolutely gracious and sweet. She asked me about my life. The truth is I was never a fan of her fiction. But I had read *The Summer of the*

---

*L'Engle returned to Smith on several occasions. These events most likely occurred in 1981, on the occasion of the awarding to her of the Smith College Medal.

*Great-Grandmother*, her memoir about her dying mother, at the time when my father was living with us and was dying. That book had meant a great deal to me, and I told her that.

Prior to her all-college lecture, there was a tea in her honor at the Alumnae House. Tea is always served at Smith, along with little cakes! Madeleine took her place in a comfortable high-backed stuffed chair and was surrounded by young women, all Smith girls. Some were seated in chairs, others were sitting on the floor, and a few tried to scoot up as close as they could, hoping literally to touch the hem of the garment. There were probably a half dozen of these girls who were sitting right by her feet. The event was planned as an informal discussion, as a kind of "at home," at which the students could ask her about anything. At one point, the conversation turned to the Numinist spiritual tradition and the question of the inexplicable in life. One girl at the very front said, "When I was little, *really* little, I could go up the stairs without my feet ever touching the treads." She was telling this to Madeleine but also to the assembled masses. Madeleine leaned over and patted her on the shoulder and said without the slightest hint of irony in her voice, "I could do that too, darling."

It was at that moment that I realized I was in the wrong place! When I write fantasy, I use metaphor as a deliberate literary device, and there it was as if everybody in the room but me believed in the *actuality* of the metaphors, Madeleine included. It was a very strange moment. I did not sense that she was pandering, that she was responding as one might to a small child, you know, by saying, "Yes, yes, I did that too, little girl." She sounded as if she was absolutely serious.

I remember her from that weekend as someone who seemed fully *present*. When she talked to people, she engaged them. She looked them in the eye. Very often someone who is that famous tends to look right past you, or to look about nervously, eyes darting, as though searching for the exit. She was not like that at all.

She was absolutely there for whomever she was talking to. It's as if she cocooned that person. I thought that was a great gift. Somehow I don't have any memory of her formal lecture, which would have been held in the large hall that seats twenty-five hundred people.

The funny thing to me is that it's almost as if *A Wrinkle in Time* and its sequels were an aberration in her career, that her strongest books were the nonfiction books and the books about the religious life. She was a great Christian apologist in the same way that I think C. S. Lewis was, except that not being an academic, she is a far more accessible writer. I think that she was as bemused as were many other people, especially people in her religious life, that the Time quartet books were seen as so significant in children's literature.

I had first read *A Wrinkle in Time* soon after it won the Newbery Medal. I was working as an editor in children's book publishing, at Knopf, and *everybody* in the industry felt obliged to read the Newbery winner. I recall being singularly unimpressed. Had I been sent it in manuscript, I am sure I would have been one of the twenty-nine editors (or however many it was!) who turned it down. First of all, I was a big science fiction and fantasy reader, and from that point of view *A Wrinkle in Time* struck me as naive and old-fashioned. It was not clever or button pushing like the science fiction and fantasy I found compelling. It had more the flavor of Charles Kingsley's *Water-Babies*, in which Mrs. Doasyouwould-bedoneby is the fairy queen and presiding presence. Likewise, in *A Wrinkle in Time* you have those great female presences who are a combination of goddess, schoolmarm, and Virgil leading you through the gates of hell and heaven. It harked back to the nineteenth century, even as it purported to be forward-looking. Going back even further in time, you could say it had a *Pilgrim's Progress*–y feel, which of course is the classic Christian journey book. So for me *A Wrinkle in Time* was a little too I-am-going-to-lead-you-through-the-gates-of-paradise. I didn't particularly like the kids in the book either. I thought that Meg was such a whiner!

I took my science fiction very seriously and was kind of a snob about it. The science fiction writers I cared about, like Ray Bradbury, had moved past stuff like "tessering" a long time ago. Madeleine seemed to be stuck in the old days. If you were going to take a naive stance as a science fiction writer, I thought it would have to be through the device of a "holy fool" character, which in a sense is what Ray Bradbury was doing. But that isn't what Madeleine L'Engle was doing. That said, I can still understand the book's success. There had been very little children's science fiction until then, and what little there was tended to have characters who were little more than place holders for whatever scientific ideas the writer was spouting. Madeleine's book broke that mold, and I think that for readers who did not know any science fiction, it must have seemed a great find. It may well have been a gateway book for them. I've always said that middle-grade and young adult books are really about the getting of wisdom. And certainly Madeleine L'Engle's books are about the getting of a kind of wisdom, in her case wisdom rooted more in religious experience than in science. I would say that I feel close to some of her ideas, her sense, for example, that as part of the universe we owe something to the universe.

My longtime agent and friend Marilyn Marlow used to tell this story about the 1963 Newbery-Caldecott dinner, where Madeleine was presented the Newbery Medal for *A Wrinkle in Time*. At the break during the banquet after Madeleine gave her acceptance speech, Marilyn went to the ladies' room, where she encountered one of the editors—twenty-six? twenty-nine?; it had definitely been a lot—who had turned down the book. This editor was very in her cups and was sobbing as she leaned over the sink and spoke into the mirror. "And to think I turned down that fucking manuscript!" For the editors of the day there was clearly much consternation and astonishment that Madeleine's book had won.

# PAUL MORAVEC

Paul Moravec, winner of the 2004 Pulitzer Prize in Music, is University Professor at Adelphi University and has served as artist in residence at the Institute for Advanced Study, Princeton, New Jersey.

*Q: How did you meet Madeleine L'Engle?*

A: I met her, I think, in the fall of 1989, a few months after reading *Walking on Water: Reflections on Faith and Art*. I'd bought a copy in June of that year, and the book had made a big impression on me. In it, she writes about spirituality, religion, and art and how they are all intertwined. She writes about the arts as a response to the pressure of reality and the pressure of mortality. She is very perceptive about music. About Bach's music, for example, she writes: "Along with reawakening the sense of newness, Bach's music points me to wholeness, a wholeness of body, mind, and spirit, which we seldom glimpse, but which we are intended to know." This struck me as exactly right. I too had come to see the act of making music as having the power to integrate all the disparate aspects of our being—the intellectual, the sensual, the physical, the emotional—to believe that music had the power to make us whole. *Walking on Water* is full of such wise observations.

Even so, after reading a book that has had a strong effect on me, I don't normally say, "All right, now I've got to meet the author." But this time there was something special. I found myself wondering: Who is this person who produced such a remarkably articulate description of the spiritual and creative life? This person who conceives of her art in terms of the spirit and ritual? Like Madeleine, I had been raised an Episcopalian. I had been a choirboy, and I had been seduced by the iconography of the Episcopal Church and by the beauty of the language and the music and the ritual, what some people call "the smells and the bells." Whatever one might think of church dogma, I regarded this aspect of the Anglican tradition as one of the great cultural forces in the world.

As a composer, I thought of the act of making music, whether or not it was sacred music, as a kind of ritual act, and of a well-planned concert as a kind of secular ritual. It interested me that music by its nature is nonideological and nondogmatic, that it cannot be invoked to argue an intellectual proposition, or articulate anything other than itself, but rather that it is its own irreducible expression of the ineffable and of the spiritual. My own view of music was all tied up with Madeleine L'Engle's core ideas, and I suppose it was partly for that reason that I wanted to know the actual spirit behind the book.

There is a quality of intimacy about the writing in *Walking on Water* that perhaps also made me want to meet its author: a distinctly welcoming, and accepting, note in the writing voice. It is almost as though L'Engle takes on the role of the confessor as she writes. Reading her, you want to go to her and confess!

I think I also believed that one could learn more about a book, or any work of art, by meeting the person who had made it, that it could be an enhancement of one's understanding of the work to do so, even if only in ways that could not be articulated. Reading *Walking on Water* had left me wanting to find out more.

So one day I called the library at the Cathedral of St. John the Divine and got Madeleine L'Engle on the phone. I explained that

I was a fan of her book, and I asked if I might stop by to meet her. She simply said, "Sure," and a few days later I went to see her after lunch. We sat together in the library and for an hour or so had a friendly chat.

She struck me as a generous person and as a person of firm convictions. You asked her a question, and she looked you directly in the eye and gave her response. She was an Episcopalian, but she seemed rather ecumenical in every way. We talked about the issues in the book, and basically she summarized what she had already written so well about them. There were no new revelations!

In fact, I didn't learn anything new from our conversation, which, I am sorry to say, is the only time I ever talked with her. But looking again at *Walking on Water* now for the first time in years, I'm struck all over again by the impact she had on me. So many of her memorable turns of phrase still run through my head. I had forgotten where they came from.

Amy Kellman retired in 2009 from her longtime post as coordinator of children's services, Carnegie Library of Pittsburgh.

*Q: How did you meet Madeleine L'Engle?*

A: I hosted Madeleine L'Engle when she came to Pittsburgh in 1993 for the Carnegie Library's Fall Festival of Children's Books, which I was responsible for planning. I had met Madeleine previously at various big library gatherings but had never spent time with her before. As far as I knew, this was her first visit to Pittsburgh.

Pat and Fred McKissack were the other two speakers. Needless to say, when it was Madeleine's turn to speak at the festival, she played to a full house and was surrounded by fans the entire time she was there. "Noble" is a word that comes to mind to describe how she struck me. She did not seem to me to be all that relaxed with the many people who hovered around her, but she was every bit the gracious lady.

We had some free time the next day and were going to see the Frank Lloyd Wright house Fallingwater, but the weather was just too wretched for the one-and-a-half-hour-long drive to Mill Run. Here in town, the Henry Clay Frick house had recently opened to visitors, so we decided to go there instead. In the end, we had time to do just half the tour. I knew that Pat McKissack would be interested in learning all about what life was like for the servants who had worked in the Frick mansion. What interested Madeleine turned out to be the really good grand piano that we came upon as we toured the house. When Madeleine saw the piano, she turned to our guide and asked, "Does somebody play it?" "No," said the guide. At which point a serious look came over Madeleine's face and she said with great emphasis, "But it will *die!*" Of course, she was quite right about that. "You *have* to play it," Madeleine admonished the guide, making her point one last time before letting go of it. I didn't know exactly what Madeleine's musical background was, but from the way she spoke about that piano, I assumed there had to have been some background.

After our three speakers had checked out of their hotel, I had them over to my house for a little downtime prior to my driving them to the airport. I remember Pat and Madeleine sitting in my kitchen and chatting away about religion. I could see they had really bonded over religion, and I remember thinking to myself with a little laugh—because their style of religion was so different from mine—that in a way they deserved each other! I suppose that sounds irreverent, but I was glad they were enjoying each other.

## BETSY HEARNE

Betsy Hearne is professor emerita in the Graduate School of Library and Information Science, University of Illinois at Urbana-Champaign. She is the author of *Beauties and Beasts*, *Seven Brave Women*, and other books and is a former editor of *Booklist* and *The Bulletin of the Center for Children's Books*.

*Q: How did you meet Madeleine L'Engle?*

A: I didn't know Madeleine L'Engle in the way that I knew other writers, artists, and other book people well: Virginia Hamilton, Trina Schart Hyman, and my dear friend and editor for thirty-seven years, Margaret McElderry. Aside from reading almost all her books, I came to know Madeleine when I interviewed her for the June 1998 issue of *School Library Journal*. It was a telephone interview, and she was in her apartment. This was almost ten years before she died. I had prepared very carefully, and I had a long list of questions, some of which were what I would call challenging. I felt that she was a complex thinker and writer, but I also felt that sometimes she cast her characters into either all-good or all-evil roles, and I couldn't believe that with her sense of moral complexity she could have made that decision without some reason. I was curious to know whether the reason was that she was writing for children or whether it was that, as a writer, this was simply how she needed to develop her plots.

My first question to her was one that people had asked her many times before: why it had taken so long for her to get *A Wrinkle in Time*, the first of her fantasy or science fiction books, published when her earlier novels, for example, *Camilla Dickinson*, which is a realistic story and a young adult bildungsroman, had been fairly quick to find a publisher. She talked about this very straightforwardly, and then I asked her another question about how she reconciled the conflicts between raising a family and being a professional writer. She was also matter-of-fact about that, saying basically that she found it hard and sometimes extremely frustrating. That led me to a question that I felt she stonewalled. I asked her about all the professional superstars in her books who were also parents—the famous scientists and doctors, people who were great at something or other—and she flatly denied that that was true. She said she saw them all as being ordinary people. It seemed to me that she had always written about special people. *Camilla Dickinson* was about a privileged young person whose special background presented both problems and opportunities for her. I didn't have any theory about this aspect of her fiction and was just probing a bit. But Madeleine was so insistent that these were not superstars but just ordinary people who did good solid work. Yet Meg's father and mother were no ordinary scientists.

I asked how the two principal families in her books compared. I had noticed what I thought were a great many similarities between the Austins and the Murrys. She replied that she did not see them as being at all alike. I began to feel that this was not the time to argue with Madeleine! As a critic, I might have said, "Look at this, look at that," and built my case, but what was interesting to me was the fact that she really *did* see the families as being very distinct. Of course, I realized, she had developed their voices over a period of many, many years, so each of their voices was bound to seem very distinctive to her. And that led me to the question about her good and evil characters, which again she kind of sidestepped. I asked, "Would you ever have a character that was morally ambiguous?" Looking back at it now, I think my original goal for the interview had been to get her to complexify in a way that I thought she was capable of, and that perhaps she was already doing in her head, although it did not always come through on the page. She was such a strong personality, with such strong opinions. She thought carefully about things, and she was in many ways unshakable, which can be both an advantage and a disadvantage. Another thing that amazed me about her was that she seemed able to keep all these chronologies in her head, that her various books, which she did not necessarily write in the order in which their ongoing story elements unfolded, all somehow made sense and hung together. I don't know how she managed that except that she must have had an incredible fantasy life and was able to develop a world so credibly that even before she translated it into a narrative, it all stayed in place in her mind.

I don't know what it was like to edit her, but I would be curious to know that. It would be interesting to work with someone with that kind of strong-willed determination, which she had to have in order to have played out the various roles that she played and to stick with a kind of literature that was not popular at the time, or at least immediately recognized in editorial circles.

I found all that very admirable. At the same time I felt there was an element of control that I might not get past. She talked a little about her family, and it seemed to me that in her life, as in her books, family was the dominant force, even though she had somehow managed to carve out a big space for herself as a creative writer. I also sensed that her energies were waning and that she felt that her time was short. It was harder for her now than in the past to concentrate and to do all the things she was used to doing. When I asked her how she was able to keep writing, given the demands of her becoming a superstar, she said in reply that an airplane was the place to be if you wanted to write because nobody could get at you.

She talked about St. John the Divine. One of the things that I have always liked about her writing is that she was not afraid to be mystical, although I believe she would have argued with that opinion because, as she told me that day, her idea was that science and religion are not at odds, that they reinforce each other and fit well together.

I asked her about *Many Waters*, which I thought was a powerful book. I wanted to probe her a little bit about the freedom she felt to take the Bible in various directions and play around with it, and how people responded to that, sometimes through protests and censorship. To me the Bible is very sexist, and I would have thought that for a believer like herself there must have been conflicts, but it wasn't clear that she saw the conflicts, and I was really interested in that. I would have liked to have had that long conversation with her.

There are people in the business I can argue and debate with, but I had realized by then that I could not argue with Madeleine. As we talked, I felt I was being managed. I don't want to put her down, because she was really such an amazing person, but I think she managed her audience as well as her characters, and if I was trying to get at anything in the interview, it was that she over-managed—or let's say, stage-managed—her characters at times. I decided that my job for the interview was simply to get her thoughts and words out to the reader and not to push her into areas that I might have wanted to go if we had been having a personal conversation.

*Q: When had you first read* A Wrinkle in Time?

A: I first read Madeleine's books in graduate school. I was swept up by her writing, and of course *A Wrinkle in Time* was what everybody read. It was such a fresh kind of book for that time, and the fact that it won the Newbery Medal was quite a remarkable thing.

*Q: Where do you see* A Wrinkle in Time *in the science fiction spectrum?*

A: She objected to the categorization of her work as fantasy, but it does strike me that when you compare her books with more hard-core science fiction—Ray Bradbury, for example—it really was fantasy. I don't mean to say that it was "softer," but there is a distinct difference. My theory about her work is that she wrote differently for children and for adults, especially in terms of moral complexity and of shades of difference in plot development and character development. That of course is something she explicitly denied.

*Q: Why do you think* A Wrinkle in Time *was rejected repeatedly before it was published?*

A: I hadn't entered the field quite yet in 1962, when it came out. But in 1964, I took my first library job at the Wooster Public Library—also known as the Wayne County [Ohio] Public Library—where the children's librarian, who did not have a library degree, refused to put *Where the Wild Things Are* on the shelf. It had just won the Caldecott Medal, and she was very disgruntled that it had won the award. That was my first exposure to issues of censorship in libraries and by libraries, to fear on the part of adults of exposing children to things that might be alarming or scary or irreverent. Then, in 1965, I entered library school and saw almost immediately that *Harriet the Spy* was also up for grabs. At a conference I attended at the University of Chicago, someone from Bruno Bettelheim's Orthogenic School got up and gave a paper denouncing the title character in *Harriet the Spy* as a bad role model for kids and said how Harriet's example could create all kinds of problems. That was when, as a lowly student at a gathering of scholars, I stood up and made my first public statement. I said I had to disagree. I said, "This is literature. Children's literature *is* literature, and how can you have every character be a good girl or a good boy and still have any sense that this is real literature?" A year or two later, soon after I had gone to work at *Booklist*, I was looking in the back files one day and discovered that *Booklist* had rejected—that is, decided not to recommend—*Harriet the Spy*. What I'm getting at is that while I don't know from experience what exactly was going on in terms of editorial consideration in 1962, I do know that around that time there was tremendous resistance to books that had ventured a little beyond the pale. After all, America was just coming out of the 1950s, which had been such a conservative era. And although there were certainly fearless editors in the 1950s, there was still plenty of resistance to the new.

Henry Rinehart is the proprietor of Henry's, an Upper
West Side Manhattan restaurant frequented by Madeleine
L'Engle in her later years.

*Q: How did you meet Madeleine L'Engle?*
A: When I opened Henry's in 1999, Madeleine was a neighbor. She'd been a resident here for a long time, with a large apartment upstairs. When I first met her, I did not know who she was.
She was still walking, and I recall a very tall, imposing, patrician
woman with an unexpectedly easy, engaging smile that she
flashed often and to great effect. She didn't strike me as a writer.
She struck me as a performer.

When she came down for a meal, she was often surrounded by
her busy, bustling family. Other times, she would be here sharing
a table with one or two friends. Henry's is considered a kid-friendly
restaurant, and I noticed that Madeleine would always be very
watchful of the children and families at the tables around her. But
it wasn't that she was bothered by the noise they sometimes made.
She was curious about them. She had an incredible social fluidity,
an ease and grace, with everyone. When fans approached her, she
always seemed as thrilled as they were.

Madeleine and I would talk about her life in the theater. I had
grown up as a juvenile actor and had traveled in a touring com-

pany in England for a time. We talked about building a life as an actor and about building a family life as an artist in New York.

I had not grown up with her books, but my sisters had, and I certainly knew the impact her books had had. I liked her immediately, but when I began to see how she and her public responded to each other at the restaurant, which was probably about as comfortable a public space as she had in her life then, I was totally taken with her. She was not a writer who was looking to disengage from the world. She seemed to see her work as a way of connecting directly with people. She seemed to actively seek it out, to treat it as a part of her job that she enjoyed. At Henry's, we are always striving to create an experience of ease and grace for our customers. These are the qualities I saw in Madeleine. We are always trying to build a sense of community. That is what Madeleine was all about.

Later, she would arrive in a wheelchair, which put her at her younger fans' eye level. Knowing that children are often nervous about approaching anyone in a wheelchair, but especially an older person, she would always have a smile for them and an inviting "Yes?" to encourage them to come closer and meet her. In her very last years in New York, she wasn't as talkative and our conversations became more perfunctory, but Madeleine was still intensely present. I used to have several vintage French posters up on the restaurant walls, including one with an image of a smiling elephant. It was an ad for Le Nil cigarette papers. Madeleine loved that poster, and when I told her I was planning to replace all the art on the walls, Madeleine asked if she could have it. One of my investors had bought the posters for the restaurant, and I didn't know if he would want them back, so I told her, "Let's see what happens." As it turned out, the investor agreed that Madeleine should have the poster, and when I presented it to her, she was thrilled. She not only admired that poster, she said. She had been making up stories about that grinning elephant all those years.

CYNTHIA ZARIN

Cynthia Zarin is a poet, journalist, and senior lecturer in English at Yale University.

*Q: How did you meet Madeleine L'Engle?*

A: I had known her a little before I wrote the profile in *The New Yorker.** I met her because I had been affiliated with the cathedral for a long time.

*Q: Had you ever visited her at the cathedral library?*

A: She was no longer at the library when I started to know her. By then, her granddaughter Charlotte had taken over there.

*Q: Had you ever asked her to read your work, as so many younger writers did?*

A: No. I never did.

*Q: How good was her memory when you interviewed her for the profile? When I spoke with her around 2003, she was focused part of the time, but at other times she seemed distracted or even disengaged.*

A: I think that Madeleine was a lot sharper than she let on at that time. She was extremely sharp when she wanted to be present. She did seem to fade in and out, as you say, but I think that like so much about Madeleine, she was probably aware of doing that most of the time.

*Cynthia Zarin's article, titled "The Storyteller: Fact, Fiction, and the Books of Madeleine L'Engle," appeared in the April 12, 2004, issue of *The New Yorker.*

*Q: How helpful was she to you as you worked on the profile?*

A: She was enormously helpful. I did the reporting for it on and off over a couple of years, and I saw Madeleine many, many times. I had been a huge fan of hers when I was a kid—a real *Wrinkle in Time* devotee—and I felt that she had greatly influenced my sense of the world: my idea of good and evil; my idea of the possibilities of family life; my idea of what it might mean to be a writer *and* have a family. I think that Madeleine probably had a good deal to do with my participation in the Anglican Church. These are all positive things. I was a great admirer.

*Q: As you got further into your work on the profile, how much of what you learned came as a surprise to you, perhaps even caught you unawares?*

A: I was completely unaware. It all came as a tremendous shock to me because I had thought I was going to write a kind of appreciation, and it quickly became clear that I could not do that.

The picture that Madeleine painted of herself—and this is often true of writers—was not necessarily who she was. Madeleine presented a picture of a halcyon life that wasn't entirely true. That in turn brought forth a charge of hypocrisy, though I think it would be kinder to say denial. She painted in her nonfiction books a picture of her life as she wished it to be. Then, in her fiction, she painted a life that in some ways was closer to the truth. As a writer, I don't feel there's anything wrong with that, in that she wrote the books she wanted to write. They're good books, most of them, and they're coherent. The fact that Madeleine did not want to make certain things in her life public was really up to Madeleine. And it's the responsibility of readers and admirers to understand that hagiography is a dangerous business, because there's no way that anybody can live up to it.

*Q: Diane Johnson wrote that biographers go through three stages in their relationship to their subject: first comes infatuation, then disillusionment. The third stage is synthesis, when the real person finally comes into view. Does this come close to describing your experience of writing the profile?*

A: Yes, I think so. I wasn't writing a biography, however: a profile does not pretend to be a biography. I hope that it was a synthesis at the end. The reactions to the profile were very interesting.

*Q: Did you become a kind of lightning rod?*

A: I think that her most adoring fans truly couldn't read it. In an almost shocking kind of way, they could not read what was there. But I think the people who knew her were pleased. There was a sort of schadenfreude in some of their reactions. You know: finally, after all these years . . .

*Q: How do you understand Madeleine's need to project such a polished version of her life not just through her books but also through her very public persona?*

A: I think that it kind of snowballed. When Madeleine first began writing, she was really writing fairy tales in the modern sense, and she did not yet have such a public persona. But when she wrote *A Wrinkle in Time* she was already forty-two—not so young—and by then her identity as a person was pretty well set. By the time she wrote *Two-Part Invention*, it would have been pretty groundshaking for her to revise that persona, which had proven to be so helpful to people, in the same way that her Christian writings were helpful.

There was also a generational issue. I think that for Madeleine as a woman of her generation it would have been impossible for her to speak frankly about Hugh. It would have been literally impossible for her to speak about her son. Those were not things that you were brought up to speak about. The culture now is completely different in its attitude toward revelation and self-revelation.

*Q: What did you make of her need to take so many young people under her wing?*

A: I think she was a natural teacher. And in some very basic ways, Madeleine was about fourteen in her perception of the world.

*Q: You told an anecdote in your profile about her making a joking comment at her apartment one day about an alligator that might show up at any moment. Did you feel she was just being playful in front of you, or what?*

A: You know, there's also a parallel moment about the dog, when she says, "This is the first time I haven't had a dog [to protect me]." I think that Madeleine was extremely conscious of what I was doing—that the jig was up—and that she had decided to participate in it. It's all in the last paragraph of the profile: "'There's really no such thing as nonfiction'"; "'I had a friend . . . She thought she could control everything.'" I think she knew that I was the messenger that would tell this truth. It was partly because I had come out of the milieu of the cathedral. Charlotte was adamant that this story be told. The family had not talked to anyone before. Charlotte said, "We've all talked about it, and we've decided that you can write this profile, but you must tell the truth." I think her words were "We're not participating in any more hagiography." So I became for them a kind of channel, and I was very concerned about this because I was concerned about my ability to be that channel. I thought that they might feel very differently about what they had said when it appeared in print. And I also felt, although in the end it didn't matter so much, that here were all her somewhat obsessive fans who might be hurt by this. The family all loved Madeleine very much. We were not in *Mommie Dearest* territory. I think they felt that because their own lives had been depicted and perhaps even used in the books, they had the right to set the record straight, to tell the truth as they understood it. People of course would draw their own conclusions. Family relationships are very complicated. Everyone knows that.

## A NOTE ON SOURCES

To verify factual statements contained in the interviews and in Madeleine L'Engle's own books, I consulted a variety of sources. For information about Charles Wadsworth Camp and the Camp family, I consulted the Mudd Library, Princeton University; Crosswicks Library Company, Crosswicks, New Jersey; the Century Association Archive; the Players Club Archive; and *The New York Times*. On the website www.metrojacksonville.com, I found fascinating local-history research focusing on the L'Engles and the Barnetts. To learn more about L'Engle's time at Smith College, I contacted the Alumnae Association of Smith College and benefited from reading portions of Daniel Horowitz's biography *Betty Friedan and the Making of "The Feminine Mystique"* (University of Massachusetts Press, 1998). For the background of New York's Episcopal Diocese, I found Honor Moore's memoir, *The Bishop's Daughter* (W. W. Norton, 2008), a great help as well as selected essays in *The University and the Church: Essays in Honor of William Alexander Johnson*, edited by James Proud and Karl Johnson (Hudson, 2008). I drew as needed on the resources of my own extensive archive on the history of American children's book publishing. My interview with Madeleine L'Engle was published in my book *The Wand in the Word: Conversations with Writers of Fantasy* (Candlewick, 2006).

## ACKNOWLEDGMENTS

In addition to each of the individuals whose voices are heard in this book, I wish to thank the following people who provided background information, research materials, and other help: Allison Jane Bruce, Ellen Cousins, Nancy Drew, Jeff Faville, Anita Fore, Elise Gibson, Claudia Barnett Gordon, Simon Green, Ann Hastings, the late Esther Hautzig, Edward Jones, Leslie Mason, Spencer Mason, Beth Nelkin, Judy Olsen, Rosalba Recchia, Ellen H. Ruffin, Barbara Scotto, Linda Gramatky Smith, Martha Walke, and Yvonne West.

Thanks too to my editor, Margaret Ferguson, and her assistant, Susan Dobinick, for their consummate professionalism and timely assistance at every stage of the work. A tip of my hat goes to Jean Feiwel for her enthusiastic support of this project from the very beginning.

I thank my agent, George M. Nicholson of Sterling Lord Literistic, for being a good guide, advocate, and friend. And, as always, my love to my family.